Dictatorship, Disorder and Decline in

Myanmar

Dictatorship, Disorder and Decline in

Myanmar

Monique Skidmore and Trevor Wilson (eds)

ANU
THE AUSTRALIAN NATIONAL UNIVERSITY

E PRESS

E PRESS

Published by ANU E Press
The Australian National University
Canberra ACT 0200, Australia
Email: anuepress@anu.edu.au
This title is also available online at: http://epress.anu.edu.au/myanmar02_citation.html

National Library of Australia
Cataloguing-in-Publication entry

Title: Dictatorship, disorder and decline in Myanmar / editors,
                  Monique Skidmore ; Trevor Wilson.

ISBN: 9781921536328 (pbk.)
                  9781921536335 (pdf)

Subjects: Government, Resistance to--Burma.
                  Military government--Burma.
                  Dictatorship--Burma.
                  Human rights--Burma.
                  Burma--Politics and government.
                  Burma--Social conditions.
                  Burma--Economic conditions.

Other Authors/Contributors:
                  Skidmore, Monique.
                  Wilson, Trevor.

Dewey Number: 303.609591

Cover design by ANU E Press
Cover photo of monks marching in 2007 from Mizzima News Agency

Table of Contents

Editors' note

This publication uses 'Myanmar' in its title because that is the official name of the country and is accepted as such by the United Nations. It has, moreover, been adopted increasingly in common usage inside the country, especially when using the Burmese language. Its use in this publication does not represent a political statement of any kind. We, however, adopt the common practice of allowing authors in their own chapters to use whichever terminology they prefer for the country. With less well-known place names, where historical names have been used, we have added the current official names in parentheses where they are first used in each chapter in order to avoid confusion.

The Editors also gratefully acknowledge the support of the Australian Agency for International Development (AusAID) and the Institute of South East Asian Studies (ISEAS) in Singapore for their support of the 2007 Myanmar/Burma Update Conference and the publication of the papers from that conference in this edition.

Contributors

Wylie Bradford is Lecturer in Economics at Macquarie University in Sydney, and researcher at 'Burma Economic Watch'

Richard Horsey is an independent consultant in Bangkok, and was interim ILO representative in Myanmar from 2003-07.

Toshihiro Kudo is Director, Southeast Asian Studies Group II, at the Institute of Developing Economies, in Chiba, Japan.

Marie Lall is Lecturer in Education Policy at the Institute of Education, University of London, specialising in education issues in South and Southeast Asia.

Jasmin Lorch is a doctoral candidate at the Department of Political Science, Albert-Ludwigs-University Freiburg on civil society in Bangladesh and the Philippines.

Mahn Mahn is the Director of the Back Pack Health Workers Team in MaeSot, Thailand, and responsible for data analysis and data collection systems across the border.

Win Min is an independent researcher based in Chiangmai, focusing on civil-military relations, who writes, lectures and comments on Burma affairs.

U Myint is a former Economic Adviser to the Economic and Social Commission for Asia and the Pacific (ESCAP), Bangkok, who writes on the Myanmar economy from Yangon.

Monique Skidmore is a medical anthropologist and Dean of Communications and International Studies at the University of Canberra, and has been co-convener of The Australian National University's Myanmar/Burma Update Conference since 2006.

Mohammed Mohiyuddin Mohammed Sulaiman is a Myanmar citizen and a PhD candidate at the International Islamic University of Malaysia in Kuala Lumpur.

Han Tin was Rector of the Institute of Education, Yangon from 1992-2001, when he retired. He now lives in Sydney.

Sean Turnell is Senior Lecturer in Economics at Macquarie University in Sydney, where in 2001 he founded the online journal 'Burma Economic Watch'.

Alison Vicary is Lecturer in Economics at Macquarie University in Sydney, and researcher at 'Burma Economic Watch'.

Trevor Wilson is a Visiting Fellow at the Department of Political and Social Change at The Australian National University and co-convener of the Myanmar/Burma Update Conference since 2004.

1: Overview

Trevor Wilson and Monique Skidmore

The military government in Myanmar, operating as the State Peace and Development Council (SPDC), maintains a firm, but increasingly contested hold on power and the country continues to stagnate economically and politically, while its social infrastructure deteriorates. The regime manages to hold out against various campaigns by its political opponents inside and outside the country, and in particular has been successful in expanding its presence into areas where it negotiated cease-fires in the 1990s and in consolidating its control over much of Karen State in eastern Myanmar. It also survived a UN Security Council vote in January 2007, but achieved this only through continued repression and abuse of power, and through loyal support from its UN Security Council backers, China and Russia.

There was little movement in the political situation between the end of 2005, when the government relocated to a new capital, Naypyitaw near Pyinmana in the centre of the country, and the end of 2007, when the military regime finally began work on a new constitution. No plausible reason has ever been given for the move to the new capital, although judging by official statements and behaviour, a primary reason seems to be to provide the security-obsessed regime with greater security and to present a more dignified and impressive 'front' to the Burmese people and to the outside world. The move to a new government/military headquarters in a remote site where access by the ordinary population can be controlled symbolises the extent to which the regime has become isolated from the people and the extent to which its priorities diverge from pursuing the wellbeing of its people.

Not surprisingly, international and media attention has focused on Myanmar in the past year, and in particular on the widespread non-violent mass street protests that occurred in towns and cities across the country without warning between late August and early October 2007, and the savage crackdown against protesters eventually authorised by the military regime. Nominally, and initially, these protests were in response to excessive price increases for fuel imposed by the SPDC, but in reality they were the result of longstanding, pent-up frustration on the part of the people with what they generally saw as the hopeless situation of their country and the reckless economic mismanagement of the military. The protests provided the world with unmistakable 'live-to-air' evidence of the extent to which the military had lost the support of the normally submissive population. It also demonstrated the extent to which ordinary people were now willing to express their opposition to the military regime without resorting to violence while knowing the likely cost to their personal liberty. In this volume, chapters by Richard Horsey (Chapter 2) and Win Min (Chapter 3) provide in-depth analyses of these events, and of the attitudes and actions of the military leadership in response to these developments.

The 2007 protests were not isolated events, although they were larger than any protests before or after the nationwide pro-democracy uprising in 1988. They were not just a momentary explosion of pent-up frustration; they reflected the accumulated animosity of the people, and now the Buddhist *Sangha*, towards the economic mismanagement of their military rulers. During the previous two years, new political groups, such as the '88 Generation Students Group, had been increasingly occupying the centre ground of opposition to the military regime, as the National League for Democracy (NLD) slipped into decline with Aung San Suu Kyi's prolonged detention and the continuing campaign of harassment of NLD members by the security forces.

On a political level, lacking any alternative strategy, the SPDC persevered with what it described as its national reconciliation 'road-map'. The National Convention, resuming in May 2004 after being suspended for eight years, concluded in September 2007 after adopting guidelines for a new constitution. A constitutional drafting commission was set up by the SPDC in October 2007, comprising 54 members nominated by the SPDC. These members represented a highly selective cross-section of the population, including several lawyers. It was by no means an 'independent' body and was even less democratic in its membership and processes than the earlier National Convention. In February 2008, before the text of the constitution had even been made public, the SPDC announced that a referendum on the new constitution would be held the next May. When it finally appeared, the text of the constitution ran to 300 pages, but was not made widely available, and voters were expected to endorse it without seeing it.

Free campaigning and debate were not permitted ahead of the referendum, with detention, arrest and incarceration instead for any public opposition to it. This did not stop opposition groups from making their views known and calling for a 'no' vote or, in some cases, a boycott. The vote was initially scheduled for 10 May 2008 and voting in most of the country occurred on that day. In some areas devastated by Cyclone Nargis (which made landfall in the Irrawaddy Delta on 2 May), voting was postponed until 24 May. International condemnation of the military regime ensued when it became clear that the referendum and not immediate and widespread disaster relief was the top priority for the ruling council.[1]

The Myanmar Government refused to allow independent election monitors to witness and verify the voting process, and few international observers (such as journalists or other experts) were present. Not surprisingly, there were widespread and plausible reports of intimidation of voters and of pre-stamped 'yes' votes being handed to voters. It is also alleged that considerable electoral fraud occurred, but this has not been independently confirmed. According to the Myanmar authorities, the final vote resulted in 92.9 per cent support for the constitution from 90 per cent of eligible voters—neither figure being credible nor adding any legitimacy to the process.

The National Convention and the referendum were seen as fundamentally flawed by opposition groups and the international community alike. The SPDC ignored pleas from the UN Secretary-General to make the process more inclusive, by including legally registered leading opposition groups, such as the NLD, the Shan Nationalities League for Democracy and the Karen National Union. The main opposition groups and Western governments dismissed the process as a sham. As the only path towards political change permitted by the military, the SPDC's national reconciliation process is still reluctantly supported (or not actively obstructed) by some Myanmar citizens as being at least a way forward. It is, however, being met by increasingly high levels of cynicism from a population that does not expect any real transfer of power to occur or any improvement in its situation. In view of the widespread and undisguised use of intimidation employed in the conduct of the referendum, however, the SPDC's national reconciliation road-map lacks credibility more than ever before—inside the country and internationally.

As for the constitution, the text contains no surprises and enshrines military control of the State through the head of state, who has the power to dismiss the parliament and appoint the chief justice. Through the military holding 25 per cent of the seats in the parliament, it can block amendment of the constitution, which is, in some ways, the most important power of all. Not surprisingly, the consensus of expert opinion seems to be that the greater formal concentration of authority in the head of state, with no apparent checks or balances on this power, represents a greater predisposition to dictatorial power than any previous Myanmar constitution. While this might reflect a historical pattern for former Myanmar monarchical rulers, it in no sense reflects the greater diversity and democratically inclined attitudes that are increasingly evident in modern Myanmar society, however suppressed they might often be. Indeed, the special status conferred on the military in national and regional assemblies, when the military is neither a pluralistic nor a transparent institution, legitimises a perpetuation of de facto military control of the affairs of state. Concerns focus on the fact that the head of state can be selected only with the support of the military (constituting one-third of the 'electoral college') and that the head of state, once chosen, can then unilaterally declare a state of emergency, suspend the parliament and dismiss the chief justice.

Always a major obsession of the SPDC, internal security remains somewhat fragile but no real threats to the State are evident. After the abolition of the military intelligence organisation in 2004, the regime's political controls under the special branch of the police and Military Affairs Security (MAS) remain tight. In the first few years of the MAS, Myanmar citizens, especially in Yangon, reported less overt pressure from the authorities. This has changed since the 2007 street protests, and the security forces have reverted to knee-jerk arrests and detention whenever any sign of dissent is detected. If anything, the number of political prisoners who have only ever protested peacefully is larger than for many years, even though token releases are occasionally made. More importantly, the regime still stops short of bringing formal charges against its main opponents, Aung San Suu Kyi and leaders of the '88 Generation Students Group, illustrating just how insecure and unsure of its political ground it remains.

It goes without saying that there is little sign of opening up or genuine relaxation of government policies of any kind. Government practice alternates between familiar repression and occasional relaxation, without any clear indication of a strategy for the future. Although it continues a half-hearted relationship with the UN Special Envoy Ibrahim Gambari, its overall relations with the United Nations deteriorated after Cyclone Nargis, when it initially refused and then delayed permission for UN agencies to undertake normal relief efforts. The SPDC's curmudgeonly attitude over these matters has seriously alienated public opinion everywhere: even the Association of South-East Asian Nations (ASEAN) and Myanmar's neighbours felt moved to criticise the regime's unwarranted negative approach to relief. Its own people felt so disgusted that they took to the road themselves to take relief supplies to cyclone victims in the affected areas. How the military authorities envisage managing such challenges under a new political arrangement after the promised 2010 elections is not clear.

Myanmar's economy continues its slow decline, saved only by a few resource projects and only partially regulated exports of raw materials. There is evidence that poverty has increased (World Food Program 2007) and employment prospects remain extremely limited. There are still no signs of badly needed, meaningful economic reforms even though the International Monetary Fund (IMF) continues its consultation processes with the SPDC. The SPDC's tight control and exploitation of all national economic assets, despite a growing private sector, are made more essential as Western financial sanctions curtail trade, tourism and investment levels and significantly complicate the country's international economic transactions. U Myint (Chapter 4) illustrates how erroneous data are used to create a false sense of progress, while Sean Turnell, Alison Vicary and Wylie Bradford (Chapter 5) offer a case study of the informal remittance system as evidence of how the majority of the population has abandoned (and in many cases has never been a part of) the conventional banking system. They argue compellingly that the growth of the remittances system is a direct result of the lack of trust and confidence in the official financial system, which is essentially dysfunctional for these purposes. Denied access to normal multilateral assistance, the SPDC has increasingly been forced to rely on China and other neighbours for investment and trade. In Chapter 6, Toshihiro Kudo explains the impacts of Myanmar's growing economic dependence on China, and how it has been blocked from receiving more beneficial and more sustainable outcomes from international assistance.

While the country still lacks the volume of international assistance going to other least-developed countries, levels of assistance to Myanmar have increased significantly since the European Union and other donors relaxed their approaches to assistance. Concerns are growing about the cumulative effect of years of neglect of Myanmar's education and health sectors. More than 30 per cent of children under five suffer from malnutrition; the HIV/AIDS epidemic has spread from high-risk groups into the general population, affecting at least 1.3 per cent of the adult population and claiming an estimated 37 000 lives in 2005 alone; and morbidity and mortality rates for malaria and tuberculosis remain very high, with incidences of drug resistance rising for both diseases.[2] Life expectancy in Myanmar is lower than most countries in South-East Asia. Clearly, a comprehensive system of public welfare and health care is urgently needed (Duffield 2008). How serious is the crisis affecting the public health system? What are the prospects for improving if not eliminating the main diseases undermining people's health and for a normal healthy lifestyle? Will the military government's 2010 health plan have an effect on the health statistics of the nation? What effect will the 'Three Diseases Fund' have on the statistics?

Although universities have remained open more or less continuously since 2000, and many new institutions of higher education have been set up, the quality of learning and teaching and overall academic standards have declined noticeably. Primary education is beset by problems of poor attendance rates, lack of educational materials, increased costs for parents and poorly trained, unmotivated teachers. Nearly half the school-age children never enrol and about only 30 per cent complete five years of primary education. In addition, there is still considerable discrimination in education against minority groups. Han Tin (Chapter 7) explains how the drive for better education can be a vehicle for change and identifies the frustrations that are leading parents and students to go outside the public system in their quest for quality learning. While he sees advantages in this as far as it adds to the diversity of education, he nevertheless calls for specific international assistance to overcome some of Myanmar's educational deficits. Will restoring ethical values to an important place in the education system bring other badly needed societal improvements, as he claims?

Many Myanmar citizens seeking a decent education still find other countries far more attractive, so the country's 'brain drain' continues. This phenomenon clearly has implications for the nation's education system, as well as for the fostering of the important capacities needed for national development. One visible impact is that many secondary students are moving to alternatives to the government schools (private or monastic education), as the chapters by Marie Lall (Chapter 8) and Jasmin Lorch (Chapter 9) outline. Lall describes a rather chaotic situation as commercially driven schools proliferate, because the state system no longer provides for basic needs. She outlines how this happens with government controls and regulation often quite unclear. Lall demonstrates that while the regime has allowed educational institutions to decay by denying resources to the state education system, this has had the perverse effect of loosening the regime's control over society.

Lorch describes the decline of the state system and attempts by civil-society groups such as the monastic networks to step into the gap. She highlights the capacity shortfalls that persist. She argues that, from the perspective of increased demands imposed on monastic education, the September 2007 uprising can be seen as 'the outcome of an overstrain of community self-help networks to cope with the pervasive failure of the welfare state'. She demonstrates how civil society is emerging where the State is weak or failing for all its authoritarian characteristics, namely in welfare-support institutions and in cease-fire areas generally, but she does not see Myanmar as a unique case. Her chapter also explains how young monks from monastic institutions came to lead the protests in 2007. In areas outside the formal system, however, such as extra tuition, early childhood development, specialised community-based schools and Christian seminaries, Lorch describes a highly confused situation as communities struggle to bridge gaps. Surprisingly, this confusion extends into the policy and regulatory frameworks that govern the operation of non-government education, where an unexpected degree of tolerance of different approaches exists alongside considerable uncertainty. In Lorch's words, 'The rigidity of the regime's educational policies certainly does not reflect the [blurred] reality on the ground.'

A consistent theme across the non-government education system is the strong push for access to international education and international recognition of qualifications. This is, of course, one of the major deficiencies in the current state-run system. The same pressure is evident in Mohammed Moyuddin Mohammed Sulaimon's chapter (10) on Islamic education, which presents a comprehensive picture of that little-known sector. He also shows how little effort is being made to allow Muslims to find a meaningful role in Myanmar society without seeking higher educational qualifications overseas. Madrasah learning seems to exist in isolation of any practical goals it could achieve either for its students or for Myanmar society. He claims that the Myanmar regime 'has never made any serious attempt either to reform madrasahs or to incorporate them into the mainstream of the present national education system', despite their constant security concerns about Muslims. Somewhat surprisingly, he paints a regulatory picture of considerable disarray and asserts that there are 'no clear-cut rules and regulations as to what a madrasah could do or not do'.

Monique Skidmore (Chapter 11) portrays a confusing array of health options available as many of the population seek alternatives to the over-stretched public health system. She highlights the ethical dilemmas faced by international donors obliged to work with an omnipresent, but often ineffectual government apparatus that deals out retribution rather than effective health services. Even before the advent of Cyclone Nargis in May 2008, Skidmore drew attention to the comprehensive inadequacy of the government's emergency health mechanisms. She points out how, as with education, affordability is limiting access to a great deal of health care and placing it beyond the reach of ordinary people. Worse, she catalogues the lack of trauma and psychological care, and makes a case that massive abuses against humanity are occurring through the deliberate withholding of health care.

Mahn Mahn and his colleagues Katherine C. Teela, Catherine I. Lee and Cara O'Connor (Chapter 12) provide empirical evidence of the widespread adverse impact on health-service delivery of chronic insurgency, authoritarian administration, increased militarisation and the abuse of human rights in Myanmar's eastern border area with Thailand. The Back Pack Health Workers' Team represents a significant alternative approach, based on grassroots operations working to a clear and effective strategy, but without any government direction or regulation. In other words, it is an approach that succeeded in a situation in which a central government role was entirely absent. Of course, the backpack system exists alongside the chaos of the country's continuing civil war.

These were among the main themes covered in the 2007 Myanmar/Burma Update conference. The chapters in this publication provide an analysis of recent developments and some examine more closely the policy implications of these developments. One striking feature of the conference was the parallel phenomena of a population increasingly opting out of participation in government-backed services. Just as people have abandoned the banking system, preferring informal mechanisms, they have been observed leaving the public education and public health sectors in favour of more reliable alternatives. This does not foreshadow the disappearance of 'the State' by any means, but it represents the spread of alternatives that are generally less susceptible to state control and orthodoxy.

The final significant development is the clearly demonstrated inability of the military regime to control media coverage of unfavourable events inside the country. This is occurring even though no foreign journalists are permanently stationed inside the country, and journalists based in neighbouring countries are refused visas to cover events such as the 2007 demonstrations or Cyclone Nargis. The phenomenon of 'citizen journalists' using mobile-phone and web-based technologies (such as 'twitting' and 'blogging') brought Myanmar citizens and international audiences some of the most frightening and inspiring images of the 2007 popular street protests. The image of detained NLD leader, Aung San Suu Kyi, appearing from her compound to greet protesting monks who had marched to her house shows the power of political persuasion that ordinary Myanmar citizens can create through their use of these outlawed technologies. Who can predict where these trends might lead? As we have seen in other countries, such transforming technologies can be immensely valuable for desperate and frustrated citizens determined to oppose excessive and inhuman authoritarian controls.

While we can expect the years 2009–10 to bring significant political developments in Myanmar at a superficial level, it is by no means clear that these will bring any substantive change. Most observers doubt that this so-called 'reconciliation' will achieve any satisfactory accommodation between the regime and its opponents, with protests and other forms of resistance inevitably continuing. The appointment of a minister for relations with the NLD could have presaged a new approach, but the complete inactivity in this role by Major-General Aung Kyi suggests that in reality the military leadership has no intention of engaging directly with the NLD, or for that matter with any of the other opposition groups. The refusal of Aung San Suu Kyi to meet with the UN Special Envoy in August 2008 shows the lack of credibility the reconciliation process has for the main opposition party. There continues to be almost no political 'space', and virtually no meaningful or credible public space or process, within which differing views might be tolerated by the authorities or some form of political negotiations attempted.

What kind of accommodation can be forged between the military leadership, cease-fire groups and non-military elements, as is now being advocated in some quarters? Can some continuing relationship be formed that acknowledges the reality of the military's intention to continue to control the country, while allowing greater freedom for individuals to improve their socioeconomic conditions? With the continued inability of the United Nations to play a meaningful reconciliation role, can the international community have any influence over the Myanmar authorities and, more importantly, can any alternative way emerge from inside the country? Although the new constitution (on paper) provides for something close to a federal system, with regional assemblies deciding local matters—which would appeal to many of the cease-fire groups such as the Wa, the Kokang, the Mon and the Kachin—unparalleled scepticism prevails about whether the military will really allow the regional dispersal of real power in this way. If it does not, tensions between the SPDC and minority populations will continue and could escalate, as expectations for genuine power sharing on the part of cease-fire groups are unfulfilled.

Finally, there is little or no evidence of long overdue policy reforms for the economy being foreshadowed. In critical sectors such as health and education, as increasing numbers of citizens flee the state-run systems, state capabilities and policies are becoming increasingly irrelevant. As young Burmese leave the country in growing numbers because of the lack of career or professional opportunities, or alternatively turn to working with international non-governmental organisations (NGOs), state institutions and mechanisms are again being marginalised. As long as these alternatives to state institutions remain, even if they are not palatable to all, any incentives or pressures at work to reform failing state institutions will continue to diminish, making true reform all that more difficult to achieve, especially in the absence of effective international pressure for such reforms. The comprehensive failure of the State, however, and therefore its abandonment by a justifiably cynical population cannot be ignored indefinitely. Moreover, the increasing poverty and depressing lack of economic and social opportunities for its citizens are sources of concern even for Myanmar's neighbours. Fundamental to the task of creating a better life for the people and the country is political reform that should be enshrined in the constitution. Unfortunately, the continued ineffectiveness of the United Nations and the international community to press for change, and the continuing repression of all peaceful protest within the country, mean that there continues to be no progress in efforts to improve the lives of Myanmar people.

References

Duffield, M. 2008, *On the edge of 'no man's land': chronic emergency in Myanmar*, Working Paper No. 01-08, Centre for Governance and International Affairs, University of Bristol.

Safman, Rachel 2007, Presentation, 2007 Myanmar/Burma Update Conference, Canberra.

World Food Program 2007, Press release, 18 October 2007, <www.wfp/English>

Endnotes

[1] The SPDC eventually yielded to some of the demands of the international community for better access as a trade-off for increased assistance, but the international community committed little such assistance. See the Post-Nargis Joint Assessment (<www.asean.org/21765>), which, 'in addition to being the first post-disaster assessment to be led by a regional organization, is also the first assessment to attempt to provide an integrated and sequenced approach to humanitarian, including relief and early recovery, and medium and long term recovery needs, closely focused on providing direct assistance to families and communities.'

[2] For comprehensive health-indicator data, see the World Health Organisation web site (<www.who.org/int/eng>), although some figures are dated. For recent data on HIV/AIDS, see Safman (2007).

Political Update

2: The dramatic events of 2007 in Myanmar: domestic and international implications[1]

Richard Horsey

Introduction

In the second half of September 2007, events in Myanmar exploded onto television screens around the world. The pictures—first showing ordered columns of orange-robed monks marching through the streets of Yangon, then showing the brutal response by security forces—generated surprise and shock. The events took place while the UN General Assembly was meeting in New York, amplifying their international political impact.

No-one seemed to have anticipated the sudden involvement of the monks or the speed with which the demonstrations gathered pace. In particular, the regime itself appeared to be taken by surprise. Then, once the demonstrations had been effectively put down, there was a sense that this was a watershed moment, and that the situation in Myanmar could never be quite the same. In the words of the Special Adviser to the UN Secretary-General, Professor Ibrahim Gambari, 'a return to the *status quo ante* is unsustainable'.[2]

In part one, this chapter explores the origin of the demonstrations, in particular the fuel-price protests of August 2007, in an attempt to understand the events that ultimately led to the large-scale demonstrations in September. It investigates why it was that the recent increase in fuel costs gave rise to persistent (if small-scale) demonstrations, when even sharper fuel-price increases in 2005 prompted no public reaction.

In part two, the chapter looks at how the September demonstrations by the monks evolved, and at the nature of the response of the security forces. It discusses the reasons why the monks took to the streets in such large numbers and the domestic impact of the regime's violent response. It then discusses whether a return to the *status quo ante* is inconceivable, and whether it would indeed be unsustainable.

The fuel-price protests of August 2007

On 15 August 2007, the Myanmar authorities significantly increased the retail price of fuel by up to 500 per cent. The extent of the price increases, compounded by the fact that no advance warning was given, resulted in a significant shock to livelihoods. This in turn led to rare expressions of dissent and acts of civil disobedience on the part of the population. This section looks at Myanmar's fuel policy, and explores the reasons why the regime felt confident in instituting such sharp, unannounced price increases. It also explores the evolving nature of political opposition in Myanmar, which can help shed some light on the reasons why the regime might have been taken by surprise by the public reaction to the price rises.

Myanmar fuel policy

Like a number of other developing countries, Myanmar has a tradition of heavily subsidising fuel prices. In 2004, before the current series of price increases, retail fuel prices in Myanmar were the cheapest in the region (and among the cheapest in the world), at US4 cents a litre for diesel and 4.4¢ for petrol. To give some idea of the extent of subsidisation implied by such prices, consider that this was less than one-sixth of the cost of unrefined crude oil on international markets at that time.[3] Such prices are all the more striking given that Myanmar has very limited domestic refining capacity and thus has to import refined fuel products.

In comparison, during the same period, retail fuel prices in Thailand (which also had small fuel subsidies) were 37¢ a litre for diesel and 54¢ a litre for petrol. Even in Indonesia, which at the time was heavily subsidising fuel, the prices were 18¢ a litre for diesel and 27¢ a litre for petrol (Metschies 2005).

The role of the black market

In 1980, Myanmar introduced a rationing system, with a limit of 60 gallons (273 litres) per vehicle per month. This immediately created a black market for fuel, with vehicle owners selling their excess to brokers, who sold it in turn to taxi drivers and others who exceeded their quotas, or in some cases smuggled it to neighbouring countries. By 2005, the black-market price had reached 67¢ a litre for diesel and 44¢ a litre for petrol. A number of private-sector bus lines began to convert their engines to run on cheaper compressed natural gas, with the encouragement of the authorities.

Given the large fiscal deficits Myanmar was running, it is hardly surprising that successive World Bank and International Monetary Fund (IMF) missions recommended that fuel and other subsidies be reduced and in due course eliminated. By 2005, with increasingly high world oil prices and a continued depreciation in the market value of the kyat against the dollar, the high level of fuel subsidies had become impossible for the Myanmar authorities to sustain.

The October 2005 price rises

On 20 October 2005, the government dramatically increased fuel prices. Diesel prices rose from 160 to 1500 kyat per imperial gallon (from 2.8 to 26¢ a litre) and petrol prices from 180 to 1500 kyat (from 3.2 to 26¢ a litre). This represented an increase of more than 900 per cent in the price of diesel, the main fuel used for the transport of goods to market and for the ubiquitous small electric generators.

The result was that private bus lines immediately quadrupled their fares, taxi charges doubled and the fares on state-run buses increased sixfold. The knock-on effects of increased fuel costs were reflected in the prices of basic commodities, which jumped 10 to 20 per cent within a week (probably in part as a result of stockpiling by consumers and speculation by traders). Prices then continued to rise gradually as the effects of higher fuel costs filtered through.

The Myanmar authorities made no attempt to prepare the ground for the increase in fuel prices and issued no public statements in advance. Public information was limited to small notices pasted on the pumps at official government outlets on the day before the price increases took effect. The contrast with expert recommendations on how such price rises should be implemented is obvious but nonetheless striking:

> Fuel policies that are rational in the long run may meet emotional opposition when they are implemented at short notice…Therefore careful strategic planning is needed. The reaction of target groups must be considered and financial and economic arguments have to be prepared as part of public awareness campaigns in the mass media…Fuel price increases should never exceed 10 per cent of the pump price at any time in real terms. (Metschies 2005:82)

Such price increases were all the more bold given the events in Indonesia earlier that month. Barely three weeks before, in a move that had been voted through parliament and explained to the public in advance, Indonesia introduced a cap on government spending for fuel subsidies, causing retail fuel prices to rise by (a comparatively modest) 120 per cent. This sparked a wave of angry demonstrations across the country.

Given what had just happened in Indonesia (and the fact that fuel-price increases had been the spark for the 1998 riots that led to the overthrow of the Suharto regime), such sharp and essentially unannounced price increases suggested either a failure on the part of the Myanmar authorities to consider the implications of such a move, or an extreme level of confidence in their ability to control popular unrest. While the ad hoc and sometimes bizarre nature of economic decision making in Myanmar makes it possible to believe that the decision to raise fuel prices was taken without any thought being given to the socioeconomic impact, the security obsession of the regime makes it harder to contemplate that the security implications would not have been considered. This suggests that the regime was extremely confident in its ability to keep a lid on any unrest. Indeed, despite their immediate and significant impacts on transport costs and commodity prices, the 2005 fuel-price increases prompted no public reaction at all.

Why a different reaction this time?

On 15 August 2007, diesel prices were increased from 1500 to 3000 kyat per imperial gallon (from 25 to 51¢ a litre) and petrol prices from 1500 to 2500 kyat (from 25 to 42¢ a litre). In addition, prices for compressed natural gas, increasingly used by buses and taxis as well as for cooking, were increased by 500 per cent.

The absence of any public protest in October 2005 would have reinforced the regime's belief that it was in firm control of the situation, and could explain why it felt confident about repeating the step, this time with no advance public information of any kind.[4] Although the impact of the price rises was very similar this time—an immediate, sharp increase in public transport costs and a (fairly small) spike in the price of some basic commodities—the public reaction was very different. In order to understand why, it is necessary to examine what has changed in the intervening two years. Two key factors can be identified.

The first factor is economic. Across Myanmar, impoverishment is increasing, with ever-larger proportions of the population unable to meet their basic needs. In the past several years, wages have failed to keep pace with high inflation. The huge increase in the price of fuel in October 2005 certainly contributed to this. On 1 April 2006, the government dramatically increased salaries for public-sector employees, by up to 1000 per cent. While this move—undoubtedly financed in part by the earlier reduction in fuel subsidies—reversed years of gradual erosion in the real value of government salaries, it was itself highly inflationary. The worst hit were the poorest segments of the population, such as day labourers, who did not benefit from the government salary hike and who were in a weak position to demand higher wages. This same group was the most seriously and quickly affected by the second round of fuel-price increases in August 2007, given that they lived in the poorer townships on the outskirts of Yangon and therefore had to travel relatively long distances to work,[5] and because, as daily wage earners, they spent a large proportion of their income on basic commodities (rice, cooking oil), which they often purchased daily.

The second factor is political. The house arrest of Daw Aung San Suu Kyi since 2003, and her inability to meet or even communicate with the National League for Democracy (NLD), has been a significant blow to the party. The NLD Central Executive Committee has become increasingly cautious and politically reactive (to the frustration of many rank-and-file party members), issuing statements but avoiding political mobilisation and action. This vacuum has been gradually filled by the emergence of two new kinds of political actor.

- **The 'social activists'**: individuals or small groups who, since 2006, have been airing grievances about high prices and the socioeconomic situation more generally, but who have deliberately avoided more political issues such as governance or the release of Daw Aung San Suu Kyi. They have staged public demonstrations, but until now the regime has been reluctant to crack down hard, perhaps fearful of sparking wider unrest.[6] One group of social activists formed the Myanmar Development Committee in early 2007.

- **The '88 Generation Students Group:** these former student activists were released from jail in late 2004. Initially careful to avoid rearrest, they maintained a relatively low profile and concentrated on re-establishing contacts and acquainting themselves with the current situation in the country (several had been in solitary confinement for more than 15 years). It was only in August 2006 that they formally established the '88 Generation Students Group, and it was the subsequent arrest of several of its key leaders that prompted the network to embark on a series of protest campaigns, first for the release of the leaders (which was obtained in January 2007) and then on a range of social issues with the aim to 'give people access to political actions'.[7]

The fuel-price increases in October 2005 came at a time when neither of these elements had fully emerged. By August 2007, however, both groups were mobilised and had been testing these issues, and so were well placed to quickly give public voice to popular discontent about the price increases.

On the Sunday after the price increases, several dozen people, including prominent '88 Generation leaders, marched through downtown Yangon in protest. Two days later, as small sporadic protests continued, the '88 Generation leaders and a number of other prominent activists were arrested. During the week, more than 100 people were taken into custody.[8] There were indications that these arrests were more than a temporary measure to take the steam out of the protests. First, the number and range of people arrested were indicative of a broader crackdown. Second, the security forces searched the residences of those who were arrested, seizing documents and computers, presumably to be used as evidence in building a legal case against them. (State media published detailed allegations against the '88 Generation leaders the next day in an effort to justify the arrests.)

Despite the many arrests, including almost the entire leadership of the '88 Generation Students Group,[9] demonstrations continued through the next week, which were reported heavily internationally. The reality on the ground was much less dramatic than the impression conveyed by the media; the demonstrations were rather small and did not appear to be particularly broad based (with bystanders generally sympathetic, but not participating actively). The government responded to these demonstrations not by deploying the riot police (Lone Htein) or the army, but with Swan Arr Shin—a militia comprising mainly hired civilians (some reportedly released convicts), apparently under the control of the regime's mass organisation, the Union Solidarity and Development Association (USDA).

Although the demonstrations were very persistent, by the end of August it appeared that they were losing momentum. The protest leaders were unable to galvanise broader public participation behind their demonstrations and the authorities continued deploying civilian militias (the Swan Arr Shin) to quickly break up any gatherings of activists. What happened next was unexpected.

The events of September 2007 and their impact

The events of September 2007

On 5 September, a street demonstration took place in the town of Pakokku (south-west of Mandalay). This demonstration was not particularly different from any of the protest marches that had been taking place in recent weeks, although it was fairly large and several hundred monks from a local monastery joined in. The authorities responded in the usual way, by deploying the security forces as well as Swan Arr Shin militia to break up the demonstration. A number of live rounds were fired over the heads of the monks and members of the militia and the security forces then severely beat a number of monks, some of whom were first tied up. Rumours circulated that one of the monks had subsequently died, but this was never confirmed.

The location was significant: Pakokku is a major centre of Buddhism in Myanmar, with several large teaching monasteries that produce theological leaders who are known to espouse strong views on the rights and responsibilities of the Buddhist clergy. The next day, a group of senior local officials visited the monastery (to apologise and to request that the monks refrain from further demonstrations). They were taken hostage by the monks for several hours and their vehicles set on fire, before eventually being released. Later, a number of monks reportedly ransacked a shop and a house owned by Swan Arr Shin members. The situation had clearly escalated significantly.

On 9 September, a newly established group called the All Burma Monks' Alliance issued a statement presenting four demands to the authorities: that they apologise for the Pakokku incident; reduce commodity and fuel prices; release all political prisoners, including Daw Aung San Suu Kyi and those detained for the recent protests; and enter into a dialogue with democratic groups with a view to achieving national reconciliation and resolving the suffering of the people.[10] The statement indicated that the authorities had until 17 September to comply with these demands or face a religious boycott. This choice of deadline was politically symbolic, as 18 September is the anniversary of the 1988 coup that brought the current military regime to power.

The deadline passed and monks began taking to the streets of cities and towns in Myanmar in protest. On 18 September, some 300 monks gathered at the southern stairway of Shwedagon Pagoda in Yangon. They found their way blocked by plain-clothes 'security' personnel. The authorities were probably concerned about the symbolism of a demonstration on the prayer platform of Myanmar's most revered Buddhist shrine, a historical focus of dissent; they were also no doubt aware of the intention of some of the monks to perform a religious ceremony declaring an alms boycott of the military. The monks marched instead to the downtown Sule Pagoda, then to Botahtaung Pagoda, gathering several hundred lay followers as they went.

Similar marches were held on subsequent days, gaining momentum every day despite torrential monsoon rains. One monk at the front of the procession held an upturned alms bowl—a symbol of religious boycott. There was no visible uniformed security presence, although plain-clothes personnel photographed and videoed the marchers. On the weekend of 22–23 September, however, the nature of the demonstrations shifted, becoming much larger in scale and more overtly political, thus posing a level of challenge to the regime that it must have found impossible to ignore. A highly symbolic moment in this regard occurred on 22 September, when a group of protesting monks was permitted to pass a police checkpoint and approach the house of Daw Aung San Suu Kyi, who briefly appeared at her gate to pay her respects.

By 24 September, the demonstrations in Yangon involved up to 100 000 people, led by tens of thousands of monks. The general population was becoming more defiant, increasingly taking part in the demonstrations rather than watching the monks or escorting them. Students, prominent political actors (from the NLD, the opposition Committee Representing the People's Parliament or CRPP and ethnic political parties) and well-known personalities (actors, artists, writers) were joining the demonstrations, in some cases carrying red 'fighting peacock' flags, a traditional symbol of political resistance in Myanmar.

That evening, the authorities issued their first reaction to these events, announcing on television that further demonstrations would not be tolerated and that action would be taken 'according to the law'.[11] This warning, and similar warnings announced subsequently by speaker-trucks, failed to curb the demonstrations and, the next day, tens of thousands of people again took to the streets in protest. On the evening of 25 September, the authorities announced a night-time curfew and, by the next morning, had positioned truck-loads of armed riot police and troops at key locations in Yangon, including at a number of monasteries, which they sealed off in order to prevent other monks from joining the demonstrations. Monks and civilians nevertheless continued to gather in large numbers on 26 September and the authorities used violence for the first time (smoke grenades and baton charges, followed by use of rubber bullets and live rounds)[12] in an attempt to prevent the demonstrations continuing, and in tense confrontations with local people at monasteries. There were many arrests, numerous injuries (including of monks and nuns) and several reported fatalities.

That night, troops stormed and occupied a number of prominent monasteries, beating and arresting a large number of monks.

It is important to note the rapid escalation in the response of the authorities, from baton charges to the use of rubber bullets and live rounds. It was in essence a military response, with the clear aim of removing opposition from the streets, as opposed to a policing response (the aim of which would be to maintain law and order while ensuring public safety and minimising loss of life). The authorities have claimed that they exercised 'maximum restraint'; while this is clearly not the case, it is true that the death toll could have been much higher.

On 27 September, despite a heavy presence of the security forces and the use of lethal force the previous day, the demonstrations continued in Yangon. There participation by monks was smaller, no doubt due in part to the large number of arrests and the continuing security presence at monasteries. The security forces responded to the continuing demonstrations with further violence, with the army now playing a more prominent role. State media acknowledged that evening that nine demonstrators had been killed, including a Japanese photojournalist, although many observers were suggesting that the real figure was several times higher.

That night, further raids on monasteries were reported and the surrounding areas were declared no-go zones. There were also raids on a number of residential areas and many arrests were reported. The next day, the demonstrations had become much smaller and were quickly broken up by security forces, with several further fatalities reported and a large number of arrests. The main public Internet link to Myanmar was apparently closed down, which significantly reduced the flow of media information coming from the country.[13]

By 1 October, the heavy security presence in Yangon had succeeded in preventing any significant demonstrations from continuing. Under cover of the night-time curfew, security forces continued to conduct large-scale raids on residential neighbourhoods, searching for protest leaders who were on the run and arresting thousands of people suspected of participating in demonstrations or merely showing support to the demonstrators. These detainees were held in makeshift detention centres in several locations in Yangon, which were overcrowded and lacking in sanitation facilities. Based on information from those who were subsequently released, it appears that detainees were interrogated and then classified into different categories (those who were active in the demonstrations, those who participated in the demonstrations and those who displayed support or sympathy for the demonstrators). Those considered to have played a relatively minor role were registered and then released (among these were many people who had never been involved in political activities and were not part of any political or activist networks). As this phase of mass detentions came to an end, the curfew was shortened and then lifted altogether on 20 October.

The significance of the involvement of Buddhist clergy

It was the incident at Pakokku on 5 September, and the subsequent lack of an apology for the actions of the security forces, that galvanised the monks into action. Beyond these perceived insults to Buddhism, however, the monks had more fundamental and longstanding grievances.

Monasteries form the only social safety net that exists for most communities in the country. As such, monasteries have been feeling the direct impact of accelerating impoverishment. As the communities they serve have become poorer, donations to the monasteries have declined.[14] At the same time, the demands on the social services they provide have increased—whether it is primary schooling, care for orphans, palliative care for AIDS patients or providing meals for the destitute. This has placed an impossible burden on monasteries, depleting their reserves and in many cases reducing monks to one meal a day, according to reliable sources in Yangon.

It was this situation that led a number of monks to join in some of the demonstrations that followed the fuel-price increases in August 2007. Although the statements of the All Burma Monks' Alliance were explicitly political from the outset, the majority of monks went to some lengths to show that their purpose in taking to the streets was to express the socioeconomic hardships that they and the people were facing, rather than the pursuit of any political agenda. During the first days of the monks' demonstrations in Yangon after 18 September, therefore, the lay population was requested to keep separate from the demonstrations and not to chant political slogans. In addition to reinforcing the message to the authorities that the monks' actions stemmed from genuine social and religious grievances, this was important to ensure the broadest possible participation of monks, including the apolitical and more conservative elements.

Note that, in this context, after the third day of demonstrations in Yangon, on 20 September the monks had announced that there would be a break in the demonstrations, which would continue each Sabbath.[15] This move was possibly aimed at avoiding confrontation with the authorities and providing space for some accommodation to be reached, and apparently reflected the counsel of some senior abbots. Monks congregated again, however, at Shwedagon Pagoda on 21 September, and the demonstrations continued, with a group of young activist monks gradually assuming a leadership role on the streets. The size of the demonstrations continued to grow, with the increasing involvement of students, political parties, civil-society groups and the general population; they also began to take on a more overtly political character.[16]

With the 17 September deadline announced after the Pakokku incident, the monks also proclaimed a religious boycott, known as the 'overturning of the alms bowl' ('*pattam nikkujjana kamma*' in Pali). This is the ultimate act of disapproval provided for in the Buddhist canon, and it permitted the monkhood (or, at least, those monks who aligned themselves with the boycott) to refuse all contact with military families, thus denying them access to religious services and merit-making opportunities. This had a powerful impact because of Myanmar's devoutly Buddhist culture. (A previous alms boycott of the military occurred in Mandalay in 1990.)[17]

The scale of the demonstrations and the leadership role of the monks took everyone by surprise. A number of exiled political groups have at various points suggested that they were involved in instigating these events (claims that have been echoed by the official Myanmar media). While there were undoubtedly many contacts between those involved in the events and dissidents overseas—demonstrated, for example, by the timely, detailed and generally accurate coverage of the events in the exiled media—it seems clear that the demonstrations were domestic in origin, and grew organically.

Domestic implications

The use of violence against monks can have profound domestic implications. The events generated a great deal of anger against the leadership and the regime as a whole, and further damaged the institutional reputation of the army. It should be noted, however, that the use of violence against monks is not unprecedented. In 1988, a number of monks were killed on the streets and many were arrested. In 1990, the authorities responded violently to the announcement of an alms boycott in Mandalay (which had been prompted by the failure of the military to hand over power to the winners of the elections held that year); many monasteries were raided and hundreds of monks arrested. There is, however, a crucial difference between those events and the recent crackdown. In the previous cases, it was easier for the authorities to justify their actions as being directed not at Buddhist monks *per se*, but at radical elements who had violated the Buddhist disciplinary code by entering the political realm ('bogus monks', in the regime's parlance). While hardly convincing to most, such an explanation does have a certain resonance with conservative abbots and laity, who believe that monks should be completely disconnected from worldly affairs. In the present case, not only was the level of violence and insult against monks and monasteries particularly shocking, the essential grievances expressed by the monks were non-political and widely shared.

Another important factor is that the recent events themselves represent a significant socioeconomic shock. Many businesses had to close their doors for days and it took some time for commerce to begin slowly picking up. The events all but shut down tourism at the start of the peak season. This had a significant impact on the large number of people who rely on the industry for income, which resulted in a knock-on effect for the economy as a whole. The economic conditions—a significant factor underlying the recent protests—therefore underwent a further decline in the months after the protests. The business elite, many of whom were closely associated with the military leadership, were doubly hit: first, by the impact of the events themselves on key sectors such as tourism; and second, by the increasing difficulties in conducting international financial transactions as a result of US financial sanctions (as well as more informal US pressure on banks, particularly in Singapore, not to provide services to Myanmar's military and business elite).

The regime, which was already deeply unpopular, therefore risked alienating two very important groups of people: conservative social and religious elites, and the business community. Taken together with the anger and fear felt by large sections of the population, the events therefore created a potentially much more challenging domestic environment for the regime. At the same time, the regime faced a more difficult international environment.

The impact on the regime's political program

The country has been left traumatised by recent events. People are angry about the violent response to the demonstrations and the failure of the authorities to acknowledge the grievances of the population, but more than anything they are angry about the brutal treatment of the monks. In addition, the use of violence together with the subsequent campaign of mass arrests created a climate of fear in the country.

What happens next will depend in part on the interplay between these dominant emotions of anger and fear. The authorities are maintaining a significant, if largely hidden, military presence in Yangon. This security presence, and the fear among the population, makes it unlikely that there will be any major public demonstrations in the short term. The underlying grievances, however, compounded by anger about recent events, have not gone away. (Indeed, if people see no hope for the future, and no prospect of bringing about change through peaceful means, there is the disturbing prospect that extremist elements could start to emerge for the first time and pursue a more radical and violent agenda.)

There has been speculation that recent events have created tensions or divisions within the regime. There are no clear indications of this being the case, and it appears that, as in the past, the perceived threats have tended to make the regime more cohesive rather than amplifying divisions.[18] The limited reshuffle of the State Peace and Development Council (SPDC) and cabinet after the death of Prime Minister Soe Win in October 2007 provides some insight in this regard. Lieutenant-General Thein Sein, who was acting Prime Minister during Soe Win's illness earlier in the year, was confirmed in the position and promoted to full (four-star) general. He is known to be close to Than Shwe. Another longstanding SPDC member, Lieutenant-General Thiha Thura Tin Aung Myint Oo (the Quartermaster-General), replaced Thein Sein in the important position of

Secretary Number One. In the cabinet, the only change was the appointment of Major-General Aung Kyi as Minister for Relations with Daw Aung San Suu Kyi and also as Minister for Labour (he was formerly the Deputy Minister). This confirmed that the hardline former Minister for Labour, U Thaung, had been sidelined.[19] In addition, the commanders of Light Infantry Divisions 77 and 33 were appointed to deputy ministerial portfolios.[20] Given that these were the two divisions initially deployed to Yangon and Mandalay to put down the protests, there could be some truth in rumours that the transfer of these two commanders to civilian positions was punishment for failing to follow orders to use force against the protesting monks, although, as always, it is difficult to know for sure.

Given that the changes have so far been limited, despite the fact that a reshuffle of regional commanders and cabinet posts is long overdue, it appears that there has been no major immediate fallout from the events of September 2007. If there had been significant internal opposition to the crackdown within the regime, a purge would have been expected; if the events had significantly altered the balance of power among the leadership, moves to consolidate this might have been expected, particularly at the key regional commander level.

The political landscape of Myanmar for the past several years has been defined by two parallel transitions: a generational transition in the leadership and a political transition in the form of the seven-step road-map. In looking at the impact of recent events, it is important to assess their impact on each of these transition processes. It is also critical to recognise that these transitions are not merely proceeding in parallel; rather, they are critically interlinked.

To understand why, it is necessary to recall that in post-independence Myanmar there has never been an orderly transfer of power. Rather, in each case there has been some form of coup accompanied by a purge of officers and businessmen associated with the former leaders. In this context, the current leaders will feel comfortable to transfer power to the next generation only if they are confident that their legacy and personal interests will continue to be respected after their departure. Achieving this is the main aim of the road-map, since it cements the legacy of the current leaders (and itself represents a key part of that legacy) and provides a framework for the predictable transfer of power to a chosen successor. (The recent top-level appointments of prime minister and secretary-one have been of trusted people within the current generation of leaders, rather than the elevation of younger officers, and are not therefore part of any generational transition; Thein Sein, at 62, for example, is older than the previous prime minister.)

What, then, is the impact of recent events on this picture? As discussed above, the information currently available suggests that these events have not fundamentally altered the balance of power within the regime, nor have they forced any fundamental reassessment of the political way forward. In the eyes of the regime, the process of change that they have defined is the only conceivable one. The impact of recent events will have been to complicate the process of moving ahead with the dual transitions while at the same time reinforcing to the leadership the urgency of doing so. This means that their focus will be on removing the obstacles (new and old) to implementing the transitions—not in their view a return to the *status quo ante*, since the situation *ante* was not for them *status quo*, but transitional. Such a focus requires them to project an image of strength and unity, and it is in this light that their response to recent initiatives by the international community should be seen.

The forthcoming constitution

The new constitution is the linchpin in the seven-step road-map and it is therefore unlikely that the regime will be willing to revisit the outcome of the National Convention. The 54-person constitutional drafting commission, comprising historians, linguists and jurists, gives some indication of this: it has the sort of composition well suited to detailed debate about the finer points of constitutional lexicography, rather than matters of content. One of the obvious obstacles created by recent events, however, relates to the referendum on this new constitution. Clearly, in the current situation, the regime is unlikely to gain major support at a constitutional referendum and its vehicle for grassroots mobilisation, the Union Solidarity and Development Association (USDA), has been damaged by its role in putting down the demonstrations. No doubt a positive referendum result could still be arranged, but its credibility, domestically and internationally, would be limited.

Socioeconomic issues

Since the demonstrations, the regime has been particularly sensitive to any discussion of socioeconomic issues, rejecting the proposal made by Professor Gambari for a poverty-alleviation commission to be formed. The above analysis can shed some light on this. It was perhaps reasonable to expect that the regime would be more open to a technical discussion on the socioeconomic improvements called for by the monks than a discussion of the demands for reconciliation and political reform. In fact, the opposite appears to be the case.

It could be that socioeconomic reform is threatening to the regime for the same reason that observers see it as so crucial: it can create pressures for change in ways that are unpredictable and difficult to control. More specifically, straightening out some of the distortions in the economy makes good economic sense, but it makes little political sense for the leadership, given that it relies precisely on these distortions to derive income for its members and their cronies, which is crucial to maintaining their patronage networks.

The reluctance to engage in discussions on socioeconomic reform could also have to do with the way in which the regime perceives itself. The military is convinced that it is the only institution capable of the decisive leadership necessary to keep the country together and strong (this view has become self-fulfilling to the extent that other institutions—such as parliament, the judiciary and the civil service—have been dismantled or weakened with decades of military rule). It follows that for them any problems are attributable not to military rule, but to the obstacles preventing the military from implementing its vision—that is, domestic political opposition, ethnic conflict, international opposition and sanctions. A poverty-alleviation commission would risk opening a discussion of the military's inherent lack of capacity to run the economy. Their response to this proposal—saying that what is needed is the lifting of sanctions—focuses precisely on external constraints rather than inherent weaknesses. This could also explain why the authorities reacted so strongly to the UN Country Team's statement about the socioeconomic aspect of the demonstrations, declaring the United Nation's Resident and Humanitarian Coordinator *persona non grata*.

Dialogue with Daw Aung San Suu Kyi

The somewhat unexpected willingness of the authorities to begin (again) a process of dialogue with Daw Aung San Suu Kyi should perhaps also be interpreted in a similar light. The regime feels relatively more comfortable engaging in a political dialogue with Daw Aung San Suu Kyi than dealing with socioeconomic issues; they have experience of doing this in the past and are confident that they can keep tight control on the process. We should, however, be cautious in interpreting their willingness to enter into this process as a sign that they are ready to compromise on key aspects of their political program. Rather, all the signals are that they see her as a major obstacle domestically and internationally to the implementation of that political program and are trying to explore the extent to which that obstacle can be reduced or removed. (They could also hope that such a process will buy them time, particularly domestically; this could be why they have given fairly extensive coverage in state media to the meetings that Daw Aung San Suu Kyi has had.) This analysis does not give grounds for much optimism.

To conclude, then: is a return to the *status quo ante* inconceivable, and what would be the prospects of the regime achieving it? If by the *status quo ante* we mean the regime's political program—the seven-step road-map and a changing of the guard at the top—the above considerations suggest that it is anything but inconceivable. The regime is certainly trying hard to give the impression that it is strong and united and will be able to achieve its aims. The extent and depth of anger in the country must, however, raise a serious question mark over their prospects for success in the medium term.

References

Houtman, Gustaaf 1999, 'Mental culture in Burmese crisis politics', *Monograph Series*, vol. 33, Institute for the Study of Languages and Cultures of Asia and Africa.

International Herald Tribune 2007, 'Myanmar official defends fuel price hikes that sparked protests', *International Herald Tribune*, 26 August 2007.

Metschies, G. P. 2005, *International Fuel Prices*, Fourth edition.

New Light of Myanmar, 8 November 2007, p. 1.

Endnotes

[1] This chapter is based in part on two briefing papers written for the Conflict Prevention and Peace Forum (*The implications of the fuel-price protests in Myanmar*, 18 September 2007; and *The impact of the events of September 2007 in Myanmar*, 12 November 2007). Only minor editorial and stylistic revisions have been made to the version of this chapter presented to the Myanmar/Burma Update conference in December 2007, and it therefore does not take into account developments in the situation since the beginning of 2008.

[2] Author's meeting with Professor Gambari, Bangkok, 15 October 2007.

[3] At the end of 2004, subsidised retail rates for diesel and petrol in Myanmar were 160 and 180 kyat per imperial gallon, respectively. An imperial gallon is equivalent to 4.55 litres. At that time, the 'market' exchange rate was about 900 kyat to the US dollar. Crude oil was about $US43 a barrel (a barrel = 159 litres).

[4] In the wake of the fuel-price increases, the only explanation the authorities offered was on 26 August in some comments from the Myanmar ambassador in Manila—clearly more for international than domestic consumption. Ambassador Thaung Tun told The Associated Press on the sidelines of a regional ministers meeting in the Philippine capital that Myanmar could no longer afford to subsidise fuel so heavily because of the steep increases in oil prices worldwide (International Herald Tribune 2007).

[5] Indeed, after the most recent fuel-price hikes, there have been reports of workers either walking long distances to work (for up to three hours) rather than taking the bus or sleeping on the streets of Yangon at night because they cannot afford the bus fare home. The government quickly intervened to force a reduction in bus fares in Yangon, and UN data suggest that wages for day labourers have been rising.

[6] One such group started a demonstration near a market in downtown Yangon in February 2007 with shouts of 'Long live Than Shwe!', before calling for lower commodity prices and more reliable electricity supply.

[7] '88 Generation leader Min Ko Naing in an interview with *Irrawaddy* magazine, 30 April 2007.

[8] A list of names of those arrested was quickly circulated by the Thai-based Assistance Association for Political Prisoners.

[9] The only prominent member to avoid arrest at the time was Htay Kywe, who went into hiding; he was eventually arrested on 12 October.

[10] According to the statement, the alliance was formed from a number of existing organisations of Buddhist monks in Myanmar.

[11] Statement by Minister for Religious Affairs, Brigadier-General Thura Myint Maung, carried on state television. No details were given concerning which laws he was referring to, but authorities later cited Section 144 of the Myanmar Penal Code relating to unlawful assembly. The Penal Code (Section 141) defines 'unlawful assembly' as assembly of five or more people with the common object to, inter alia, 'overawe by criminal force, or show of criminal force, the Union Parliament or the Government'. Paragraph (b) of Order 2/88 of 18 September 1988 prohibits unauthorised public assembly of five or more people (it is not clear whether this more general provision remains in force, as other provisions of Order 2/88 have been abrogated). Order 6/90 of 20 October 1990 bans all unlawful *Sangha* (Buddhist monk) organisations, except the nine legal Buddhist sects. A number of other laws prohibit criticism of the government or otherwise curtail freedom of expression.

[12] There were media reports of tear gas being used, but information from eyewitnesses interviewed by the author indicates that these were most likely to have been smoke grenades, since the fumes did not cause the usual physiological reactions of tear gas. Reports from demonstrators and photographs of spent cartridges carried in the media suggest that the rubber bullets used were not the large 'baton round' type, but metal ball bearings coated with a layer of rubber, capable of inflicting fatal injuries, particularly at short range (less than 40 metres).

[13] The two Internet service providers in the country are state-controlled. The only other Internet access is by dedicated satellite links (such as those operated by foreign embassies, the United Nations or multinational companies) as well as possibly through a small number of data-capable satellite phones. People who departed the country through Yangon airport at that time reported no apparent increase in checks on baggage, suggesting either that there was a lack of coordination on the part of the authorities or that the main aim of the Internet block was to prevent people *within* the country (including perhaps the civil service in Naypyitaw) from viewing information about the situation.

[14] A UN Development Program (UNDP) survey of household living conditions in Myanmar paints a worrying picture of poverty and vulnerability in the country. It is based on data collected in 2004 and 2005 by the UNDP together with the government's Central Statistical Organisation, the analysis of which was finalised in 2006. Overall rates of poverty are high, at 32 per cent, with a further 10 per cent of the population vulnerable to falling into poverty; 90 per cent of the population lives on less than US65¢ a day. These figures should be considered conservative and reflect the situation in 2005, before the two rounds of fuel-price increases and the (inflationary) hike in public-sector salaries.

[15] In Myanmar Buddhism, the Sabbath falls four times in a lunar month, or approximately once every seventh day.

[16] The All Burma Monks' Alliance issued a statement on 21 September calling on people from all sectors of society to join the demonstrations on 24 September.

[17] The Buddhist canon permits a boycott of laity who commit any of eight offences—namely: striving for that which is not gain; striving for that which is not benefit; acting against a monastery; vilifying and making insidious comparisons between monks; inciting dissension among monks; defaming the Buddha; defaming the Dhamma; and defaming the *Sangha*. See Houtman (1999:ch. 10). In the wake of the boycott and demonstrations, the military authorities were at pains to demonstrate that they retained the support of senior monks and the *New Light of Myanmar* showed regular images of senior regime and government figures making donations to monasteries. Anecdotal reports suggested at the same time that not all abbots were prepared to accept donations from the authorities.

[18] See also Win Min's chapter in this volume.

[19] U Thaung remains in the cabinet with the Science and Technology portfolio. In addition to being removed as Minister for Labour, he no longer has the de facto foreign-policy role he once had. Previously, he had significant influence on a wide range of foreign-policy matters (for example, taking charge of the visits by UN Undersecretary-General Gambari to Myanmar in 2006), in part because of his close ties to the top two leaders (he is from the same home town as Senior General Than Shwe and graduated from the first intake of the Defence Services Academy together with Vice-Senior General Maung Aye). He had good foreign-policy credentials, having been Myanmar ambassador in Washington in 1996–97. In contrast, neither the then Prime Minister, Soe Win, nor the Foreign Minister Nyan Win, both newly appointed from the ranks of the army, had any significant international or foreign-policy experience. U Thaung's generally belligerent approach to international issues, however, including relations with the International Labour Organisation, and his sidelining of the Foreign Ministry and its professional diplomats, hardly served Myanmar's interests abroad and made him significant enemies at home, resulting in his eventual sidelining.

[20] On 6 November 2007, the commander of Light Infantry Division 33, Brigadier-General Tin Tun Aung, was appointed Deputy Minister for Labour, and the commander of Light Infantry Division 77, Brigadier-General Win Myint, was appointed Deputy Minister for Electric Power No. 2 (see New Light of Myanmar 2007).

3: Internal dynamics of the Burmese military: before, during and after the 2007 demonstrations

Win Min

Introduction

Since the military takeover in 1962, the internal dynamics in the Burmese military, which is not monolithic, have greatly affected the way successive military governments have organised themselves and operated. Top military leaders have devised their ideas, built up their power bases and purged rival factions in order to maintain their hardline approaches and their hold on power. This chapter explains how the internal dynamics of the Burmese military played out before, during and after the September 2007 demonstrations and analyses their impact, especially on political and socioeconomic reforms. It also considers possible future internal dynamics, how they might play out and the potential impacts for the country as a whole.

Historical antecedents

The internal dynamics apparent in the regime today have their roots in the period of General Ne Win's rule. The former top leader General Ne Win (1962–88) had the idea of using the military as a vehicle to unite the country. This idea led him to carry out the 1962 coup, ending the post-independence period of democratic constitutional rule.[1] He first placed the country directly under military rule (the Revolutionary Council, 1962–74), but the country later came under his personal rule. He oversaw the indoctrination of military officers through the use of military curriculums that asserted that only military might could ultimately save the ethnically diverse country from disintegration and disunity. At the same time, he enforced unity in the military and was quick to remove anyone he perceived as having an opinion different from his own.

A year after the coup, the number two in the junta leadership, Brigadier-General Aung Gyi, and his faction were dismissed or transferred to inactive posts because Aung Gyi disagreed with Ne Win's economic policies of nationalisation (Lintner 1994). This was the beginning of the military's economic mismanagement of the country, which ultimately resulted in great poverty in one of the most promising and resource-rich countries in South-East Asia.

In the mid-1970s, the Defence Minister and Chief of Staff of the Armed Forces, General Tin Oo (the current Vice-Chairman of the main opposition party), who was regarded as the third-ranking member of the ruling oligarchy, and his faction were also dismissed (Silverstein 1977).General Tin Oo's popularity as a real soldier was growing in the military and among the population. It appeared that Ne Win suspected that Tin Oo preferred an apolitical professional military.[2] A group of young military officers, frustrated with the military's mismanagement of the economy and who were close to Tin Oo, made a failed coup attempt against Ne Win. Tin Oo was officially accused of withholding knowledge of the plot. After the purge, indirect military rule with a constitutional one-party socialist system (from 1974–88), led by retired General Ne Win, was instituted without any internal resistance, because other generals were afraid of being sacked.

In 1983, former Military Intelligence Chief Brigadier-General Tin Oo and his faction were also sacked for becoming too powerful, although they were charged publicly with corruption (Selth 2002). Tin Oo was often referred to as 'number one and a half', and he and his faction were perceived as rivals to Ne Win and his family's power and privileges.[3] After that, Ne Win severely reduced the power of the military intelligence. Perhaps as a result, the military intelligence was not able to prevent the North Korean assassination attack against the South Korean official delegation in Rangoon in 1983. The weakened capacity of the intelligence service to gather and report information and coordinate their work seems to have made it easier for underground activists to network secretly. At the same time, the government's economic failures set the stage for the countrywide pro-democracy uprising that took place in 1988. The uprising was sparked by the government's desperate decision to demonetise major bank notes, which severely affected the general population. The ensuing demonstrations were violently suppressed by the military.

Characteristics of the SLORC period (1988–92)

A different pattern of power dynamics can be seen in the first few years after the 1988 coup among the next generation of army officers, known at the time as the State Law and Order Restoration Council (SLORC). Unlike in the past, when power was concentrated in the hands of the top leader, until the mid-1990s power was shared among the SLORC members together with some residual influence from General Ne Win. In 1992, the top junta leader, General Saw Maung, was forced to retire by other SLORC members on 'health grounds', seemingly for his public promise to transfer power to the elected party.[4] Other SLORC members were opposed to transferring power to the National League for Democracy (NLD) led by Aung San Suu Kyi. This ended any remaining hopes for a democratic transition after the elections.

General Than Shwe, who replaced Saw Maung, and who has a background in psychological warfare, is considered to be a good tactician. He has regularly used divide-and-rule tactics to weaken not just the opposition's power, but the power of other top generals. He has had huge statues of three prominent Burmese kings, who demonstrated great military might and held absolute power, erected in the new capital, Naypyitaw, which means 'royal city' in Burmese.[5] Besides desiring absolute control, he is known for being xenophobic and is influenced by astrology.[6]

In 1997, a group of SLORC members, including Lieutenant-General Tun Kyi, Lieutenant-General Kyaw Ba and Lieutenant-General Myint Aung, was sacked because of their growing power, which challenged the top three generals. After that, the SLORC renamed itself the State Peace and Development Council (SPDC) and power was concentrated among the remaining top three leaders. The growing popularity of the third-highest ranking officer, Military Intelligence Chief and Prime Minister General Khin Nyunt, made Than Shwe uncomfortable. Khin Nyunt was a pragmatic leader who had subtly suggested to Than Shwe that the civil service and economic policymaking should be demilitarised in order to improve the administration of the country.[7] He also encouraged engagement with the international community and the opposition, including the NLD. Than Shwe, however, appeared to see the opposition as an enemy and an obstacle to his achieving absolute power. According to many reports, Than Shwe hates Aung San Suu Kyi and he does not even want to hear her name (Jagan 2003). In 2004, Khin Nyunt and his military intelligence officers were purged. The reason given was corruption and disobeying Than Shwe's orders. In fact, they were purged because of their growing power and their attempts to push for gradual economic reform, which could lead to political reform. Than Shwe feared that he would lose his absolute control.

Internal dynamics before the August–September 2007 demonstrations

Since the 2004 sacking of General Khin Nyunt and the military intelligence officials who made up his power base, power has been concentrated in the hands of the two top generals, who are hardliners in dealing with the international community. Without Khin Nyunt there to suggest a different approach, the hardliners have restricted the role of the international community in encouraging a gradual democratic change and in alleviating social problems. The International Committee of the Red Cross (ICRC), which has been monitoring the condition of political prisoners, has not been able to access the country's prisons since 2005. Some health-related non-governmental organisations (NGOs), such as the Global Fund and Médecins sans Frontières, left the country in 2005 because of government-imposed restrictions on their access to project areas.[8] In 2006, the Center for Humanitarian Dialogue, which had been trying to facilitate a dialogue between the SPDC and Aung San Suu Kyi, had to leave the country. In 2006, the SPDC announced new guidelines for international NGOs, which placed several new restrictions on their activities.

The purge of Khin Nyunt also resulted in greater economic mismanagement without any checks and balances from the military intelligence. As a result, in 2005, gasoline prices were increased eightfold. In 2006, the salaries of civil servants were also increased by a factor of five to 12 times, with military officers receiving the highest increases. They did not feel the effects of the diesel-price increase so much, but ordinary citizens whose salaries were not increased were hurt. The government overspent its budget to cover for the sudden and huge salary increase. At the same time, it sped up its plan to move the capital to Naypyitaw in late 2005 in order to isolate itself from the people and the international community, partly on the advice of astrologers, in order to maintain its power. Since the construction of new buildings was not complete, they spent a huge amount of money to expedite the completion of the construction projects. In addition, the construction of residences for the top generals began in Pyin Oo Lwin. As a result, the government had little money left to continue subsidising fuel prices while international fuel prices continued to rise. Rather than increasing the fuel price gradually, as other countries had, the SPDC increased the price fivefold overnight in August 2007. Consequently, thousands of people took to the streets in August and September because of their difficulties making ends meet. The junta, however, responded by cracking down violently on the peaceful demonstrations.

Since the purge of General Khin Nyunt, the junta has made a number of attempts to discredit him and to improve its own image. An indirect result of this was that there were opportunities for some non-violent actions by activists and anti-corruption efforts by a faction in the military. A few months after the 2004 purge of Khin Nyunt, the junta released several imprisoned 1988-generation student leaders, including Min Ko Naing, who was considered to be the second-most popular leader after Aung San Suu Kyi. The junta claimed that military intelligence had treated these prisoners incorrectly and detained some of them longer than they should have. On the other hand, the junta appeared to believe that after spending more than 10 years in prison, the student leaders would have no popular support from younger people and would not have the capacity to organize, and therefore they could not pose a direct threat to the regime's power. The junta might also have hoped that the releases would gain them some praise from the international community, despite ignoring repeated international calls for the release of Aung San Suu Kyi from house arrest.

Soon after being freed, Min Ko Naing and his colleagues set up the '88 Generation Students Group and tested the waters by engaging in symbolic activities. Examples included attending the NLD's annual ceremonies, launching a letter campaign for people to express their feelings and a 'white campaign' in which people wore white to demonstrate their support for the release of political prisoners and political reform. In 2007, they organised a street demonstration on Aung San Suu Kyi's birthday and an event marking the day her house arrest should have expired. At this stage, the regime began to feel that the former student leaders could pose a threat to their power. Min Ko Naing and his colleagues were detained again in late 2006, right before the resumption of the National Convention, which was tasked with drafting the principles for the constitution in 1993 but finished this task only in September 2007. They were released, however, after the convention took a break in early 2007. The release could be attributed to a faction in the military that wanted to respond to increasing international pressure to release the prisoners after Burma was placed on the UN Security Council's agenda.[9] In the August–September 2007 demonstrations, the '88 Generation Students Group leaders and other underground activists took advantage of the intelligence gaps after the dismantling of Khin Nyunt's military intelligence to network in secret and to mobilise the people (Hlaing 2008).

After the junta accused General Khin Nyunt and his military intelligence of being involved in corruption, it launched a series of crackdowns against corruption. Corruption has been widespread in the military, but it has also often been used as a pretext for purges. Some generals who were not sacked were believed to be more corrupt than those who were sacked. Prime Minister Soe Win, who replaced Khin Nyunt, made public announcements calling for clean government and declared that fighting corruption was one of his main missions. During the anti-corruption campaign, action was taken against most of the businessmen close to Khin Nyunt. Than Shwe wanted them to provide testimony to justify the removal of Khin Nyunt and his military intelligence faction on the grounds of corruption. High-level businessmen very close to Than Shwe, including Tay Za (Htoo Trading Company) and Nay Aung (IGE Pty Ltd and Aung Yee Phyoe Company Ltd), a son of Than Shwe's protégé, Aung Thaung, were exempted from the anti-corruption campaign although they appeared to be more corrupt than those arrested.[10] Tay Za can be considered the only representative of Than Shwe's family businesses and he can influence the heads of two of the country's biggest conglomerates, the Union of Myanmar Economic Holding and the Myanmar Economic Cooperation. Nay Aung has a monopoly on procurement for almost all government ministries.[11]

Then Prime Minister General Soe Win also tried to address the country's economic problems. He encouraged the setting up of a new system to process passports, which would be quicker than the way the military intelligence had managed the process and would be free from corruption. This would make it easier for people to work abroad, which could help ease economic problems in the country by increasing the amount of remittances sent back to Burma. Soe Win also tried to bring down prices by reducing corruption. This did not work, however, because he had no control over other macro-economic measures. Later, he set up his own economic body—namely, a purchasing committee for government projects—although it was not announced publicly. This committee was to manage imports for government projects and was to be led by the Trade Minister, Tin Naing Thein, who was relatively close to Soe Win. He expected that he could reduce the corruption associated with government projects in this way. Soe Win's family is less corrupt compared with other generals.

Using the opportunity of General Soe Win's anti-corruption campaign, the second-highest junta leader, Vice-Senior General Maung Aye, who is considered to be a relatively less corrupt and more professional soldier than Than Shwe, attempted to pursue cases of corruption involving officers close to Than Shwe.[12] After Khin Nyunt was removed, the factional struggle between Than Shwe and Maung Aye became more apparent (Clapp 2007). He had some success in punishing middle-level officers, but not the high-level officers. The customs chief, who was close to Than Shwe's wife, was imprisoned on corruption charges and officers under him were also imprisoned or sacked in 2006. Maung Aye, however, was not able to take action against the Home Affairs Minister, Major-General Maung Oo, despite the fact that his close friend and crony, a famous diesel tycoon, was found guilty and punished for his corrupt business practices in early 2007. It appears that Than Shwe protected Maung Oo, who was close to him. Than Shwe appeared to use Maung Oo, who also commands the police intelligence agencies (including the special branch), to balance the power of the new military intelligence branch, Military Affairs Security (MAS), under Lieutenant-General Ye Myint. Ye Myint is considered to be close to Maung Aye (Callahan 2007).

It was also impossible for Maung Aye to go against Than Shwe's wife, although the former agriculture minister, Nyunt Tin, who was also close to Than Shwe's wife and who was imprisoned for corruption, testified in 2005 that he had to give her bribes of jewellery, including several diamonds.[13] Than Shwe was disappointed with Nyunt Tin's testimony, which Maung Aye also learned about. Than Shwe fainted after the testimony and stayed in bed for days, not going to his office (Jagan 2005).

General Maung Aye appeared to use his involvement in the clean-government campaign as a reason for continuing to stay in the military and not retiring. He seemed to be hoping that Than Shwe would retire because of health problems or possibly even die, giving Maung Aye a chance to replace him. (Than Shwe was hospitalised in Singapore in 2007 for chest pain, but he appeared to recover.) According to sources close to his personal doctor, Than Shwe has a heart problem and diabetes (Jagan 2008c). There have been reports that Than Shwe wants his loyalist, General Shwe Mann, the third-highest ranking junta officer, to succeed him, rather than Maung Aye. Than Shwe has already used divide-and-rule tactics between Maung Aye and Shwe Mann. It appears that Than Shwe already urged Maung Aye to retire together with him, but Maung Aye has managed to resist the suggestion so far.[14] The official retirement age for the Burmese military is sixty. Both generals are well beyond retirement age, with Than Shwe in his mid-seventies and Maung Aye in his early seventies. It appears that Maung Aye wants to remain in the military in order to pick someone loyal to him to become number one in the future. This would ensure his family's wellbeing and security in the future.

General Than Shwe has tried to reduce the power of Maung Aye, with the aim of gradually pushing for their joint retirement. Starting from 2006, Than Shwe did not go to his office regularly, except for special meetings such as the four-monthly special operation meetings and monthly joint SPDC cabinet meetings. He also asked Maung Aye not to go to the office regularly and just attend the special meetings. Maung Aye still attended the weekly meetings of the Trade Council, of which he was the chairman until the August–September 2007 demonstrations. In August 2007, however, Than Shwe removed Maung Aye from his position as chairman of the Trade Council (Jagan 2008b). It appears that Than Shwe later let Maung Aye propose one of his men, Lieutenant-General Thiha Thura Tin Aung Myint Oo (the Quartermaster-General), as his replacement on the Trade Council.

While Maung Aye has been considered a hardliner in fighting against ethnic armies, he could be more open-minded about dealing with the NLD than Than Shwe. According to an NLD member, Maung Aye had a good conversation with Aung San Suu Kyi in one of their secret meetings.[15] In contrast, Than Shwe did not listen or talk much in that meeting. Although Maung Aye appears to believe that the military's institutional integrity is the only important factor in holding the country together, he is seen as relatively less ambitious about becoming a political leader than Than Shwe.[16] He and his men have not been involved much in the activities of the pro-military mass organisation, the Union Solidarity and Development Association (USDA), which is expected to be transformed into a political party before the elections come. In contrast, Than Shwe initiated the USDA, and he and his men, particularly the Agriculture Minister, Major-General Htay Oo (Secretary-General of the USDA), and the Industry No. 1 Minister, Aung Thaung (secretariat member of the USDA), have been very involved in the USDA's activities.

After the sacking of Khin Nyunt, who was considered to be relatively friendly with the Association of South-East Asian Nations (ASEAN), ASEAN stopped defending Burma. This was due in part to international pressure and occurred despite the fact that ASEAN members traditionally did not criticise one another in public. One ASEAN member, the Philippines, even supported the United States' call to put Burma on the UN Security Council agenda. Later, ASEAN also started publicly criticising the regime for its foot dragging regarding the constitutional convention, which was only the first step of the regime's seven-point road-map to a political transition. China, which also considered Khin Nyunt to be a reformist, became the sole country in the region to defend Burma at international forums. China came under pressure itself to do something about Burma and pushed the junta to expedite the road-map process.

In the post-Khin Nyunt era, the top two generals have taken a different stance towards relations with foreign countries. Than Shwe visited India right after sacking Khin Nyunt, but he has not been to China since 2003. During his trip to New Delhi, he sought aid and indirect relief from Chinese pressure. Maung Aye also rarely visits China. Although he understands the importance of having Chinese backing, he seems to be less interested in a close relationship with China than Khin Nyunt (International Crisis Group 2000). This could be due to his experience fighting against the Burmese communists, who were supported by China in the past. Instead, Maung Aye has been keen to develop better ties with Russia and India. He visited Russia in 2006 and India in April 2008. China also appears to be less interested in engaging with Than Shwe and Maung Aye. After Khin Nyunt was sacked, China instead invited the third-highest ranking officer, General Shwe Mann, to meet with the Chinese Prime Minister early in 2007.

Internal dynamics during the August–September 2007 demonstrations

Amid the demonstrations, General Shwe Mann, who is Chief of Staff of the Army, Navy and Air Force, chaired most of the National Security Council meetings, without the presence of Than Shwe or Maung Aye (Jagan 2008a). The National Security Council is tasked with managing the country's day-to-day security operations. Shwe Mann had maintained a low profile until September in order not to be seen as a threat or rival to Maung Aye. He has become more prominent in his new role as the acting chair of the National Security Council meetings. The new arrangement could be another attempt by Than Shwe to reduce the power of Maung Aye by limiting his day-to-day management of security operations. In future, Maung Aye might be able to intervene in security affairs only in emergency cases. In such instances, however, there could be a problem of overlapping orders from Maung Aye and Shwe Mann. By delegating regular security operations to Shwe Mann, it is also likely that Than Shwe and Maung Aye will focus more on how to deal with international pressure on Burma in the future, since this pressure is likely to increase.

Asking Shwe Mann to serve as the acting chairman of the National Security Council could also signify that Than Shwe does not completely trust Maung Aye to be tough in quelling demonstrations. The new situation will give Than Shwe the opportunity to bypass Maung Aye and go directly to Shwe Mann with certain orders. There have been reports that Maung Aye did not support the idea of using pro-military mass organisations, such as the USDA and the Swan Arr Shin (Masters of Force) militia, to crack down on protesters.[17] According to sources close to the military, he even pushed for the release of a detainee whose leg was broken but who was denied medical treatment after being attacked by the USDA and Swan Arr Shin in August 2007.[18] He also appeared to disagree with the use of large-scale violence against unarmed civilians, especially the beating and shooting of monks as well as causing bloodshed when raiding the monasteries at night.[19] Sources close to the military also said that the army's standing orders for suppressing the demonstrations were to use firepower as little as possible.[20] This is in direct contrast with the orders issued in 1988 when the troops were told to shoot indiscriminately, and killed thousands of demonstrators. This time, Maung Aye told the regional commanders to use as little violence as possible.[21] Sources close to the military said that, in contrast, after 25 September, Than Shwe encouraged the regional commanders to use violence decisively.[22] This contravened the army's standing orders.

Regional commanders also appeared to respond differently to the army's standing orders. This is seen in the varying levels of violence used in different regions. This could be due partly to the competing commands from Than Shwe and Maung Aye. The worst violence—including the shooting and killing of demonstrators and raids on monasteries—happened in Yangon, although a curfew was imposed in Yangon and Mandalay. Soldiers shot directly at the demonstrators on the streets of Yangon on 26 and 27 September. Although the government admitted that 15 people, including a Japanese journalist, were killed in Yangon, the real numbers could be much higher than that. More than a dozen monasteries in Yangon were violently raided during the night of 27 September. Ngwe Kyar Yan Monastery in South Okkalapa township in Yangon was the worst hit, with video footage showing smashed windows and blood stains on the floor.

The mother of the Yangon Regional Commander, Major-General Hla Htay Win, used to regularly visit Ngwe Kyaw Yan Monastery. This could have influenced Hla Htay Win, who is considered to be close to Maung Aye, to avoid resorting to the use of violence against the monks in that monastery. The Bureau of Special Operations chief for Yangon region, Lieutenant-General Myint Swe, who is close to Than Shwe, is likely to have been under great pressure from Than Shwe to use violence decisively. Myint Swe is the nephew of Than Shwe's wife. Myint Swe led the command centre established at Kone Myint Thara at Eight Mile, in Yangon, together with the Yangon Regional Commander and the Deputy Home Affairs Minister, Brigadier-General Phone Swe. The commander of Light Infantry Division (LID) 77, Brigadier-General Win Myint, based in Bago (Pegu) but assigned to Yangon during the crackdown, appeared to have been lenient towards the demonstrators on 25 September, the first day of the curfew, since there was no shooting or raiding of monasteries by the military on that day. Tens of thousands of people continued to march on the streets in Yangon on 25 and 26 September. The relative lack of shooting into the crowds by the military on 26 September could also be because LID 77 did not have enough troops to deal with many demonstrators. On the evening of 26 September, LID 66, based in Pyay (Prome), was called into Yangon. The pre-dawn raids of the monasteries and serious shooting began on 27 September.

The level of force used in Mandalay (under the Central Regional Command), unlike in Yangon, was modest. In Mandalay, a curfew was also imposed on 25 September, but almost no monasteries were raided during the nights of 26 and 27 September. Also, there was no significant shooting (mostly warning shots above people's heads) or beating of demonstrators on the streets. According to an eyewitness, on 26 September, soldiers in Mandalay paid their respects to the monks by worshipping them and requesting them to disperse, rather than beating or shooting at them (Gray 2007). On the evening of 26 September, troops from LID 99, based in Meiktila, were moved into Mandalay. Still no significant shooting occurred. Although troops were posted around the perimeter of the monasteries, the monasteries were not violently raided during the night. Troops asked the monks not to come out of their monasteries, telling them that they had been ordered to shoot if the monks did come out (Hlaing 2008). As a result, the monks decided to stay in. Although the Bureau of Special Operations chief for Mandalay, Lieutenant-General Ye Myint, and the Central Regional Commander, Major-General Khin Zaw, are close to Than Shwe, they appeared to want to use as little force as possible in controlling and stopping the demonstrations in Mandalay. The troops in Mandalay could also have been worried about a backlash if they used excessive violence since the strength of the monks there was greater than in Yangon. (Mandalay has the highest number of monks studying at teaching temples.)

Although there was no curfew and relatively fewer demonstrations in Kachin State, the northern regional commander, Major-General Ohn Myint, responded very harshly. He ordered troops to raid the monasteries in Myitkyina, the capital of Kachin State, and in Bamaw on the night of 25 September. These were the first night-time raids in the country. More than 200 monks were arrested during the raids and more monks were detained the next day (Saw Yan Naing 2007). Ohn Myint, who is close to Than Shwe, is considered to be one of the most hardline regional commanders. His response seemed out of proportion with the situation, as there were only a few hundred monks and people on the streets in Kachin State, while there were thousands of demonstrators on the streets in different towns in upper Burma.

For instance, in the upper Burma town of Pakokku, where the first beatings of monks by the security forces occurred, there were thousands of demonstrators on the streets. The brutal treatment of monks in Pakokku sparked demonstrations in other cities. In Sittwe (Akyab), the capital of Rakhine (Arakan) State, where the monks started the demonstrations, there were also thousands of demonstrators on the streets. The military authorities did not, however, order the shooting of demonstrators or the raiding of monasteries in either Pakokku or Sittwe to stop the demonstrations. As in Mandalay, troops in Pakkoku and Sittwe could have been worried about the relatively greater strength of the monks in those towns. Pakkoku has the second-highest number of monks studying after Mandalay. Sittwe has a history of activism by monks, starting with Burma's struggle for independence, during which a famous Arakanese monk, U Ottama, took the lead. In Sittwe, when demonstrators surrounded their compound, the authorities even made a concession and released two people who were arrested in late August and had already been sentenced to two years in prison for providing water to the marching monks. The authorities appeared to make this concession in order to defuse the protestors' anger and prevent the situation getting worse.

During September, the SPDC's four-monthly meeting was postponed at the last minute, with some of the commanders already on their way to Naypyitaw. General Maung Aye also postponed his scheduled visit to Bangladesh for the third time. Although it was apparent that Maung Aye needed to supervise the security operations in case even bigger demonstrations broke out, he also appeared to be worried that he might lose more authority if he were away. After being removed from the chairman's position of the Trade Council, Maung Aye appeared to be worried that the person replacing him might be a Than Shwe loyalist rather than someone loyal to him. Than Shwe had previously promoted his own supporters and placed them in important positions while Maung Aye was away. For instance, Than Shwe's special military advisor, Major-General Nay Win, and the Defence Headquarters Security Commander, Major-General Hla Aung Thaung, were both promoted from brigadier-general to major general while Maung Aye was away a few years earlier. In fact, Maung Aye had opposed their promotions while he was at the military headquarters.

During the demonstrations, family members of the hardliners were sent abroad. They might have been worried that a faction in the military would stop listening to Than Shwe's orders and remove him. According to a businessman close to a few regional commanders, this could have happened if the demonstrators had continued their marches despite the threat of being shot.[23] In 1988, none of General Ne Win's family members left the country, since Ne Win and his family appeared confident that the whole of the military was united behind him. This time, however, it seems that Than Shwe and his family did not have the same degree of confidence as Ne Win had in 1988, although the demonstrations in 2007 were smaller than those in 1988. Than Shwe's closest crony, Tay Za, arranged for his airline to send Than Shwe's family abroad and for their stay outside the country. Another crony, Zaw Zaw (the owner of Max Myanmar Co. Ltd), who is close to General Shwe Mann, also helped Than Shwe's family during their stay abroad.[24] In a snowball effect, other hardliners' immediate family members also flew out to Singapore. For instance, hardliner U Aung Thaung's son, Nay Aung, left for Singapore during the demonstrations. U Aung Thaung is not just close to Than Shwe, he has a family connection to Maung Aye; one of U Aung Thaung's sons, Major Pyi Aung, married Maung Aye's only daughter, Nandar Aye.

Internal dynamics after the August–September 2007 demonstrations

A hardline faction under Than Shwe organised USDA rallies to regain some legitimacy after losing much of what it had through its violent crackdown on the monk-led demonstrations. Although Shan State was the most favourable place to start organising the rallies, since there had been no significant demonstrations there, the first rallies to denounce the 2007 demonstrations and to support the junta and its road-map took place in Kachin State on 29 September. It appeared that the northern regional commander, Major-General Ohn Myint, was aggressive not just in the use of force against the monks, but in forcing people to come to mass rallies in his region. Ohn Myint is also known to be close to Than Shwe. Maung Aye wanted to take action against Ohn Myint because of his corruption, but Maung Aye could not do this since Than Shwe protected Ohn Myint. Ohn Myint also pressured the ethnic cease-fire groups in Kachin State, including the Kachin Independence Organisation, to join the mass rallies. In fact, the mass rallies frustrated many people as they had to wake up at five in the morning to be prepared for the marching.

Later, the USDA's mass rallies were organised in different cities and towns throughout most of the country. The junta used these mass rallies to prove to the international community and military personnel that the SPDC had the support of the majority of the people and that the people were against the 2007 demonstrations. General Than Shwe used to tell world leaders, including then UN Secretary-General Kofi Annan, that the USDA rallies showed how the people of Burma were supporting the junta and its road-map. For the same reason, when the UN Secretary-General's special advisor, Ibrahim Gambari, visited Burma from 29 September to 2 October, right after the demonstrations were suppressed, he was taken to Shan State for a day to witness the USDA rallies. At the 2007 UN General Assembly meeting, the Burmese delegation also referred to the USDA rallies, claiming that the majority of the people in Burma supported the SPDC and its road-map, and opposed the 2007 demonstrations.

The USDA rallies denounced the 2007 demonstrations saying they were instigated by the United States and the NLD. This appeared to be one of the signs that Than Shwe, also the patron of the USDA, did not recognise people's survival problems after the fuel-price hikes or their demand for national reconciliation, which were the main underlying causes of the 2007 demonstrations. This indicates that Than Shwe is unlikely to move forward towards a substantive dialogue for reconciliation between the junta and the opposition, although the junta appointed a liaison minister to hold preliminary talks with Aung San Suu Kyi to reduce increasing international pressure. Major-General Aung Kyi, who was appointed the Minister for Relations in October 2007, appears not to be close to Than Shwe. Before this, Than Shwe also sought to appease the International Labour Organisation (ILO) by appointing Aung Kyi as Labour Minister. The ILO had been displeased with the former Labour Minister, U Thaung, a hardliner who was also close to Than Shwe. Maung Aye and Shwe Mann prefer Aung Kyi to U Thaung, and he has subsequently had a good relationship with the ILO.[25] Aung Kyi has talked to Aung San Suu Kyi a few times, although no results have come out of the meetings yet.

After the demonstrations, Than Shwe did make some changes inside the military, including in its economic bodies, in order to provide some hope that things would improve and to buy more time. Only the personnel, however, were changed—not the policies. In early November, Maung Aye's protégé, Lieutenant-General Tin Aung Myint Oo, was appointed to take up the chairmanship of the Trade Council, the position formerly held by Maung Aye. In fact, Maung Aye had agreed to give up this position only if someone loyal to him was appointed in his place, and Maung Aye remained the army chief. Tin Aung Myint Oo demonstrated his hardline attitude when managing the aftermath of the banking crisis in 2003 and the construction of the new capital. Tin Aung Myint Oo is also one of the richest generals in the SPDC. Many businesspeople feel that his appointment as chairman of the Trade Council will not result in any needed policy changes.

After the death of Prime Minister Soe Win, General Thein Sein, who was considered to be loyal to Than Shwe, was appointed Prime Minister in October 2007. Thein Sein is not a hardliner, but he does not have the capacity to initiate policies and it is expected that he will simply follow Than Shwe's orders. So, unlike former Prime Minister Khin Nyunt, he will not take any initiatives for gradual economic or political reform. He is already 62 and has a heart pacemaker and appears not to have the energy to be a dynamic actor. Unlike Soe Win, however, he will not simply take orders from Than Shwe to implement brutal operations such as the 2003 Depayin massacre.[26] Although the Prime Minister's post was taken by someone loyal to Than Shwe, Tin Aung Myint Oo replaced Thein Sein in the powerful position of Secretary No. 1 in the SPDC. Tin Aung Myint Oo could check the power of Shwe Mann and Thein Sein in the future. In October 2007, two former regional commanders—Mandalay Commander, Major-General Khin Zaw, and North-West Commander, Major-General Thar Aye, both of whom were close to Than Shwe—were also promoted to the SPDC as Bureau of Special Operations (BSO) chiefs. One other commander, the South-West Commander, Major-General Thura Myint Aung, who was considered to be neutral between Than Shwe and Maung Aye, was also promoted and replaced Thein Sein as Adjutant-General, another powerful position in the SPDC, bypassing other senior generals who were BSO chiefs. This appointment of a neutral figure indicates some resistance from Maung Aye to Than Shwe's plans to put people loyal to him in all the important positions.

Since the 2007 demonstrations, which resulted originally from economic problems, there have been mixed signals with regard to military removals and appointments within SPDC economic bodies. While General Maung Aye was removed as chairman of the Trade Council, the hardliner who led the other economic body, the Myanmar Investment Commission (MIC), was also removed. U Thaung, who is considered to be close to General Than Shwe, was replaced as chairman of the MIC by the Livestock and Fishery Minister, Brigadier-General Maung Maung Thein, who appears to be a pragmatist, and who has a good reputation among businessmen for listening to them relatively well. He is reputedly close to Shwe Mann, so the change of leadership of the MIC could benefit the latter.

After the changes in the economic bodies, the generals told businessmen that the main plan for new economic bodies was to give businesses more breathing space and to figure out how to change from euro-based trade to Chinese yuan-based and Indian rupee-based trade. They also warned them to be prepared for the worst in resisting Western pressure. This is another negative sign that Than Shwe is unlikely to negotiate seriously with Aung San Suu Kyi, since he and his hardliners have been determined to resist Western pressure for substantive negotiations. Businessmen were also given hints that there would be policy changes in the business bodies, including the Trade Council, after personnel changes were made, on the grounds that the former heads, including Maung Aye, had mismanaged the economy. Many businessmen are, however, frustrated with the continued mismanagement of the economy and do not expect the situation to improve with these personnel changes without a significant policy shift. They also do not feel much confidence about the possible switching of trade payments to the yuan and rupee. They have been worried about increasing US pressure on the financial transactions of Burmese businessmen, especially after these sanctions hit the banking operations in Singapore of the airline owned by Than Shwe's closest business crony, Tay Za. As a result, Tay Za had to temporarily shut down the services his airline, Air Bagan, was flying between Burma and Singapore.

According to sources close to the military, the MAS submitted a confidential report that the Burmese people were facing a big gap between their income and their expenditure after the fuel-price hikes.[27] The report also suggested that this problem should be resolved immediately. Than Shwe, however, and his hardliners believed that this problem was not serious and did not need urgent attention. They even expelled the UN Development Program (UNDP) resident coordinator, Charles Petrie, in December 2007 for highlighting socioeconomic problems as the main cause of the 2007 demonstrations and asking the junta to address them urgently. Despite the hardliners' position, some generals agreed with the MAS report. The MAS chief, Lieutenant-General Ye Myint, is closer to Maung Aye than to Than Shwe. It is likely that Maung Aye will agree with the MAS report and Shwe Mann could also be alarmed by the seriousness of Burma's economic problems, since he has been listening to the views of businessmen. Apparently to overcome their internal differences about the assessment of the state of the economy and to divert attention from economic problems, Than Shwe announced a political initiative in October 2007, offering to meet personally with Aung San Suu Kyi if she agreed to dissociate herself from sanctions against the regime, which Than Shwe considers to be the main problem for the economy. Than Shwe seems to believe that Aung San Suu Kyi will not agree to give up sanctions and he can use this rejection to explain away the country's economic difficulties.

Since November 2007, Than Shwe has also shown his lack of interest in serious dialogue with Aung San Suu Kyi in various ways. First, in early November, he refused to see UN envoy Gambari, who hoped to mediate between Than Shwe and Aung San Suu Kyi during his visit. Second, Gambari's proposals to make constitutional compromises and set up a poverty-alleviation committee were rejected by the designated government spokesman, Brigadier-General Kyaw Hsan, who served as the Information Minister. Kyaw Hsan is a hardliner close to Than Shwe. In his meeting with Gambari, Kyaw Hsan also said that the opposition would be allowed to vote in the referendum for the constitution, but would not be allowed to participate in the constitutional drafting committee, which was set up in October and met for the first time in December. Third, at the last minute, Than Shwe ordered Prime Minister, Thein Sein, to block Gambari's briefing at the 2007 November ASEAN summit in Singapore, although the Minister for Foreign Affairs, Nyan Win, had already agreed to Singapore's proposal for the briefing. Fourth, in his address to the USDA annual conference in November 2007, Than Shwe reiterated that the government's seven-point road-map was the only way forward, which seemed to reflect a rejection of any constitutional compromises with the opposition. To make matters worse, the junta had pro-junta political parties and ethnic cease-fire groups attack Aung San Suu Kyi's statement, which was read out on her behalf by Gambari in November 2007. The groups issued public statements denouncing Aung San Suu Kyi's statement and asserted that Aung San Suu Kyi could not represent them.

Although it appeared that Than Shwe wanted to use the road-map as a tool to buy more time and to maintain a distance from the international community, he had a contingency plan to expedite the process if necessary. Surprising many people, including many other generals, Than Shwe announced in February 2008 that the referendum on the draft constitution would be held in May 2008 and the elections in 2010 (Jagan 2008a). Than Shwe could have moved forward with the road-map because of increasing international pressure after the 2007 demonstrations and also because of a desire to avoid engaging in political dialogue and economic reform. He could have been worried when even China, which had traditionally insisted on non-interference in Burma's internal affairs, signed off on the UN Security Council President's statement criticising the junta for its brutal crackdown and demanding that it start talking to the opposition. China also sent a number of missions to Burma after the 2007 demonstrations to expedite the road-map and economic reform. By holding the referendum, Than Shwe could also have intended to reduce Maung Aye's power by giving more authority to the USDA and transforming the USDA into a political party to contest the 2010 elections. Sources close to the military said that Than Shwe made it clear that he expected the constitution to pass in the referendum. Officials guaranteed that the constitution would be approved using various means, including persuasion, intimidation and donations to various communities (such as churches in Kachin State).

After the referendum, there was another reshuffle, in June 2008. Again, Than Shwe apparently tried to reduce Maung Aye's power. Although the BSO chiefs, most of whom were close to Than Shwe, were retired, they were replaced with regional commanders who were closer to Than Shwe than to Maung Aye. Than Shwe's loyalists, Ye Myint (BSO No. 1) and Khin Maung Than (BSO No. 3), and Maung Aye's loyalist, Kyaw Win (BSO No. 2), were retired. Their replacements, Major-Generals Ohn Myint and Ko Ko, are both close to Than Shwe, while the other new BSO chief, Major-General Min Aung Hlaing, appears to be neutral. Although one of Maung Aye's followers, Hla Htay Win, was promoted to the headquarters, his position is not that powerful as he is now the chief of military training. Maung Aye's brother-in-law, Maung Maung Swe, also lost one of his two ministerial posts, as Immigration Minister. The Industry No. 2 Minister, Major-General Saw Lwin, who was close to Maung Aye, was also moved to a less powerful ministry, immigration.

Future scenarios

Increasingly hardline positions on policy issues are likely to emerge in the immediate future since a series of military appointments shows that Than Shwe and his hardliners are still in control. It appears that Than Shwe will continue to make critical decisions and demonstrate his authority by appearing at important meetings from time to time. Than Shwe is likely to also continue to play Maung Aye off against Shwe Mann in order to maintain his centrality as a balancing figure, as he did with Maung Aye and Khin Nyunt in the past.

At the same time, Than Shwe will probably delegate more power to Shwe Mann, whom he considers to be loyal to him. Than Shwe is, however, also likely to keep hold of the purse strings, rather than handing monetary power to Shwe Mann. General Ne Win also held onto this power after he retired from the military. By giving more power to Shwe Mann, Than Shwe appears to believe that more and more generals will side with Shwe Mann than with Maung Aye. This is a tactic Ne Win used to pave the way for men loyal to him to rise through the ranks.

Although Than Shwe has a succession plan, he might not be able to follow through with it if his health deteriorates further. Than Shwe reportedly fainted after his November 2007 meeting with the Chinese Vice-Minister of Foreign Affairs, who brought a confidential letter from the Chinese Prime Minister urging Than Shwe to expedite the road-map process and economic reform.[28]

Than Shwe's reluctance to initiate economic reform is likely to result in greater socioeconomic hardship for the Burmese people. His refusal to cooperate with the international community has increased various governments' frustration with the regime and will likely lead to increased external pressure.

For the intermediate term, there are three possible scenarios.

- Than Shwe will stay in the military even after the referendum and elections. He will, however, appoint Shwe Mann president after the 2010 elections. In this scenario, he could keep Maung Aye in the military as long as he is still in the military himself. He could also keep his hardliners, such as Aung Thaung and U Thaung, in the new government. This is the most likely scenario.
- Than Shwe will give up control gradually, while ensuring that Maung Aye retires from the military at the same time as he does. This would probably happen after the 2010 elections. Than Shwe is likely to then appoint his protégé, Myint Swe, as the new military leader and another of his protégés, Shwe Mann, as the president.
- Maung Aye will take over power. This could happen if Than Shwe dies suddenly. As Than Shwe gradually delegates more power and as his health declines, it is also possible that he might be forced to retire just as General Saw Maung had to in the first years of the SLORC, when power was more dispersed.

The third scenario could still come to pass if demonstrations break out again. Than Shwe's refusal to make the country's socioeconomic problems a priority and to enter into a dialogue with the opposition could make people increasingly frustrated and lead them onto the streets again. Many activists, including the monks who organised the 2007 demonstrations, are in hiding in the country and are waiting for another opportunity to take to the streets. Unlike in 1988, many did not flee to the border. If mass demonstrations happen again, and if Than Shwe orders the use of violence against peaceful demonstrators, some authorities could refuse to comply and Maung Aye might be in a position to take over. The morale of many officers has been low, since the regime has not been able to convince them why the military had to use violence against revered monks in the 2007 demonstrations.

If Than Shwe steps down or is removed, there will be no dominant figure like him to dictate hardline positions, as power is likely to be distributed among the top leaders. Although Than Shwe might perceive Shwe Mann to be loyal to him, it is likely that he could become more pragmatic when Than Shwe's influence over him diminishes. This is what happened to Ne Win's protégé, Khin Nyunt, when Ne Win's power gradually waned after 1988. It is likely that any post-Than Shwe junta will be more vulnerable to pressure from the pragmatic officers in the military, from citizens, from the opposition parties, including the ethnic minority groups, and from the international community, and it could be compelled to make gradual economic and political reforms.

References

Callahan, Mary P. 2007, 'Of *kyay-zu* and *kyet-su*: the military in 2006', in Monique Skidmore and Trevor Wilson (eds), *Myanmar: The state, community and the environment*, Asia Pacific Press/ANU E Press, Canberra.

Clapp, Priscilla 2007, *Burma's long road to democracy*, Special Report No. 193, November, US Institute for Peace, Washington, DC.

Gray, Denis 2007, 'Myanmar's monks, 1988 activists linked', *Associated Press*, 26 October 2007.

Hlaing, Kyaw Yin 2008, 'Challenging the authoritarian state: Buddhist monks and peaceful protests in Burma', *The Fletcher Forum of World Affairs*, vol. 32, no. 1, Winter, pp. 125–43.

International Crisis Group 2006, *Myanmar: new threats to humanitarian aid*, Asia Briefing No. 58, 8 December, Brussels.

Jagan, Larry 2003, 'Suu Kyi and democracy divide junta's generals', *Bangkok Post*, 8 April 2003.

Jagan, Larry 2005, 'Rangoon's generals prepare for the changing of guard', *Bangkok Post*, 12 October 2005.

Jagan, Larry 2008a, 'Intrigue and illness in Myanmar's junta', *Asia Times* (online), 26 February 2008.

Jagan, Larry 2008b, 'Burma stonewall', *Bangkok Post*, 6 March 2008.

Jagan, Larry 2008c, 'Burma: junta split may hasten civilian rule', *Inter Press Service* (online), 31 March 2008.

Lintner, Bertil 1994, *Burma in Revolt: Opium and Insurgency since 1948*, Westview Press, Boulder Colorado.

Saw Yan Naing 2007, 'Burmese troops fire on Rangoon protestors; unconfirmed reports say five monks, one woman dead', *The Irrawaddy* (online), 26 September 2007.

Selth, Andrew 2002, *Burma's Armed Forces: Power Without Glory*, Eastbridge Press, Norwalk.

Silverstein, Joseph 1972, *The Political Legacy of Aung San*, Cornell University Press, Ithaca, New York.

Endnotes

[1] Interview with a family member of a close associate of General Ne Win, 10 November 2007.

[2] Interview with a former military intelligence officer who was close to Brigadier-General Tin Oo, the former military intelligence chief, 30 July 2007.

[3] Interview with a former military intelligence officer who was close to Brigadier-General Tin Oo, 30 July 2007.

[4] Interview with a former military medical officer, 30 June 2007.

[5] It can also be translated simply as 'capital'.

[6] Interview with a former military intelligence officer, 15 November 2007.

[7] Interview with an insider from General Khin Nyunt's former military intelligence faction, 10 November 2005.

[8] According to the International Crisis Group (2006), the real reason why the Global Fund refused to fund health care in Myanmar was an objection from the Bush Administration in the United States, which was itself under pressure from Congress.

[9] Interview with a UN official from Rangoon, 23 August 2007.

[10] Interview with a businessman close to the military, 16 January 2008.

[11] Interview with a former military intelligence officer, 20 April 2008.

[12] Interview with a former Burmese diplomat, 30 March 2008.

[13] Personal interview with a former military intelligence officer, 15 December 2006.

[14] Personal interview with a businessman close to the generals, 20 March 2007.

[15] Interview with an NLD member who was close to senior NLD leaders, 15 September 2005.

[16] Interview with a former military intelligence officer, 1 November 2007.

[17] Ibid.

[18] Interview with a businessman close to the military, 21 September 2007.

[19] Interview with a senior diplomat who had close connections with the generals, 29 September 2007.

[20] Interview with a businessman close to the military, 30 September 2007.

[21] Interview with a businessman who is close to a few regional commanders, 10 October 2007.

[22] Ibid.

[23] Interview with a businessman close to few regional commanders, 30 September 2007.

[24] Interview with a businessman close to the military, 29 September 2007.

[25] Interview with a businessman close to the generals, 5 November 2007.

[26] The village where Aung San Suu Kyi and her supporters were attacked on 30 May 2003 by pro-SPDC elements while travelling through central Burma.

[27] Interview with a businessman close to the military, 2 December 2007.

[28] Interview with a businessman close to the military, 20 November 2007.

Economic Update

4: Myanmar's GDP growth and investment: lessons from a historical perspective

U Myint

Introduction

According to official figures, Myanmar has achieved double-digit gross domestic product (GDP) growth rates every year for the six years from 2000 to 2005. These figures have proved controversial. A related and another contentious issue regarding Myanmar's economic performance in the same period is that high real GDP growth rates have been achieved with comparatively low gross domestic investment (GDI) to GDP ratios.

In order to gain a proper perspective on these issues, one approach is to use cross-sectional data for a particular period to obtain a comparative view of Myanmar's performance vis-a-vis the performance of its neighbours in the same period. The comparative approach has been adopted frequently and has been useful in analysing developments in Myanmar's economic and social situation through the years.

Myanmar has, however, a rich tradition of data collection and analysis. National accounts data, for example, go as far back as 1948, when the country gained independence, and even beyond. In addition to cross-sectional analysis, therefore, the available time-series data could be used to review Myanmar's recent economic performance, as reflected in official data of the country's past experience. Such a brief review is attempted in this chapter with specific attention devoted to real GDP growth and GDI.

Myanmar's 'good' performance from a comparative viewpoint

Appendix Table 4.1 gives GDP growth rates for the first six years of the new millennium for 19 developing Asian countries, including Myanmar. The countries in the table are grouped into four categories—namely: 1) newly industrialising economies (NIEs); 2) second-tier NIEs; 3) other developing countries; and 4) least-developed countries. The table shows that Myanmar's GDP growth rate in real terms has been good compared with other countries in the region; Myanmar's average growth rate was 12.9 per cent a year for this period. Since the average annual growth rates for the four categories of developing Asian countries ranged between 4.5 per cent and 5.8 per cent for the period, Myanmar's growth performance has been more than double the growth rates of these countries.

The fact that Myanmar's higher real GDP growth rates have been achieved with considerably lower GDI to GDP ratios, compared with other countries in the region, is illustrated in Appendix Table 4.2. That table shows that while the GDI/GDP ratio averaged 24 per cent per annum for the period 2000–05 for other Asian countries, Myanmar's GDI/GDP ratio averaged about 12 per cent per annum. This means that Myanmar has been able to achieve a real GDP growth rate double the rate of its neighbours, with half their GDI ratios.

Reservations about Myanmar's growth performance

Many observers, within the country and abroad, have expressed reservations about Myanmar's official growth rates. The International Monetary Fund (IMF), for example, has a conservative outlook regarding Myanmar's economic performance in recent years, because it is of the view that other regional countries in a similar situation as Myanmar have not experienced such robust growth in the same period. The IMF has defined 'similarity' in terms of a low level of development, a large agricultural sector, a pervasive role of the State in the economy and a recent history of conflict. Bangladesh, Cambodia, Laos and Vietnam were identified as countries having such attributes. It was pointed out that Myanmar, despite its high official growth figures, did not fare well when its social indicators were compared with those for these countries. It also did not measure up to these countries in terms of per capita GDP in US dollars. Moreover, the IMF had difficulty reconciling Myanmar's high agricultural growth with its official figures on harvested acreage, irrigated areas and the reported decline in the use of fertilisers and pesticides.

Similarly, high industrial growth does not seem to be consistent with the relatively low increase in industrial power consumption, manufacturing's use of petroleum products and the decline in capital-goods imports. The IMF concludes that all these imply an implausibly large increase in productive efficiency. The IMF expected near-zero growth for Myanmar in the fiscal year 2003/04, based on its belief that constraints that would arise from a low level of imported inputs, structural rigidities, delayed effects of sanctions and the banking crisis. In sharp contrast with IMF expectations, Myanmar authorities estimated 13.8 per cent growth for that year.

Review of Myanmar's economic performance using time-series data

The time-series data for the review cover the whole of Myanmar's post-independence era—57 years, from independence in 1948 to the fiscal year 2005/06, the last year for which data were available. For convenience and ease of presentation, data are presented in Appendix Tables 4.3–4.8, with each covering a decade: the 1950s, 1960s, 1970s, 1980s, 1990s and the first decade of the new millennium. What they reveal is highlighted below.

Double-digit real GDP growth, 1948–2005

Sustained double-digit growth in real GDP began in the fiscal year 1999/2000 and continued for seven years up to 2005 (and could continue for several years more). Such sustained double-digit growth represents a sharp break with the country's development experience in its entire post-independence period, extending across half a century. Until 1999/2000, which ushered in the new millennium, there had never been double-digit real GDP growth that extended across two consecutive years.

During the 50 years since independence, there have been five instances of double-digit GDP growth: twice in the 1950s (1950 and 1956) and three times in the 1960s (1962, 1964 and 1967). In all these instances, a double-digit growth year has always been either immediately preceded by or immediately followed by a negative-growth year. For instance, real growth of 12.9 per cent in 1950 was preceded by a 10 per cent real GDP decline in 1948 and a further 5 per cent fall in 1949. Similarly, 13 per cent growth in 1962 was followed by a decline of 6.1 per cent in 1963. For three decades preceding the fiscal year 1999/2000, there had not been a single instance of double-digit real GDP growth.

Real GDP growth and the GDI/GDP ratio, 1948–2005

Table 4.1 summarises how real GDP growth and the GDI/GDP ratio have changed in Myanmar in the past five decades and in the early years of the new millennium.

Table 4.1 Myanmar: real GDP growth rates and the GDI/GDP ratio, 1950/51–2004/05

Fiscal years	Average GDP growth rate (%)	Average GDI/GDP ratio (%)
1950/51–1959/60	5.8	18.9
1961/62–1970/71	3.5	12.2
1970/71–1979/80	3.9	12.8
1980/81–1989/90	1.9	16.1
1990/91–1999/2000	6.1	13.6
1999/2000–2004/05	12.6	11.8

From Table 4.1, we can say that in the 1950s, Myanmar was not a least-developed country, and, with a GDI/GDP ratio of 19 per cent, it achieved an average annual growth rate of about 6 per cent.

In the next two decades (the 1960s and 1970s), as a consequence of command-style economic management under military rule, self-imposed isolation and the 'Burmese way to socialism', the economy deteriorated. Real GDP growth was reduced to 3–4 per cent per annum, while the GDI/GDP ratio fell to between 12 and 13 per cent.

The 1980s were, economically, the worst in Myanmar's post-independence history. Although the decade started off well with real GDP growing between 5 per cent and 8 per cent and the GDI/GDP ratio reaching 21–22 per cent, the political turmoil and social disturbances in the latter half of the decade overshadowed the good beginning. For the decade as a whole, therefore, GDP growth averaged only 1.9 per cent per annum—slightly below the 2 per cent growth in population. The GDI/GDP ratio, however, remained relatively high for this period, averaging 16 per cent per annum (Appendix Table 4.7). We could also recall that in 1987, Myanmar applied for and was granted 'least-developed country' status by the United Nations and, in 1988, a new regime came to power that abandoned the 'Burmese way to socialism' and adopted a 'market-oriented' approach for the country to become a 'modern developed nation'.

A claim could be made that economic reforms in the first half of the 1990s enabled the country to attain a respectable 6 per cent growth in this decade. This better performance has, however, been achieved with a relatively stagnant GDI/GDP ratio of about 13 per cent.

What conclusion can be drawn, then, regarding Myanmar's growth experience from independence in 1948 up to the end of the 1990s? If we wish to be unkind, we can say that Myanmar is a subsistence agricultural economy, relying on a few commodities, with a pre-industrial economic structure, which has no shock absorbers to cushion the impact of events originating within and outside the country. Natural and human-made disasters, therefore, windfalls from the bounty of nature and commodity booms that resulted from such events as the Korean War largely determined the state of the economy, rather than factors such as the GDI/GDP ratio.

Such unkind views can, however, no longer hold with the official data for Myanmar's economic performance coming into the new millennium. In biblical times, it was possible for a country's economy to enjoy seven fat years in a row and then to suffer seven lean years in a row. Not anymore! Global warming, a growing menace, has brought with it climate change that has made weather volatile and erratic. There is no way a country can expect to have seven consecutive years of good harvests in the twenty-first century. The fact that real GDP growth in Myanmar doubled from 6 per cent in the 1990s to 12 per cent at the start of the new millennium, and that this double-digit growth was sustained for seven years while the GDI/GDP ratio fell to 11–12 per cent, deserves some explanation. There are probably two reasons for this: politics and arithmetic.

Regarding politics, the powers that be in the country have a fixation with high GDP growth rates, which are believed to indicate the country's growing prosperity and wellbeing. These growth rates have therefore become highly politicised and, in the process, credibility and good sense have fallen by the wayside.

As for arithmetic, social and economic indicators for the country are normally expressed as a ratio of GDP. Now, when the GDP that is used as a denominator in these indicators is padded, inflated and made to rise proportionately more than the numerator, this will introduce a downward bias to the indicators. It is therefore not surprising that an unusually high real GDP growth rate, as reflected in official national account statistics, in the new millennium has led to a fall in the GDI/GDP ratio. This also accounts for the pathetically low export/GDP ratio and industrial value added/GDP ratio, as well as many other social and economic indicators, which are embarrassingly far below such indicators in other countries in the region.

This has not always been the case in Myanmar's post-independence history. For instance, Table 4.2 provides the ratio of exports to GDP for the 1950s, when the country did not suffer from politically inspired GDP figures. This ratio averaged 22.6 per cent per annum for the decade, which was consistent with such ratios for any country in the world judged to be in a similar economic situation as Myanmar at that time.

Table 4.2 Myanmar: GDP, exports and the export/GDP ratio, 1950/51–1959/60 (million kyat, current prices)

Fiscal year	1950/ 1951	1951/ 1952	1952/ 1953	1953/ 1954	1954/ 1955	1955/ 1956	1956/ 1957	1957/ 1958	1958/ 1959	1959/ 1960	Total	Average
GDP	3690	4084	4620	4589	4813	5144	5452	5384	5626	5999	49 401	4940
Exports	975	1093	1292	1066	1116	1174	1183	894	1002	1179	10 974	1097
Exports/GDP (%)	26.42	26.76	27.97	23.23	23.19	22.82	21.70	16.60	17.81	19.65	226	22.62

Source: Government of Burma, *Economic Survey of Burma*, 1955, 1959 and 1963.

The same exercise reported in Table 4.2, using official figures for the new millennium, yields Table 4.3, with an export/GDP ratio reduced to 0.44 per cent—a percentage that will take us back to a pre-colonial and pre-industrial era, definitely before King Mindon's reign (1853–78), when Myanmar had little regular commerce with the outside world.

Table 4.3 Myanmar: GDP, exports and the export/GDP ratio, 2000/01–2002/03 (million kyat, current prices)

Fiscal year	2000/01	2001/02	2002/03	Total	Average
GDP	2 552 733	3 548 472	5 527 000	11 628 205	3 876 068
Exports	12 627	16 350	19 955	48 932	16 311
Exports/GDP ratio (%)	0.49	0.46	0.36	1.31	0.44

Source: Central Statistical Organisation, *Statistical Yearbook 2003*: Table 14.02, p. 315.

Conclusion

The above observations lead us to conclude that Myanmar has two choices in terms of its economic data:

- continue to stick with exceptionally high and unbelievable real GDP growth rates and the associated embarrassingly poor social and economic indicators
- revise real GDP growth rates to more realistic, accurate and reasonable levels and have less embarrassing social and economic indicators.

What to choose? I think we have stuck with the first option long enough; it has been counterproductive. The good image that a high growth rate is expected to convey has proved elusive. The public data are largely ignored and are probably thought not fit to be printed, so do not appear in the major regional and world economic reviews and reports. On the other hand, the embarrassing social and economic indicators they generate attract publicity, are talked about, highlighted and published. This is not good politics.

It is time therefore to move to the second option. Improvement in quality, accuracy, credibility, reliability, timeliness and the availability of economic and social statistical data and information will be an essential first step in building a modern developed nation.

Appendix

Appendix Table 4.1 GDP growth rates, selected Asian countries, 2000–05 (per cent)

Economy	2000	2001	2002	2003	2004	2005	2000–05 Average
I. Newly industrialising economies (NIEs)							
Republic of Korea	8.5	3.8	7.0	3.1	4.6	4.1	5.2
Hong Kong	10.2	0.5	1.9	3.2	8.1	5.7	4.9
Singapore	9.7	−1.8	3.2	1.4	8.4	4.1	4.2
Taiwan	5.8	−2.2	3.9	3.3	5.7	4.2	3.5
Average NIEs	8.6	0.1	4.0	2.8	6.7	4.5	4.5
II. Second-tier NIEs							
Malaysia	8.9	0.3	4.1	5.3	7.1	5.7	5.2
Thailand	4.8	2.2	5.3	6.9	6.1	5.6	5.2
Indonesia	4.9	3.8	4.3	5.0	5.1	5.5	4.8
Average second-tier NIEs	6.2	2.1	4.6	5.7	6.1	5.6	5.1
III. Other developing countries							
China	8.0	7.5	8.3	9.3	9.5	8.5	8.5
Vietnam	6.1	5.8	6.4	7.1	7.5	7.6	6.8
India	4.4	5.8	4.0	8.5	6.5	6.9	6.0
Pakistan	3.9	1.8	3.1	5.1	6.4	7.0	4.6
Philippines	4.4	1.8	4.3	4.7	6.1	5.0	4.4
Sri Lanka	6.0	−1.5	4.0	5.9	5.5	5.2	4.2
Average other developing countries	5.5	3.5	5.0	6.8	6.9	6.7	5.8
IV. Least-developed countries							
Bhutan	5.5	7.1	6.7	6.5	7.0	8.0	6.8
Laos	5.8	5.8	5.9	5.9	6.5	7.0	6.2
Bangladesh	5.9	5.3	4.4	5.3	5.5	5.3	5.3
Cambodia	7.0	5.6	5.5	5.2	6.0	2.3	5.3
Nepal	6.0	4.8	−0.4	2.9	3.3	3.0	3.3
Average least-developed countries	6.0	5.7	4.4	5.2	5.7	5.1	5.4
Average all selected (18) countries above	6.6	2.9	4.5	5.1	6.4	5.5	5.2
Myanmar	13.7	11.3	12.0	13.8	13.6	13.2	12.9

Source: Asian Development Bank 2005, *Key Indicators of Developing Asian and Pacific Countries*, Online Edition, Asian Development Bank, Manila. Source for Myanmar: Ministry of National Planning and Economic Development, Yangon.

Appendix Table 4.2 GDI, selected Asian countries, 2000–05 (per cent of GDP)

Economy	2000	2001	2002	2003	2004	2005	2000–05 (average)
I. Newly industrialising economies (NIEs)							
Republic of Korea	28.3	27.0	26.1	29.4	30.2	30.1	28.5
Hong Kong	28.1	25.3	22.8	21.9	21.8	20.5	23.4
Singapore	32.0	26.5	23.7	15.6	19.4	18.6	22.6
Taiwan	22.9	18.4	17.4	17.4	21.5	20.2	19.6
Average NIEs	27.8	24.3	22.5	21.1	23.2	22.4	23.6
II. Second-tier NIEs							
Malaysia	27.2	23.9	24.0	21.6	22.6	19.8	23.2
Thailand	22.8	24.1	23.8	24.9	27.1	31.6	25.7
Indonesia	16.1	23.5	20.4	17.3	21.3	21.3	20.0
Average second-tier NIEs	22.0	23.8	22.7	21.3	23.7	24.2	23.0
III. Other developing countries							
China	36.3	34.2	35.2	38.0	39.3	43.5	37.8
Vietnam	23.9	31.2	33.2	35.4	35.5	35.4	32.4
India	24.4	23.0	25.3	27.2	30.1	-	26.0
Pakistan	16.0	17.2	16.8	16.9	17.3	16.8	16.8
Philippines	29.1	19.0	17.7	16.7	17.1	15.7	19.2
Sri Lanka	28.1	22.0	21.3	22.3	25.8	27.0	24.4
Average other developing countries	26.3	24.4	24.9	26.1	27.5	27.7	26.2
IV. Least-developed countries							
Laos	20.5	21.0	21.2	21.2	22.0	22.0	21.3
Bangladesh	23.0	23.1	23.1	23.4	24.0	24.4	23.5
Cambodia	17.3	18.7	20.1	25.1	25.8	26.4	22.2
Nepal	24.3	24.1	24.2	25.8	26.4	25.7	25.1
Average least-developed countries	21.3	21.7	22.2	23.9	24.6	24.6	23.1
Average all selected (17) countries above	24.4	23.6	23.1	23.1	24.8	24.7	24.0
Myanmar	12.4	11.6	10.4	11.0	12.0	-	11.5

Source: Asian Development Bank 2004 and 2006, *Asian Development Outlook*. Source for Myanmar: Ministry of National Planning and Economic Development, Yangon.

Appendix Table 4.3 Myanmar: GDP at 2000/01 constant prices, and GDI as ratio of GDP, 1999/2000–2005/06

Fiscal year	GDP (million kyat)	GDP change from previous year (%)	GDI/GDP ratio (%)
1999/2000	2 246 035	10.9	13.4
2000/01	2 553 742	13.7	12.4
2001/02	2 842 314	11.3	11.6
2002/03	3 183 392	12.0	10.4
2003/04	3 622 700	13.8	11.0
2004/05	4 115 387	13.6	12.0
2005/06	4 658 619	13.2	n.a.
Total		88.5	-
Average		12.6	11.8[a]

[a] average for years 1999/00 to 2004/05

Notes: GDI = total investment + stock changes; GDP figures are calculated from data in the *Statistical Yearbook* and using growth rates given in tables in Paras (11) and (14) of *Myanmar's Economic Development*; GDI figure for 2003/04 is from UNCTAD 2005, *Handbook of Statistics*, Table 7.3, p. 349; GDI figure for 2004/05 is from UNCTAD 2006, *LDC Report 2006*, Annex Table 6, p. 316.

Sources: Ministry of National Planning and Economic Development 2006, *Myanmar's Economic Development*, December 2006; Central Statistical Organisation 2003, *Statistical Yearbook*.

Appendix Table 4.4 Myanmar: GDP at 1947/48 constant prices, and GDI as ratio of GDP, 1948/49–1960/61

Fiscal year	GDP (million kyat)	GDP change from previous year (%)	GDI/GDP ratio (%)
1948/49	3200	−10.0	n.a.
1949/50	3038	−5.1	n.a.
1950/51	3431	12.9	12.9
1951/52	3636	6.0	18.2
1952/53	3899	7.2	19.0
1953/54	4073	4.5	22.0
1954/55	4294	5.4	21.0
1955/56	4456	3.8	18.0
1956/57	4934	10.7	19.9
1957/58	4778	−3.2	22.0
1958/59	5195	8.7	19.4
1959/60	5600	7.8	18.7
1960/61	5563	−0.7	16.3
Total		63.2	207.3
Average (1950/51–1960/61)		5.8	18.8

Sources: Government of Burma 1955, 1962, 1963, *Economic Survey of Burma*.

Appendix Table 4.5 Myanmar: GDP at 1969/70 constant prices, and GDI as a ratio of GDP, 1961/62–1970/71

Fiscal year	GDP (million kyat)	GDP change from previous year (%)	GDI/GDP ratio (%)
1961/62	7798	3.6	11.4
1962/63	8811	13.0	10.6
1963/64	8272	−6.1	10.6
1964/65	9106	10.1	18.4
1965/66	8715	−4.3	4.3
1966/67	8355	−4.1	12.2
1967/68	9200	10.1	15.8
1968/69	9503	3.3	12.8
1969/70	9976	5.0	14.2
1970/71	10 388	4.1	11.8
Total		34.6	122.0
Average		3.5	12.2

Sources: Ministry of Planning and Finance, 1972/73 and 1975/76, *Report to the Pyithu Hluttaw.*

Appendix Table 4.6 Myanmar: GDP at 1969/70 constant prices, and GDI as ratio of GDP, 1970/71–1979/80

Fiscal year	GDP (million kyat)	GDP change from previous year (%)	GDI/GDP ratio (%)
1970/71	10 388	4.1	11.8
1971/72	10 641	2.4	12.2
1972/73	10 538	−1.0	10.8
1973/74	10 812	2.6	10.2
1974/75	11 101	2.7	9.0
1975/76	11 562	4.2	9.9
1976/77	12 265	6.1	10.3
1977/78	12 996	6.0	13.0
1978/79	13 843	6.5	18.2
1979/80	14 562	5.2	22.3
Total		38.8	127.7
Average		3.9	12.8

Sources: Ministry of Planning and Finance 1979/80 and 1984/85, *Report to the Pyithu Hluttaw.*

Appendix Table 4.7 Myanmar: GDP at 1985/86 constant prices, and GDI as a ratio of GDP, 1980/81–1989/90

Fiscal year	GDP (million kyat)	GDP change from previous year (%)	GDI/GDP ratio (%)
1980/81	44 338	7.9	21.5
1981/82	47 157	6.4	22.9
1982/83	49 714	5.4	22.2
1983/84	51 878	4.3	18.0
1984/85	54 437	4.9	15.1
1985/86	55 989	2.9	15.5
1986/87	55 397	−1.1	12.7
1987/88	53 178	−4.0	11.6
1988/89	47 141	−11.4	12.8
1989/90	48 883	3.7	9.2
Total		19.1	161.5
Average		1.9	16.1

Sources: Ministry of Planning and Finance 1984/85, *Report to the Pyithu Hluttaw*; Central Statistical Organisation 1991, *Statistical Yearbook*.

Appendix Table 4.8 Myanmar: GDP at 1985/86 constant prices, and GDI as a ratio of GDP, 1990/91–1999/00

Fiscal year	GDP (million kyat)	GDP change from previous year (%)	GDI/GDP ratio (%)
1990/91	50 260	2.8	13.4
1991/92	49 933	−0.7	15.3
1992/93	54 757	9.7	17.6
1993/94	58 064	6.0	12.4
1994/95	62 406	7.5	12.4
1995/96	66 742	7.0	14.2
1996/97	71 042	6.4	12.3
1997/98	75 123	5.7	12.5
1998/99	79 460	5.8	12.4
1999/00	88 157	10.9	13.4
Total		61.2	135.9
Average		6.1	13.6

Sources: Central Statistical Organisation 1995, 1997 and 2003, *Statistical Yearbook*.

5: Migrant-worker remittances and Burma: an economic analysis of survey results

Sean Turnell, Alison Vicary and Wylie Bradford

Introduction

In recent years, great interest has awakened in the question of migrant remittances. The potential for remittances—a phenomenon hitherto regarded as of little consequence—to act as a means for poverty alleviation and economic development has increasingly come to enjoy a broad consensus. In the light of this, and the recognition that for many developing countries remittances constitute a larger and more stable source of foreign exchange than trade, investment or aid, a vast and growing literature on the topic has emerged. Notwithstanding this broad interest, there is, however, yet to appear any major study with respect to the question of migrant remittances to Burma.

This chapter seeks to at least partially redress this void by examining the extent, nature and pattern of remittances made by Burmese migrant workers in Thailand. Drawing on a survey of such workers conducted by the authors, it was found that remittances to Burma were large, were used disproportionately to ensure simple survival and were realised overwhelmingly via informal mechanisms. The last two attributes are a direct consequence of Burma's dysfunctional economy, which sadly also severely limits the gains to the country that remittances might otherwise bring.

For many developing countries, the remittances that their citizens send from abroad constitute a larger source of foreign exchange than international trade, aid or foreign investment. In 2006, such remittances, which were made by an estimated 150 million migrants across the globe, amounted to about $US300 billion. In the same year, total aid and foreign direct investment (FDI) to developing countries were about $US270 billion. The sheer volume of remittances, coupled with the fact that they are relatively stable and often counter-cyclical, makes them a potentially powerful source of development finance for receiving countries.

Many of the issues relating to remittance payments, however, are clouded by lack of data and considerable mystery as to the means by which they are made. The International Monetary Fund (IMF) records annual data for official worker remittance payments in its *Balance of Payments Statistics Yearbook*, but such data record only those payments that are made through official banking channels. Remittances that flow through private and unofficial channels, and via a variety of non-banking instruments, are not recorded. This is problematic for many countries and circumstances, but it is especially significant for migrants from countries in which trust in banks is mostly absent.

In Burma, there is all pervasive *mis*trust—not only in banks, but in just about all of the country's institutions, financial and otherwise. Add to this an oppressive, secretive state and we have a comprehensive package of circumstances that makes data for the country highly unreliable. According to the IMF, official worker remittances to Burma totalled $US81.3 million in 2004 (the latest data available), from which must be deducted the remittances of foreign workers in Burma (mostly working for multinational corporations and international aid agencies) of $US24.5 million—delivering a net remittance surplus of $US56.8 million. Of course, these official flows (the inward component of which is due largely to funds sent home by Burmese merchant seaman) greatly understate the remittances sent by Burma's estimated two million or so migrant workers and refugees who live outside its borders, and which are made (overwhelmingly) via informal payment mechanisms of various types. Such remittances are likely to be three to four times the official flows and their existence represents a lifeline that permits the survival of many thousands of families in Burma.

The importance of the remittance issue has triggered a vast and growing literature on the topic and great interest from multilateral agencies such as the World Bank, the IMF and the Organisation for Economic Cooperation and Development (OECD). Remittances have also come to the attention of international banks and other financial institutions, with their eye for market opportunities, anxious to grab a share of this potentially lucrative trade. No study, however, has yet been undertaken in relation to Burma, especially with respect to the informal remittance channels that dominate most payments into and out of the country.

The purpose of this chapter, accordingly, is to attempt to remedy this neglect at least partially by shedding some light on the nature, patterns and magnitude of the remittances sent by Burmese migrant workers and refugees in Thailand. Central to this analysis is the survey conducted by the authors across 2002–03. The use of a survey is necessary in the context of Burma since, firstly and simply, information and data scarcely exist in any other form. A survey is, however, also useful for other reasons when exploring remittances, including the fact that it can shed light on the uses of funds sent, the incentives faced by senders and recipients and other salient facts beyond simply financial data. Similar studies using household and individual survey data have yielded much information regarding remittances in other countries and regions, but this is the first such study regarding Burma and its population in Thailand.

The chapter is divided into seven sections. It begins by considering the broader context of remittances and why they are important—for the individuals directly concerned as senders and receivers and, more generally, for recipient countries. Section three considers the types of instruments and channels through which remittances are sent. The focus is particularly on informal remittance devices. As will become clear, such devices are not only the most important means by far through which remittances are sent into Burma, they are the least understood. Section four examines why migrants are often likely to choose informal remittance devices, despite the benefits formal methods confer. Section five details the results of our survey and examines the amounts sent, the costs of sending, the end uses of funds and methods of delivery, as well as the factors that determine these. Section six offers some conjectures on the survey results, relating the experiences revealed to those of other people and situations and highlighting the differences that set Burma apart. The chapter concludes with some thoughts about how Burma's economic mismanagement squanders the development potential of the country's remittance flows.

The importance of remittances

The increasing attention paid to the question of migrant remittances comes from the realisation of the important role they play in poverty alleviation and, circumstances permitting, economic development more broadly. The former is most obvious in the way the circumstances of individuals are directly transformed; the latter operates via a collective response much dependent on the existence of institutions that can leverage remittances to create true 'development finance'.

Individual poverty alleviation

Remittance payments directly alleviate the poverty of the individuals and households to whom they are sent. Forming a relatively stable source of income independent of the (often dire) local economy of recipient families, remittances offer a lifeline to millions in the most vulnerable groups across the developing world. Moreover—and unlike other financial flows to developing countries that stream through government agencies and non-governmental organisations (NGOs)—remittance payments are targeted precisely to the needs and desires of their receivers. It is not aid agencies or governments that decide when, where or why remittance incomes are spent, but the recipients themselves.

As with other 'novel' devices of promise in the field of economic development (micro-finance and civil-society promotion being other examples), relatively little in the way of empirical work has been undertaken on the impact of remittances on poverty alleviation. The empirical work that has been done, however, supports the positive picture painted above and in the countless anecdotes that dominate the literature. For instance, a 71-country study undertaken by Adams and Page (2005:1646) concluded that remittances 'reduce the level, depth, and severity of poverty' of receivers and their communities. Likewise, Ratha (2005) found that remittance flows lowered the proportion of people living in absolute poverty in Uganda, Bangladesh and Ghana by 11, 6 and 5 per cent, respectively. Gupta et al. (2007) find that a 10 per cent increase in a country's remittances-to-GDP ratio corresponds with a fall in the percentage of people living on less than $US1 a day of just more than 1 per cent. The World Bank (2003), the OECD's Financial Action Task Force (2005) and Spatafora (2005) also find reductions in absolute poverty among remittance receivers. Meanwhile, studies such as López-Córdova (2005) and Hildebrandt and McKenzie (2005) find positive associations between remittances and poverty-reduction 'proxies' such as lower infant mortality and higher birth rates.[1]

The ways in which remittances alleviate the poverty of individuals are, in the 'first round' of effects, direct and fairly obvious. They include the following.

- **'Survivalist' income supplementation.** For many recipients, remittances provide food security, shelter, clothing and other basic needs.
- **Consumption 'smoothing'.** Many recipients of remittances, especially in rural areas, have highly variable incomes. Remittances allow better matching of incomes and spending, the misalignment of which otherwise threatens survival and/or the taking on of debt.
- **Education.** In many developing countries, education is expensive at all levels, whatever the formal commitments of the State. Remittances can allow for the payment of school fees and can provide the wherewithal for children to attend school rather than working for family survival.[2]
- **Housing.** The use of remittances for the construction, upgrading and repair of houses is prominent in many widely different circumstances.
- **Health.** Remittances can be employed to access preventive and ameliorative health care. As with education, affordable health care is often unavailable in many remittance-recipient countries.
- **Debt.** Being in thrall to moneylenders is an all-too-common experience for many in the developing world. Remittances provide for the repayment of debts and for the means to avoid the taking on of debt by providing alternative income and asset streams.
- **Social spending.** Day-to-day needs include various 'social' expenditures that are culturally unavoidable. Remittances can be employed to meet marriage expenses and religious obligations and, less happily but even more unavoidable, funeral and related costs.
- **Consumer goods.** Remittances allow for the purchase of consumer goods, from the most humble and labour saving, to those that entertain and make for a richer life.

Of course, the extent to which remittances reduce poverty is explicably bound up in how they are used. Typically for poorer recipients, remittance payments are used for basic survival, consumption, housing, health and education, as per above. Once these needs are met, however, remittances can be 'invested' whereupon they provide 'second-round' impacts on poverty into the future. Of course, education and some health expenditure can legitimately be thought of as constituting investment, but important in this context is the extent to which remittances can be used to create income-generating activities. Expenditure on agricultural equipment and fertilisers, vehicles, retail stock and equipment and on land improvement are not uncommon forms of investment of remittance earnings.[3]

Broader concerns: remittances and economic development

Remittance income does not benefit just individual recipients, it benefits the local and national economies in which they live. Indeed, the spending allowed by remittances has a multiplied effect on local economies—as funds subsequently spent create incomes for others and stimulate economic activity generally. Beyond such multiplier effects, however, are other factors conducive to economic growth and stability.

- Remittances can provide receiving countries with much-needed foreign exchange. As noted at the outset of this chapter, remittances are a more stable and reliable form of foreign earnings in many developing countries than either FDI or aid flows, and help alleviate the balance-of-payments and debt crises that are often a characteristic of such countries. In this sense, they are also a potentially stabilising factor for national currencies and can provide developing countries with lower borrowing costs by presenting them with a stable flow of foreign exchange 'collateral'.[4]

- Adding to the appeal of remittance flows to local and national economies is the fact that their frequency and magnitude tend to be counter-cyclical. Economic distress in the home country—precisely the scenario least conducive to other financial flows such as FDI—inspires migrant workers (for altruistic reasons or to protect their own economic interests at home) to increase the volume of funds they remit. Thus, just as remittances allow consumption smoothing for individual households, in this sense they provide a potentially stabilising stream of earnings for national economies too.

- Remittances provide a potential boon for a country's financial development: a stream of earnings to be tapped for saving and for leveraging through formal credit and other products.[5] The existence of links between financial-sector development and economic growth now enjoys a broad consensus, and there is also growing acceptance that better financial institutions lead to lower levels of poverty and inequality.[6] 'Leveraging up' remittances through formal financial institutions (FIs) is important since, by themselves, remittance flows do not solve the structural financial constraints faced by many developing countries. FIs allow remittance recipients to access credit to finance business projects, smooth consumption and so on, and to establish a financial and savings culture more broadly. 'Banking the unbanked' is one of the prime objectives of the micro-finance 'movement', but it is an objective similarly enhanced by FIs bundling remittance payments into savings and (ultimately) loan products through which investment can be activated.[7] Of course, FIs also stand to benefit individually in the longer run through the establishment, via remittance products, of customer relationships with people who are often the most enterprising members of society. In Latin America, about one-fifth of remittance senders become bank clients (Orozco and Fedewa 2006:21).[8]

- The 'leveraging up' of remittances via financial institutions is the policy of individual FIs and micro-finance operators, as well as significant industry representative groups such as the World Council of Credit Unions (WOCCU). The latter's International Remittance Network has enabled hundreds of credit unions (in sending and receiving countries, mostly in the Americas) to participate in the remittance business in collaboration with money-transfer firms (WOCCU n.d.). These firms are relatively expensive, however, and their fees are a significant drain on the margin of funds available for saving.[9] Help is available from various multilateral agencies and NGOs in developing remittance products and linking them with micro-finance—in which context the International Fund for Agricultural Development (IFAD) of the United Nations, USAID (which is providing funds for the WOCCU initiatives) and the Ford and Rockefeller Foundations are especially prominent.

Negative aspects of remittances

The overwhelming narrative of the remittances issue is a positive one, but it is important to recognise that such payments are the flipside of what is also the loss of labour abroad. Moreover, this labour is often the most highly skilled—the manifestation of the 'brain drain' that is a characteristic of the interaction between the rich and the poor worlds more broadly. Such labour migration causes skills shortages at home and imposes great human costs that come from people forced to be away from their families and their communities.[10] The existence of substantial labour migration from a country, and the remittance flows created as a consequence, is often a most eloquent statement about the lack of economic opportunities at home.

A concern sometimes voiced about remittances is that they might promote a variant of the so-called 'Dutch disease'. A phenomenon identified with respect to the Netherlands in the 1960s, Dutch disease is the possibility that foreign exchange flows in one area (gas, in the case of the Netherlands) could result in the overvaluation of a country's exchange rate and, as a consequence, make other areas of its economy uncompetitive. Given the often-chaotic nature of foreign-exchange arrangements in developing countries, Dutch disease effects with respect to remittances are almost certainly overstated. Certainly, as a problem, it would be swamped by far more significant ones in the case of Burma's multiple exchange-rate arrangements—otherwise variously guided by government fiat (in the case of the 'official' rate) and the wild swings of sentiment that drive the unofficial value of the kyat.

Remittance channels and instruments

A characteristic of the global remittances trade is the prominence of informal as well as formal funds-transfer methods and instruments. Formality and informality are, of course, relative concepts in many developing countries (and especially in one such as Burma). For the purposes here, however, and consistent with the categories adopted in many countries and multilateral agencies, formal transfers and informal transfers are distinguished by the fact that the former operates via regulated institutions and the latter via entities that operate outside the regulated financial system (World Bank 2003:23). Typically, banks, dedicated money-transfer firms, other financial institutions, post and telegraph services and so on dominate formal transfers. Informal transfers are impossible to categorise narrowly and include everything from *hundi* systems, couriers and traders and ethnic store networks, to simply carrying money in person across borders. As the survey results show, the relative importance of formal versus informal methods varies wildly according to circumstance.[11]

Formal funds-transfer schemes

Funds-transfer schemes normally provide the least risky, but also the most expensive way of sending remittances, with charges typically ranging between 10 and 15 per cent of the principal transferred (World Bank 2006:135). The funds-transfer sector is dominated by dedicated money-transfer firms, of which Western Union (which commands an estimated 15 per cent of the global remittances business) is the giant (with more than 300 000 agents in more than 200 countries).[12] In recent times, however, formal banks have made inroads into the market share of firms such as Western Union. This is the result of a number of factors (including greater migrant familiarity with banks), but not least the aggressive entry into remittance markets by banks themselves. The latter include some of the most prominent global bank 'brands', as well as newly privatised and commercialised banks in migrants' home countries. The trend is especially apparent in the highly lucrative Latin American remittances business, hitherto very much the preserve of Western Union and its peers. Representative of the phenomenon is the situation in the remittance trade to Mexico, where banks increased their market share from 4 to 17 per cent between 1993 and 2000 (Amuedo-Dorantes et al. 2005:52).

Informal funds-transfer schemes

Informal funds-transfer schemes are used by migrants all over the world where, legal status of sender aside, they thrive because financial institutions in their home country are few, weak or not accessible. If we add to this the fact that many migrant workers come from rural areas and have no familiarity with banks in the first instance, there is a situation in which informal transfer systems have managed to survive in a world of otherwise growing financial-sector formality and sophistication. The relative importance of formal/informal transfer systems varies widely. Informal mechanisms account for probably only 5–20 per cent of remittances in Latin America, but in Sub-Saharan Africa they probably make up 45–65 per cent of the trade (World Bank 2003; Freund and Spatafora 2005).

As noted above, there are many devices that come under the informal funds-transfer rubric. The nature and *modus operandi* of the most important of these are the issues to which this chapter now turns.

Hundi

So labelled in Burma, *hundi* arrangements are known under a variety of names in the many countries and cultures in which they operate. Known variously as *'hawala'* (in the Arabic-speaking world), *'chiao hui'* (in China) and *'poey kwan'* (in Thailand), *hundi* is an ancient device in which monetary value is transferred via a network of dealers or brokers from one location to another. While much mystery is sometimes made of *hundi* schemes, the mechanics of their operations are relatively straightforward—as can be seen in the following (equally simple) example:

> Person A, a Burmese migrant worker in Thailand, desires to send money home to her family in Burma. To do this, she approaches a *hundi* dealer whom she knows and pays them, in baht, the amount she wants sent. The *hundi* dealer now contacts their counterpart (another *hundi* dealer) in Burma, who pays Person A's family in kyat. The amount received by the family will be the kyat equivalent of that paid by Person A in baht, less an amount that represents the commission charged by the two *hundi* dealers. As far as Person A is concerned, the transaction is now complete. She has sent her money home.

A number of matters remain unresolved in the above example, of course. First, the *hundi* dealer in Thailand now owes the *hundi* dealer in Burma for the remittance payment. How will this be settled? There are a number of ways, depending on the circumstances. One of the most common methods (highly applicable in the context of Burma) is that the debt between the two *hundi* dealers will be settled in goods. Many *hundi* dealers are, in fact, shops and traders of various kinds, with *hundi* dealing a 'side' activity. In the case above, therefore, goods to the value of the remittance debt will ultimately make their way from the *hundi* dealer in Thailand to their Burma counterpart. In cases such as Burma, with little in the way of domestic production of complex consumer items, the importation of goods presents a ready avenue for *hundi* settlements. Beyond such 'in-kind' settlements, however, are a number of other reconciliation devices. Most obviously, in circumstances in which financial institutions are accessible to *hundi* dealers (if not to *hundi* customers), funds could be sent directly via banks or money-transfer firms. Such circumstances are mostly unlikely, however, which opens the way for settlement in near-monetary commodities such as gold, precious stones and (sometimes) contraband such as narcotics.

A related issue is the question of foreign exchange flows—or, rather, as the example above shows, their absence. *Hundi* mechanisms, because they are characterised by 'netting' or 'book-transfer' methodologies, transfer value rather than currencies. Accordingly, and as long as settlement between the *hundi* dealers is not ultimately made in cash, *hundi* systems do not deliver foreign exchange to recipient countries. As this chapter explains, this has implications—not least in that it hinders the development potential of remittances via the 'leveraging up' of such flows through formal financial institutions. Since *hundi* systems hide financial flows between countries, they can also be used for money laundering.[13]

In practice, various complications come into the simple picture painted above, most of which, however, only add to the appeal of the *hundi* system. For instance, to ensure security, the *hundi* dealer in Thailand usually gives the Burmese migrant worker an authentication code. This code is communicated by the *hundi* dealer to their equivalent in Burma (usually by phone) and by the Burmese migrant worker to their beneficiary in Burma (also usually by phone). This beneficiary must reveal the authentication code to the *hundi* dealer in Burma in order to receive the remittance payment. Another complication to the simplified example above is that often the *hundi* 'commission' is not an explicit independent 'charge', but an implicit fee levied via discounting the (baht/kyat) exchange rate through which the remittances are calculated. Finally, and as is readily apparent from the above, at the core of the *hundi* system is trust. For the senders and receivers of remittances, such trust is won by observation of the system in successful operation and repeated dealings. Among *hundi* dealers themselves, trust is often based on kith and kin relationships. Accordingly, it is no surprise that *hundi* dealers everywhere tend to assemble networks based on ethnicity. Given too that *hundi* operations are often a sideline to trading generally, so-called 'ethnic stores' are often integral to *hundi* networks.

Personal delivery

In the age of the Internet, the delivery of remittance payments by hand—via friends, family members, couriers and traders—remains surprisingly resilient in the remittance trade around the world, and not just in the poorest of countries. Suro et al. (2002), for instance, found that personal delivery accounted for 10 per cent of remittance payments to Latin America—a market otherwise dominated by money-transfer firms, banks and other financial institutions.[14]

Internationally, personal delivery ranks among the cheapest of remittance systems, but it is also the most vulnerable to theft and accordingly requires high levels of trust. It is therefore often the case that the 'courier' is a family member, a close friend or, in the case of the Thai–Burma border trade, a trader dependent for their own security on the discretion of their customers on either side of a dangerous frontier.

Choosing between formal and informal transfer schemes

One of the major barriers to the use of formal transfer mechanisms is, not surprisingly, the legal status of the sender. If a migrant worker is without legal status in the host country, using a bank or a formal money-transfer firm (where formal identification is usually a requirement) is difficult and risky. In Thailand, foreigners wanting to access a bank need to set up a 'non-resident' baht bank account, which in turn requires the production of a passport, a long-term visa or work permit, as well as a letter of recommendation from an employer, existing bank customer or from the customer's bank abroad. In contrast, informal funds transfers require minimal paperwork and are 'anonymous' as far as government authorities are concerned.

The legal status of the sender is likely the most significant reason for the use of informal funds transfers in most circumstances. There are other reasons, however, including the following.

- A cultural or historical familiarity with informal funds-transfer mechanisms and, conversely, unfamiliarity with formal financial institutions such as banks. Naturally, many *hundi* dealers and the like are themselves members of remitting and recipient communities.
- Informal funds transfers are based on trust networks of personal contacts—precisely the same sorts of networks and contacts that are important in enabling cross-border migration (such as that between Thailand and Burma) in the first place.
- A lack of formal financial institutions in the (often predominantly rural) areas where recipients live. In the literature, this is sometimes referred to as the 'last-mile' problem (World Bank 2003:29). Such problems can dictate the use of informal funds transfers, even if formal channels are available and cost effective for the sender—that is, in the so-called 'first mile'.
- Informal funds-transfer systems tend to be extraordinarily resilient in the face of all manner of instability, including conflict and civil wars, economic crises, weak and unreliable monetary and financial systems, the levying of economic sanctions and other events than can affect the formal economy and what the World Bank (2003) calls 'national infrastructure'.

- Informal funds transfers move funds remarkably quickly. The typical experience globally is that even people in very remote areas receive payment via informal funds transfers within 24 hours.
- Informal funds transfers are often the cheapest remittance channel. Estimates vary, but informal funds transfers typically cost between 2 and 10 per cent of the transaction principal (Adams 2006; World Bank 2003). Informal funds transfers do not have to meet regulatory or compliance costs and the like, nor do their promoters typically have much in the way of expensive infrastructure.
- In many countries and circumstances, 'quasi-legal' economic activity (such as informal funds transfers) is the dominant form of business. In such circumstances, commerce runs along functional rather than strictly 'legal' channels. Informal funds transfers are illegal in many places; their functionality is a product, however, of their widespread and everyday acceptance.

Survey findings

The data underlying this analysis of Burmese migrant worker remittances are drawn from a survey of about 1000 such workers undertaken by the authors in 2002–03. The survey was conducted in 12 provinces of Thailand, selected according to their relative importance as areas of settlement and employment of Burmese.[15] By far the majority of the workers interviewed had fled the violent repression in Burma that followed the uprisings of 1988, with most arriving during the latter half of the 1990s. The survey revealed that prominent in the list of factors driving the flight of the Burmese, in addition to fleeing the country's political repression and civil wars, was Burma's grinding poverty and lack of economic opportunities. Not unexpectedly, given their proximity to Thailand and the long experience of conflict in these areas, the majority of the workers surveyed (and Burmese in Thailand generally) were from rural areas of Burma's Karen, Mon and Shan States, as well from Tenasserim Division. The median income for Burmese migrant workers employed in their first job in Thailand was about 2500 baht (Bt) a month. Only 40 per cent of the workers surveyed were in possession of a formal work permit conferring legal employment status. Workers holding work permits were over-represented in jobs earning more than Bt5000 a month, while the converse was true for those earning below Bt1000. The workers in the survey were employed across a number of industries, including fishing, construction, retail trade, hotels and restaurants, household service, food processing, agriculture, forestry and quarrying. Incomes earned varied widely across these industries, the highest paid being those engaged in quarrying and the lowest in agriculture and forestry. A majority (62 per cent) of those surveyed were men.

Results: amounts sent

As can be seen from Table 5.1, the median amount sent home by the 524 survey recipients who declared making remittance payments was Bt15 000 (about $US575). This is an annual aggregate figure, nominated by the respondents as the total they sent home for the previous 12 months. The maximum amount sent by any single worker was Bt3 million, while the lowest non-zero annual remittance total was Bt3000.

Table 5.1 Summary statistics for remittances (n = 524/1023)

Summary measure	Value (baht)
Sum	10 034 083
Mean	19 149
Median	15 000
Mode	10 000
Aggregate ratio to income	0.38

The aggregate ratio of annual remittance payments to annual disposable income of 38 per cent is quite high relative to experiences elsewhere. Moreover, the ratio is almost certainly understated since the survey includes bands of income rather than discrete amounts and the calculation here includes income at the top of each nominated band. Estimates for the United States suggest that migrant workers send home between 20 and 40 per cent of their aggregate earnings, but the concentration in most studies is between 20 and 25 per cent (Orozco 2006; Amuedo-Dorantes et al. 2005).

Should the survey results be anywhere near representative of the million or so Burmese in Thailand, the aggregate annual flows of remittances to Burma in 2002/03 from this source would have been in the order of $US300 million.[16] Such flows are nearly five times Burma's 'official' remittance payments for the year, more than twice the amount of FDI received and they would represent about 5 per cent of Burma's GDP.[17] Of course, these numbers are very rough, but they give some idea of the magnitude of the likely remittance payments to Burma and the potential they could yield for the country's economy more broadly.

Not unexpectedly, individual remittances from migrant workers tend to rise with income (de la Garza and Lowell 2004). As can be seen in Figure 5.1, the survey data are consistent with this general rule. What appear to be strong falls at various income categories in the graph is largely a statistical anomaly—due to greater sampling variability caused by small numbers of respondents at these incomes.

Figure 5.1 Remittances by income group

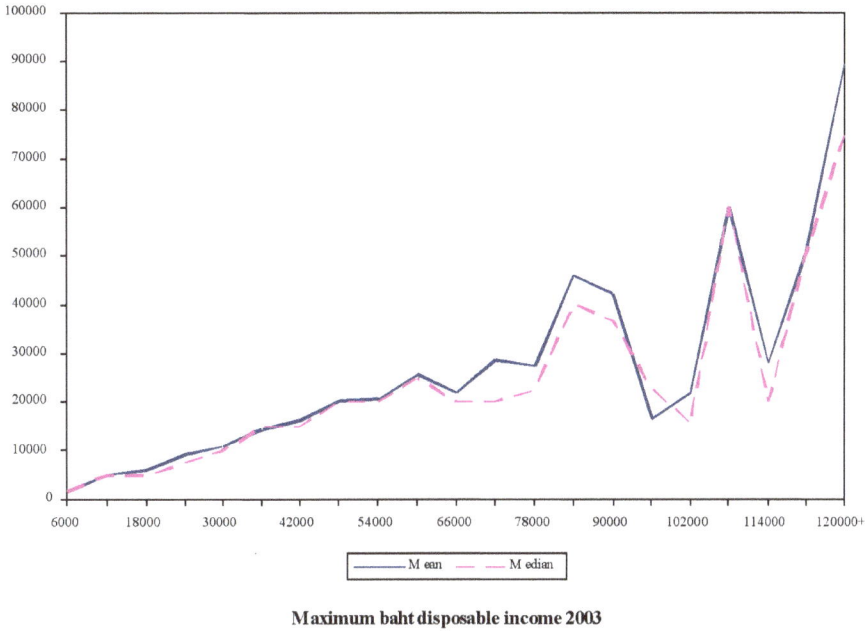

Maximum baht disposable income 2003

Figure 5.2 Remittances by duration of residence in Thailand

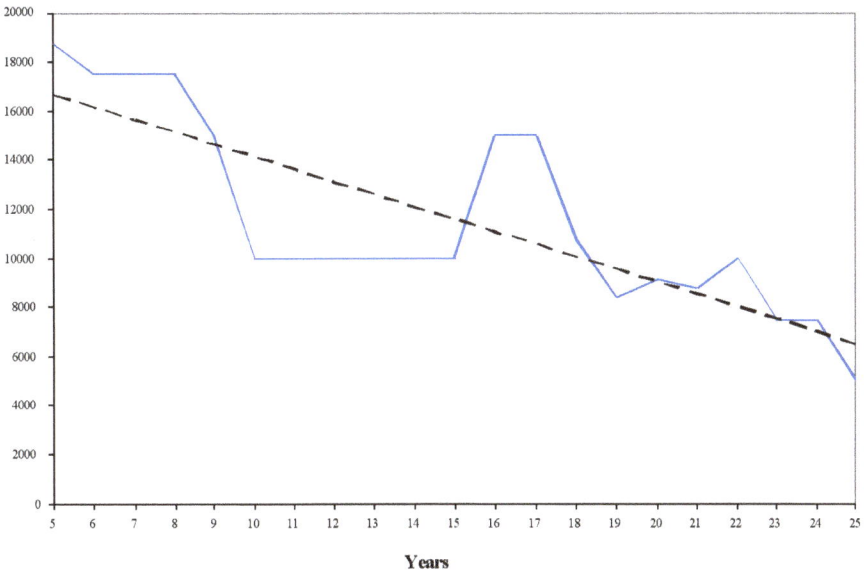

Years

A phenomenon identified in other places and contexts is that individual remittances decline with time, usually as a consequence of migrants putting down roots in their host country and losing touch with their former home. As Figure 5.2 indicates, such a decline in remittances is evident from our data too. The authors are, however, reluctant to draw the conventional inference since few Burmese establish *de jure* permanent settlement in Thailand (if not de facto residence for considerable periods). It is possible, for instance, that in Burma's circumstances the depicted decline in remittances for individuals across time is less a function of them establishing themselves in Thailand than the fact that family members might themselves have subsequently left Burma. In this case, there could be no-one left to send remittances to.

Uses for remittances

What are Burmese migrant-worker remittances used for? Migrant-worker remittances everywhere are made and subsequently spent according to a hierarchy of needs. According to this survey, the remittances Burmese workers send from Thailand are used overwhelmingly to assist their families in basic survival. Some 96 per cent of respondents nominated this as their first order of priority. Indeed, many nominated family survival as their only motivation, with some taking the opportunity to annotate on our survey documents the living conditions faced by their families back in Burma.

As can be seen from Figure 5.3, other purposes (nominated on the survey itself according to priorities common in other contexts and circumstances) were negligible motivating factors. Such motivations, however minor, included (in order of importance assigned by survey respondents): to purchase or develop farm land; to establish a business; to meet education expenses; to repay debt; to hire workers in Burma; and to purchase consumer goods.

Figure 5.3 Remittances by intended recipient use

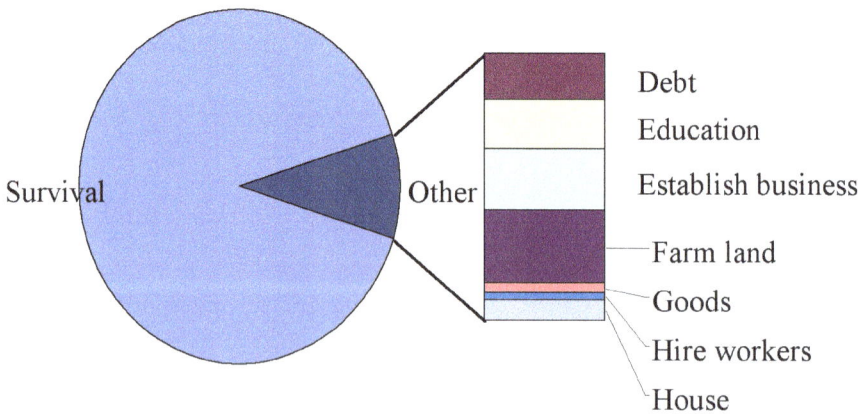

Figure 5.4 Remittance share by transfer method

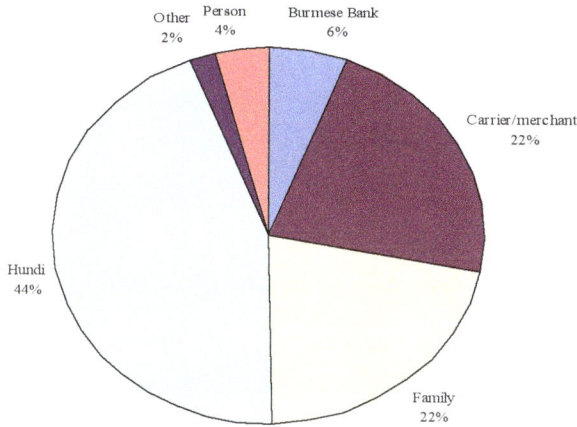

Methods and instruments

The most noteworthy fact revealed by the survey of remittance methods and instruments is the overwhelming dominance of informal funds transfers. As demonstrated in Figure 5.4, 94 per cent of respondents in the survey reported that they made their remittance payments via informal funds transfers. Within informal funds transfers, *hundi* was the dominant device (twice as large as any other), but significant proportions were simply carried into Burma by hand by either close family members or carriers and merchants. The nearly one-quarter share taken up by carriers and merchants could reflect a number of factors: most obviously, the porous nature of the Thai–Burma border, but also a possible remittance role played by brokers who bring many Burmese into Thailand in the first place. The small share (6 per cent) of migrant workers who carry their payments back into Burma themselves likely reflects the fact that Burma's political situation dictates that few migrants are in a position to return home.

The dominance of *hundi* is not unexpected since, as alluded to above, it is a device particularly well suited to the situation faced by Burmese migrant workers. Using banks is almost impossible for most Burmese in Thailand because of the level of documentation required (as noted earlier, to use banks in Thailand, foreigners must establish a 'non-resident' baht bank account, which in turn requires a passport, a long-term visa or work permit, as well as letters of recommendation). Meanwhile, Burma's political situation means that other formal transfer mechanisms (such as money-transfer firms) are not functional in the trade. Accordingly, and unless funds are physically carried across the border, *hundi* is the device preferred by most. As noted earlier, *hundi* relies on trust. Significantly then, the survey revealed no cases of fraud and numerous anecdotes of *hundi* dealer selection being based on positive word of mouth, reinforced by subsequent repeated dealings.

Other reasons for the dominance of *hundi* almost certainly include historical familiarity and cost. Hundi systems have a long history in Burma and in the colonial era they were championed by the Chettiar moneylenders, who, for nearly a century, were the country's principal financiers. The Chettiars used *hundi* systems not only to transfer funds (domestically as well as internationally), but to provide a (critically important) credit instrument to Burmese cultivators. In this context, the Chettiars provided credit simply by making payments in advance of the *hundi* sender's remittance—turning a *hundi* into something akin to the 'bill of exchange' long familiar in the West. Just like bills of exchange elsewhere, Western banks operating in Burma even 'discounted' *hundis* (that is, buying them at less than face value and thus providing the seller with finance at a discount 'rate' equivalent to an interest charge), thus connecting colonial Burma's informal financial system with that of its formal and international equivalent—and providing Burma with the finance that went towards the transformation of the Irrawaddy (Ayeyarwady) Delta into the largest rice-growing region in the world. Eventually, in its perennial quest to create a viable tax system in Burma, the colonial government even supplied a specially authorised *hundi* 'chapter', upon which was payable a stamp duty. The Chettiars were effectively expelled from Burma post independence, but the *hundi* lived on as a principal device for trade throughout the country and beyond it. With the Chettiars gone, *hundi* in Burma ceased to be identified with any particular ethnic group. This legacy today separates the experience of *hundi* in Burma from those of many other parts of South-East Asia, where the trade is greatly dominated by ethnic Chinese and their businesses.[18]

While precision in this context is not remotely possible, the authors estimate that about 40 per cent of all of Burma's 'legal' border trade is conducted via *hundi*, while more than 90 per cent of strictly illegal business (smuggling notably) is undertaken through *hundi* channels. Following the emergence of private banks in Burma in the early 1990s, *hundi* entered a period of decline as a remittance and credit device in the country. It has re-emerged strongly since the collapse of the most important of these banks in the financial crisis of 2002–03.

The survey respondents reported that the average cost of sending a *hundi* amounted to about 5 to 10 per cent of the principal sent (levied mostly via a discount/premium on the baht/kyat exchange rate). As noted earlier in this chapter, formal money-transfer firms typically charge between 10 and 15 per cent.

The small (6 per cent) share of remittances sent into Burma via formal banks is confined almost exclusively to migrant workers sending funds to Putao in Kachin State. Putao is a hill town that can be reached only by air. This, coupled with the fact that it is also home to four battalions of the Tatmadaw (army), conceivably makes the physical carrying of funds from Thailand, and that sent via *hundi*, highly vulnerable to 'official' expropriation.

Other regional variations of remittance method are also apparent in our survey data. The physical carrying of funds, for instance, is the overwhelming practice of those sending funds to Shan State. In contrast, almost 100 per cent of workers remitting funds to Tenasserim (Tanyintharyi) and Mon State use *hundi*.

Hundi is the dominant remittance device according to the number of Burmese migrant workers using it, but it is also the favoured instrument according to value. In this context, *hundi*'s lead over other mechanisms is marginal, and to some extent the most remarkable fact observable in Figure 5.5 is the high degree of equality of the various instruments by value (the numerals written in each of the columns below represent the raw numbers of individuals nominating each of the remittance devices).

Figure 5.5 Remittance magnitudes by method

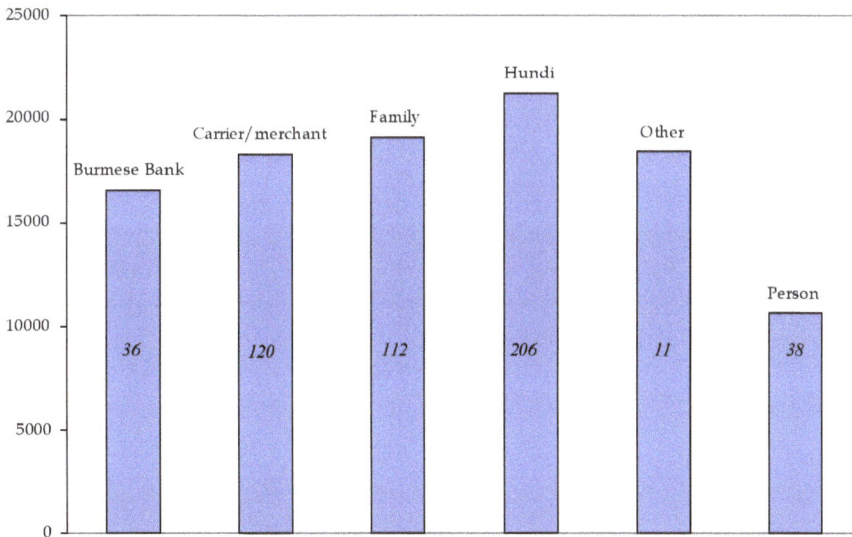

Gender differences

This survey yields some interesting differences in remittance patterns according to gender, of which the essential finding is that female Burmese migrant workers send home a higher proportion of their income (40 per cent of the maximum) than males (36 per cent). Male workers earn more, but their median annual remittance of Bt15 000 is identical to that of female workers. This finding is similar to that of other studies exploring gender differences in remittance patterns in other country pairs (see, for instance, Moreno 2005). The differences are more pronounced among lower-income workers (of which women constitute a larger proportion than the population generally) than among those earning higher incomes. Curiously, the survey also reveals differences according to gender in terms of remittance methods and instruments. Women are more likely (18 per cent) to use a bank to send their money home (though the absolute numbers here remain small) and are more likely to send money by hand through another person (25 per cent), but are less likely to use *hundi* (13 per cent).

Table 5.2 Remittances and gender

Summary measure	Female	Male
Sum	Bt3 869 100	Bt6 164 983
Mean	Bt18 966	Bt19 488
Median	Bt15 000	Bt15 000
Mode	Bt10 000	Bt10 000
Coefficient of variation	73.9%	112.1%
Aggregate ratio to income (2003 maximum)	0.40	0.36

Some conjectures

This survey reveals that remittances sent from Burmese migrant workers in Thailand directly alleviate the poverty of individuals and households to whom they are sent. Remittances are also likely to provide for individual benefits in allowing greater access to health services and education. Health and education appeared only weakly in our survey results as independent motivations for sending remittances, but it is ventured that both are likely to also reside implicitly within the survival rubric.

The survey also suggests, however, that any national economic development benefits allowed by remittances are largely absent in the Burmese context. The circumstances of Burma's political economy instead undermine the broader processes that might otherwise be apparent.

Remittances and foreign reserves

As noted at the outset of this chapter, an important benefit often yielded by remittance flows is the extent that they provide sizeable and relatively stable flows of foreign reserves. This attribute is greatly undermined in the Burmese context by the fact that *hundi* is the most common method by which remittances are made. As demonstrated, *hundi* works via 'netting' transactions that minimise the flow of foreign exchange.

Remittances and business capital

Elsewhere, remittances have provided businesses in recipient countries with otherwise scarce capital. Establishing or expanding a business is a strong motivation for remittances in many countries and circumstances. Paying remittances for the purpose of business is not, however, a strong motivating factor in the context of Burma. Even if simple survival was not an all-consuming force, Burma's dire economic and political circumstances would tell against substantial investment flows. Indeed, given the risks, it is probably in their own best interests that Burma's migrant workers are unwilling to expose their hard-earned gains in this way.

Remittances and financial development

The 'leveraging up' of the development potential of remittances through formal financial institutions is much celebrated. Similarly highly regarded is the way that remittance flows might themselves stimulate the development of financial institutions. Unfortunately, these attributes are likewise absent in the circumstances in which Burmese migrant workers find themselves. This is because, first (and as noted above), about 60 per cent of our survey recipients do not possess Thai work permits—a fact that would automatically (legally) rule them out of holding an account at a bank in Thailand. Of course, even among the 40 per cent that do hold work permits, the additional documentation hurdles for opening a bank account remain formidable.

Second, and probably more significant than first-mile obstacles, are the last-mile problems in Burma itself. Put simply, and especially since the banking crisis of 2003, Burma's formal financial system remains distrusted and dysfunctional. Burma's banks eke out a marginal existence in an environment hostile to the survival of financial institutions and they are not an effective instrument to facilitate remittances or, indeed, even to gain from them.

Impact of the 'Saffron Revolution'

In the wake of what has become widely known as the Saffron Revolution of September–October 2007, money transfers to Burma (of all types) ceased to function. Formal bank-based instruments were suspended in the days of high chaos in September, but in October the impact of US and other international sanctions made even those foreign banks normally happy to do business with Burma think twice. Even the normally extremely resilient *hundi* system seized up for a few days, including that (central to this chapter) channelling funds from Burmese workers in Thailand. There was, however, a significant difference between the problems faced by the formal and informal systems—the latter being a function not of systemic problems of *hundi* networks themselves, but of fears that Burma's military regime might resort to its time-honoured practice of suddenly 'demonetising' certain denominations of the kyat. Money transfers to Burma have resumed since the 2007 demonstrations, but the situation remains uncertain and volatile.

Concluding thoughts

The survey that informs this chapter reveals that the remittances Burmese migrant workers in Thailand send home are large and, circumstances permitting, could provide the means to accelerate Burma's economic development. Unfortunately, the survey also reveals that these remittances are employed overwhelmingly in the cause of simple survival, with little in the way of funds left over for investment and other 'productive' purposes that would maximise their development impact. Equally, this chapter finds that remittances to Burma are made overwhelmingly via various informal devices, negating the possibility that they could be 'leveraged up' via formal financial institutions and minimising the dynamic economic effects they might otherwise trigger. Of course, the fact that Burmese migrant-worker remittances are used for bare survival and that they are channelled in informal ways offers yet another window into Burma's dire political economy. In its seminal report on the development possibilities of remittances, the OECD (Straubhaar and Vadean 2005:10) noted that 'the best way to maximise the impact of remittances on economic growth…is to implement sound macroeconomic policies and policies of good governance…a sound banking system, respect for property rights, and an outward-oriented trade and FDI strategy'. In present-day Burma, such attributes are, alas, highly conspicuous by their absence.

References

Adams, R. H. 2006, 'Do remittances reduce poverty?', *id21 Insights*, vol. 60, January.

Adams, R. H. and Page, J. 2005, 'Do international migration and remittances reduce poverty in developing countries', *World Development*, vol. 33, no. 10, pp. 1645–69.

Aggarwal, R., Demirguc-Kunt, A. and Martinez Peria, M. S. 2006, *Do workers' remittances promote financial development?*, World Bank Policy Research Working Paper No. 3957, World Bank, Washington, DC.

Amuedo-Dorantes, C., Bansak, C. and Pozo, S. 2005, 'On the remitting patterns of immigrants: evidence from Mexican survey data', *Economic Review*, First Quarter 2005, Federal Reserve Bank of Atlanta, Atlanta.

Beck, T., Levine, R. and Loayza, N. 2000a, 'Financial intermediation and growth: causality and causes', *Journal of Monetary Economics*, vol. 46, pp. 31–77.

Beck, T., Levine, R. and Loayza, N. 2000b, 'Finance and the sources of growth', *Journal of Financial Economics*, vol. 58, pp. 261–300.

Beck, T., Demirgüc-Kunt, A. and Levine, R. 2004, *Finance, inequality and poverty: cross-country evidence*, NBER Working Paper No. 10979, National Bureau of Economic Research, Cambridge, Massachusetts.

Bolt, P. J. 2000, *China and Southeast Asia's Ethnic Chinese: State and diaspora in contemporary Asia*, Praeger, Westport, Connecticut.

Bradford, W. and Vicary, A. 2005, 'Preliminary survey results about Burmese migrant workers in Thailand', *Burma Economic Watch*, 1/2005.

Clemens, M. 2007, *Do visas kill? Health effects of African health professional emigration*, Center for Global Development Working Paper No. 114, Center for Global Development, Washington, DC.

Cox, E., Ureta, A. and Ureta, M. 2003, 'International migration, remittances, and schooling: evidence from El Salvador', *Journal of Development Economics*, vol. 72, pp. 429–61.

de la Garza, R. and Lowell, B. A. 2004, *Sending Money Home: Hispanic remittances and community development*, Rowman and Littlefield, Oxford.

Financial Action Task Force 2005, *Money Laundering and Terrorist Financing Typologies*, Organisation for Economic Cooperation and Development, Paris.

Freund, C. and Spatafora, N. 2005, *Remittances: transaction costs, determinants, and informal flows*, World Bank Policy Research Working Paper No. 3704, World Bank, Washington, DC.

Giuliano, P. and Ruiz-Arranz, M. 2005, *Remittances, financial development and growth*, IMF Working Paper, WP/05/24, December, International Monetary Fund, Washington, DC.

Gupta, S., Pattillo, C. and Wagh, S. 2007, *Impact of remittances on poverty and financial development in Sub-Saharan Africa*, IMF Working Paper WP/07/38, February, International Monetary Fund, Washington, DC.

Hastings, A. H. 2006, Entry of MFIs into the remittance market: opportunities and challenges, Paper prepared for the Global Microcredit Summit, 13 November, Halifax, Nova Scotia.

Hildebrandt, N. and McKenzie, D. J. 2005, *The effects of migration on child health in Mexico*, World Bank Policy Research Working Paper No. 3573, World Bank, Washington, DC.

Inter-American Development Bank (IADB) 2003, *Sending Money Home: An international comparison of remittance markets*, Inter-American Development Bank, Washington, DC.

International Monetary Fund (IMF) 2002, *Balance of Payments Statistics. Yearbook 2002*, International Monetary Fund, Washington, DC.

International Monetary Fund (IMF) 2004, *Balance of Payments Statistics. Yearbook 2004*, International Monetary Fund, Washington, DC.

International Monetary Fund (IMF) 2007, *International Financial Statistics*, August, International Monetary Fund, Washington, DC.

Kanaiaupuni, S. and Donato, K. M. 1999, 'Migradollars and mortality: the effects of migration on infant survival in Mexico', *Demography*, vol. 36, pp. 339–53.

King, R. and Levine, R. 1993, 'Finance and growth: Schumpeter might be right', *Quarterly Journal of Economics*, vol. 108, pp. 717–37.

Lapper, Richard 2007, 'Cashing in on homeward flows', *Financial Times*, 28 August 2007.

Levine, R. 1997, 'Financial development and economic growth: views and agenda', *Journal of Economic Literature*, vol. 35, pp. 688–726.

Levine, R. 2004, *Finance and growth: theory and evidence*, NBER Working Paper No. 10766, National Bureau of Economic Research, Cambridge, Massachusetts.

Levine, R. and Zervos, S. 1998, 'Stock markets, banks, and growth', *American Economic Review*, vol. 88, pp. 537–58.

López-Córdova, E. 2005, 'Globalization, migration, and development: the role of Mexican migrant remittances', *Economia*, vol. 6, pp. 217–56.

Maimbo, S. and Ratha, D. 2005, *Remittances: Development impact and future prospects*, World Bank, Washington, DC.

Moreno, C. 2005, Gender, remittances and development, Paper presented to the Conference on Women Leaders, 27 September 2005, Haifa, Israel.

Orozco, M. 2006, 'Sending money home: can remittances reduce poverty', *id21 Insights*, no. 60, January.

Orozco, M. and Fedewa, R. 2006, *Leveraging efforts on remittances and financial intermediation*, Working Paper 24, Inter-American Development Bank, Washington, DC.

Rajan, R. and Zingales, L. 1998, 'Financial dependence and growth', *American Economic Review*, vol. 88, pp. 559–86.

Ratha, D. 2005, 'Remittances: a lifeline for development', *Finance and Development*, vol. 42, no. 4, December.

Spatafora, N. 2005, 'Two current issues facing developing countries', *World Economic Outlook*, International Monetary Fund, Washington, DC.

Straubhaar, T. and Vadean, F. P. 2005, 'International migrant remittances and their role in development', *Migration, Remittances and Development*, Organisation for Economic Cooperation and Development, Paris.

Suro, R. 2003, *Remittance Senders and Receivers: Tracking the transnational channels*, Inter-American Development Bank in collaboration with the Pew Hispanic Center, Washington, DC.

Suro, R., Bendixen, L., Lowell, L. and Benavides, D. C. 2002, *Billions in Motion: Latino immigrants, remittances and banking*, Pew Hispanic Center, Washington, DC.

Terry, D. F. and Wilson, S. R. 2005, *Beyond Small Change: Making migrant remittances count*, Inter-American Development Bank, Washington, DC.

United Nations Development Program (UNDP) 2005, *The potential role of remittances in achieving the Millennium Development Goals—an exploration*, UNDP Background Note, October, <http://tcdc1.undp.org/Remittances_Oct02005B.pdf>

Vicary, A. 2004, 'Economic survey of "Burmese" working in Thailand: an overview of a BEW project', *Burma Economic Watch*, 1/2004.

Woodruff, C. and Zenteno, R. 2001, *Remittances and microenterprises in Mexico*, UCSD Working Paper, University of California, San Diego.

World Bank 2003, *Informal Funds Transfer Systems in the APEC Region: Initial findings and a framework for further analysis*, World Bank, Washington, DC.

World Bank 2006, *Global Economic Prospects 2006: Economic implications of remittances and migration*, World Bank, Washington, DC.

World Council of Credit Unions (WOCCU) n.d., *A Technical Guide to Remittances*, viewed 13 February 2008, <http://www.woccu.org/development/remittances/index.php>

Yang, D. 2005, *International migration, human capital, and entrepreneurship: evidence from Philippine migrants' exchange rate shocks*, World Bank Policy Research Working Paper No. 3578, World Bank, Washington, DC.

Endnotes

[1] Surveys of the ever-growing literature on the role of remittances and poverty reduction can be accessed at the web site of the Institute of Development Studies (<http://www.livelihoods.org/hot_topics/migration/remittancesindex.html#1>).

[2] For more on the impact of remittances on school attendance, see Yang (2005) and López-Córdova (2005).

[3] The Inter-American Development Bank (IADB 2003) found that, for Latin America, 5–10 per cent of remittances were immediately invested in business of some form (and a roughly similar proportion was used for education). Woodruff and Zenteno (2001) estimated that remittances provided about 20 per cent of the capital employed by more than 6000 urban micro-enterprises in Mexico. Yang (2005) and Aggarwal et al. (2006) likewise find evidence of remittances promoting entrepreneurship across many countries and circumstances.

[4] Gupta et al. (2007) and Ratha (2005) speculate that developing countries could raise funds on global financial markets by effectively 'securitising' future remittance flows.

[5] Empirical analysis by Aggarwal et al. (2006) reports 'a robust positive impact of remittances on financial sector development'. Their study is backed up by a growing number of others suggesting a link between remittances, financial development and economic growth. See, for instance, Guiliano and Ruiz-Arranz (2005) and Gupta et al. (2007).

[6] On the role of financial institutions and economic development, see King and Levine (1993), Levine (1997, 2004), Beck et al. (2000a, 2000b) and Rajan and Zingales (1998). With respect to the relatively new findings positing a link between financial-sector development and better outcomes in poverty and inequality, see Beck et al. (2004) and Aggarwal et al. (2006).

[7] According to the UNDP (2005), up to 40 per cent of remittance recipients save at least some of their payments. Savings rates of senders seem to be highly variable according to context. According to Orozco and Fedewa (2006:4) in their work on the Americas, 'on average, around 10% of remittances received are saved and invested'. For more on the link between savings and subsequent investment decisions, see Gupta et al. (2007:24).

[8] FIs around the world have recognised the potential of remittances. BancoSol of Bolivia, one of the world's largest and most successful micro-finance institutions, has a special savings and loan product, 'My Family, My Country, My Return', through which remittance recipients can take out housing loans (Orozco and Fedewa 2006:16). Other mainstream banks and micro-finance providers offer similar products.

[9] Nevertheless, collective deals to reduce the fees that money-transfer firms charge micro-finance institutions have been done. For more, see Orozco and Fedewa (2006:13–15). ACLEDA Bank of Cambodia is one micro-finance institution that has partnered with Western Union.

[10] For more on the damaging impact of this brain drain, particularly on national health systems, see Clemens (2007).

[11] While Freund and Spatafora (2005) nominate a ratio range of informal to formal mechanisms of between 20 and 200 per cent, in practice, almost any ratio can apply.

[12] Western Union's closest competitor (with a global share of about 3 per cent) is MoneyGram, also based in the United States. For more on these firms, their background and their rivalry, see Lapper (2007). Money-transfer firms are especially dominant in the remittances business to Latin America (their share of the important US–Mexico market is about 70 per cent (Amuedo-Dorantes et al. 2005:51).

[13] Concerns about the use of *hundi* systems for money laundering and as a possible vehicle for terrorist financing have heightened greatly in recent years. For a review of some of the issues, see Financial Action Task Force (2005).

[14] Suro (2002) also found that an additional 7 per cent of remittance payments in the region were made sending cash through the post. This mechanism could not work in Burma since the postal system scarcely exists in most of the country and, even where it does, it is greatly distrusted.

[15] For a comprehensive outline of the survey itself, its methodology and the provinces selected, see Vicary (2004) and Bradford and Vicary (2005).

[16] We have assumed an identical ratio of remittance senders to total migrant population identified by our survey. Of course, the figure of 'one million' Burmese in Thailand is not much more than an informed 'guestimate'—albeit, we expect, a conservative one.

[17] Investment and GDP data are based on that in IMF (2007).

[18] See, for instance, Bolt (2000) for one of but many studies investigating this phenomenon.

6: Myanmar's economic relations with China: who benefits and who pays?

Toshihiro Kudo

Introduction

Against the background of closer diplomatic, political and security ties between Myanmar and China since 1988, their economic relations have also become stronger throughout the 1990s and up to the present. China is now a major supplier of consumer and capital goods to Myanmar, in particular through border trade. China also provides a large amount of economic cooperation in the areas of infrastructure, state-owned economic enterprises (SEEs) and energy. Nevertheless, Myanmar's trade with China has failed to have a substantial impact on its broad-based economic and industrial development. China's economic cooperation apparently supports the present regime, but its effects on the whole economy are limited. At worst, bad loans might need to be paid off by Myanmar and Chinese stakeholders, including taxpayers. Strengthened economic ties with China will be instrumental in regime survival, but will not be a powerful force affecting the process of economic development in Myanmar.

Myanmar and China call each other *'paukphaw'*, a Myanmar word for siblings. *Paukphaw* is not used for any other foreign country, reflecting Myanmar and China's close and cordial relationship.[1] For Myanmar, China has historically been by far its most important neighbour, sharing the longest border, of 2227 kilometres. Myanmar regained its independence in 1948 and quickly welcomed the birth of the People's Republic of China in the next year. The Sino–Myanmar relationship has always been premised on five principles of peaceful coexistence, which include mutual respect for each other's territorial integrity and sovereignty and mutual non-aggression (Than 2003).

Nevertheless, independent Myanmar has been cautious about its relationship with China. In reality, Sino–Myanmar relations have undergone a series of ups and downs and China has occasionally posed a real threat to Myanmar's security, such as the incursion of defeated Chinese Nationalist (Kuomintang or KMT) troops into the northern Shan State in 1949, overt and covert Chinese support for the Burmese Communist Party's insurgency against Yangon up until 1988 and confrontations between Burmese and resident overseas Chinese, including militant Maoist students in 1967. Indeed, the Myanmar leadership, always extremely sensitive about the country's sovereignty, independence and territorial integrity, had long observed strict neutrality during the Cold War, avoiding obtaining military and economic aid from the superpowers.

Dramatic changes have emerged since the birth in 1988 of the present government, the State Peace and Development Council (SPDC), originally called the State Law and Order Restoration Council (SLORC). The United States, the European Union, Japan and multilateral aid organisations all withheld official development assistance and some Western countries imposed political sanctions and weapons embargoes after 1990. Under mounting international pressure, the military regime in Yangon had no choice but to approach Beijing for help. As diplomatic, political and security ties between the two countries grew closer, economic relations also strengthened.

The purpose of this chapter is to examine the development of and changes in Myanmar–China economic relations since 1988 and to evaluate China's growing influence on the Myanmar economy. It seeks to answer the question of whether or not the Myanmar economy can survive and grow with reinforced economic ties with China. In other words, can China support the Myanmar economy against the imposition of economic sanctions by Western countries? This question is relevant to assess the impact and effectiveness of sanctions. The chapter also tries to answer another question—namely, who benefits in what ways and who pays what costs as the two countries strengthen their ties, in spite of Myanmar's isolation from the mainstream of the international community.

The second section introduces a brief history of how the two countries have become the closest of allies since 1988. The third section examines trade relations between Myanmar and China, while the fourth section describes Chinese economic and business cooperation with Myanmar. The last section summarises the author's arguments and answers the research questions.

Historical and political background

For many years, China adopted a dual-track approach towards Myanmar by endorsing party-to-party relations between the Chinese Communist Party (CCP) and the Burmese Communist Party (BCP), in addition to maintaining state-to-state relations. The CCP's covert and overt support of the BCP, which resorted to armed struggle against the Yangon government soon after its independence, seriously hindered the two countries' state-to-state relationship for many years after Myanmar's independence.

When the military took power in a coup in 1988, thousands of pro-democracy activists, including students, fled to the border area near Thailand, where numerous ethnic insurgencies were active (Lintner 1998).[2] None of the ethnic rebels there could, however, secure a meaningful amount of armaments. On the other hand, unlike the ethnic insurgents, the BCP located along the Chinese border had access to vast quantities of arms and ammunition that were supplied by China. Hypothetically, an alliance of pro-democracy activists, ethnic rebels and an armed BCP might have posed a potential threat to Myanmar's military government, but it was not to happen.

Instead, a mutiny caused the BCP to split into four ethnic groups in early 1989. The CCP had already withdrawn its active support of the BCP after 1985 (Than 2003). Just before the end of the Cold War, China departed from its dual-track diplomacy and renounced its policy stance favouring the BCP. Having lost Beijing's backing, the BCP collapsed in the year after the establishment of the SLORC.[3] On the other hand, Yangon was fortunate to secure Beijing's backing in the midst of Western ostracism.

The mutiny inside the BCP provided a golden opportunity for the Myanmar military to neutralise the newly emerged armed groups, and they were willing to pay any price for this. Lieutenant-General Khin Nyunt, then Secretary No. 1 of the SLORC, wasted no time in going to the Chinese border and he achieved a successful cease-fire with these groups. Under the terms of the cease-fire, the Myanmar Government offered the former BCP mutineers development assistance such as roads, bridges, power stations, schools and hospitals as well as business opportunities, including mining and lumbering concessions and border trade. As Bertil Lintner, veteran South-East Asia correspondent, writes:

> Ironically, at a time when almost the entire population of Burma had turned against the regime, thousands of former insurgents thus rallied behind the ruling military. The threat from the border areas was thwarted, the regime was safe, but the consequences for the country, and the outside world, were disastrous. (Lintner 1998:170)

Than Shwe, then Vice-Chairman of the SLORC, accompanied by Khin Nyunt, visited Beijing in October 1989 and laid the foundations for the current partnership between the two countries. The visit also marked a departure from Myanmar's past policy on arms imports, whereby it eschewed large arms purchases from the superpowers consistent with its policy of strict neutrality (Jannuzi 1998). The SLORC apparently launched an ambitious plan to enlarge and modernise the Tatmadaw, the Myanmar armed forces, by late 1988 or early 1989, with heavy reliance on Chinese armaments (Selth 1996). At the same time, the military leadership successfully extracted a promise of economic and technical cooperation from China.

Without the change in China's diplomacy towards Myanmar and the break up of the BCP, the relationships and structures of power would not have reached their present points. Arms transfers and economic ties have dramatically increased China's influence over Myanmar. Indeed, a few years of military and economic aid have turned the non-aligned state of Myanmar into China's closest ally.

Today, the military government is effectively dependent on China for its survival and, some analysts say, it has become a Chinese client state (Ott 1998).

Trade relations

China as an important but unbalanced trading partner

China occupies an important position in Myanmar's external trade. Tables 6.1 and 6.2 show the major trading partners of Myanmar since 1980. According to the tables, China has consistently occupied a high ranking, since Myanmar–Chinese border trade—hitherto an activity deemed illegal—was legitimised and formalised in 1988. China's fifth position in this trade constituted 8.1 per cent of Myanmar's total exports to the rest of the world and 20.6 per cent of its total imports from the rest of the world (ranking China first in 1990),[4] although Myanmar's volume of external trade was small at that time. Since then, Myanmar's trade with China has grown rapidly.

Table 6.1 Myanmar's major export partners (per cent)

	1980		1988		1990	
1	Singapore	14.3	Africa	19.7	Africa	14.3
2	Africa	10.6	Singapore	9.7	Thailand	12.0
3	Japan	9.9	Hong Kong	9.1	Singapore	11.3
4	Indonesia	9.5	Japan	8.4	India	10.8
5	Hong Kong	7.6	Indonesia	7.0	China	8.1

	1995		2000		2008	
1	Singapore	16.0	United States	22.4	Thailand	49.0
2	India	12.2	Thailand	11.8	India	12.1
3	China	11.3	Africa	8.6	Africa	5.8
4	Africa	9.3	India	8.2	China	5.3
5	Indonesia	8.0	China	5.7	Japan	5.1

Source: International Monetary Fund, *Direction of Trade*.

Table 6.2 Myanmar's major import partners (per cent)

	1980		1988		1990	
1	Japan	43.7	Japan	39.0	China	20.6
2	United Kingdom	8.8	United Kingdom	9.1	Singapore	17.9
3	Germany	7.4	Germany	6.7	Japan	16.6
4	Singapore	6.1	United States	6.0	Germany	4.8
5	United States	5.0	Singapore	5.8	Malaysia	4.7

	1995		2000		2006	
1	Singapore	29.9	Thailand	18.3	China	34.0
2	China	29.0	China	18.0	Thailand	21.4
3	Malaysia	10.8	Singapore	15.8	Singapore	15.8
4	Japan	7.4	South Korea	10.5	Malaysia	4.6
5	South Korea	4.1	Malaysia	8.4	South Korea	4.0

Source: International Monetary Fund, *Direction of Trade*.

Myanmar's imports from China grew more rapidly than its exports to China throughout the 1990s and up to 2006. Figure 6.1 clearly shows the unbalanced nature of Myanmar's exports to and imports from China. While Myanmar's exports to China increased by 6.9 times, from $US33.3 million in 1990 to $US229.7 million in 2006, its imports from China expanded by 9.6 times, from $US137.7 million in 1990 to $US1.328 billion in 2006, resulting in a huge trade deficit of $US1.098 billion in 2006, which was 2.4 times larger than Myanmar's total trade surplus of $US451.4 million in the same year.

Figure 6.1: Trade between Myanmar and China

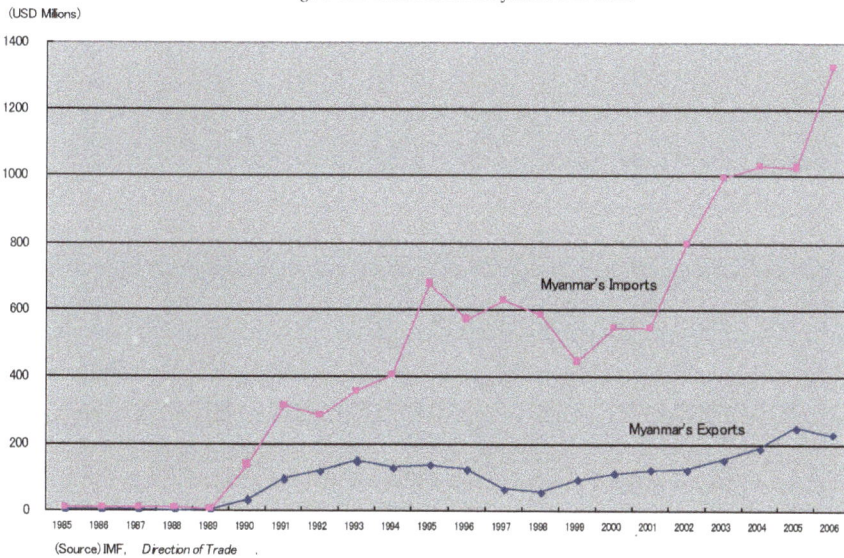

(Source) IMF, *Direction of Trade*　.

Exports: weak impacts on the economic development of Chinese trade

Myanmar's exports to China comprise mostly wood, gemstones and fruit and nuts (Table 6.3). Myanmar has, however, become more and more dependent on wood exports, the share of which occupied nearly 70 per cent of the total for the period 2000–03.[5] According to Chinese Customs data, this trend continued through 2007.[6] Wood accounted for 69 per cent of exports in 2004, 71 per cent in 2005, 60 per cent in 2006 and 51 per cent in 2007. In contrast, the share of gemstones declined to a few per cent by the early 2000s, probably because of the government's export restrictions. Wood is exported mostly in the form of logs or roughly sawn timber without much human and technical input. Such a high dependency on timber has made the levels of Myanmar's exports to China rather stagnant, since this trade is constrained by the availability of natural resources.

Table 6.3 Myanmar's major exports to China (per cent)

Rank	Items	1988–91	1992–95	1996–99	2000–03
1	24[a] Cork and wood	7.4	40.8	43.7	67.7
2	05 Vegetables and fruit	14.6	5.5	3.0	8.1
3	28 Metalliferous ores and metal scrap	3.8	4.3	6.2	4.8
4	27 Crude fertilisers and crude materials (excluding petroleum etc.)	0.2	0.2	8.0	4.0
5	66 Non-metallic mineral manufactures, n.e.s.	20.8	30.8	24.6	3.6
6	03 Fish, crustaceans, molluscs, preparations thereof	9.7	5.0	1.9	3.3
7	29 Crude animal and vegetable materials, not elsewhere specified	8.7	3.6	3.6	2.1
8	22 Oil seeds and oleaginous fruit	9.0	1.3	1.0	1.5
9	23 Crude rubber (including synthetic and reclaimed)	0.1	0.1	0.2	1.2
10	63 Cork and wood manufactures (excluding furniture)	0.1	0.5	0.2	0.5

[a] Standard International Trade Classification (SITC) numbers
Source: UN Comtrade Database.

More importantly, various studies have identified wood extraction and its export in the form of logs as having had a weak impact on broad-based economic and industrial development, because it fails to generate improved utilisation of existing factors of production, expanded factor endowments or positive linkage effects. This contrasts sharply with Myanmar's other newly emerged export products in the 1990s, such as beans and pulses for Indian markets and garments for the US and EU markets—both of which had a considerable impact on the national economy. Fujita and Okamoto (2006) explain that the cultivation of beans and pulses grew rapidly by mobilising previously untapped domestic resources, including arable land and labour in the dry season. The sudden emergence of export markets provided farmers and merchants with incentives to utilise idle resources more fully and effectively. Such an export-driven development path is termed 'vent for surplus' by Myanmar economist Hla Myint (1959). Garment exports can be described similarly, for which the United States and the European Union presented big export markets, and untapped unemployed and underemployed labour were mobilised from urban and rural areas for this extremely labour-intensive industry.[7]

Contrasting with these examples, wood extraction and log exports that dominated Myanmar–China trade have not produced broad-based economic growth with the development of value-added wood-based industries downstream. Moreover, the Myanmar Government does not seem to pay due attention to the sustainability of wood extraction and export. Some specialists warn that unless effective controls against excessive logging are implemented, Myanmar will lose one of its major exports in the foreseeable future (see, for example, Global Witness 2005).

In order to enhance imports from Cambodia, Laos, Myanmar and Vietnam (known collectively as CLMV), China began its Early Harvest Plan (EHP) under the ASEAN–China Free Trade Agreement (ACFTA) in January 2004. The EHP with the Association for South-East Asian Nations (ASEAN) covered about 600 agricultural products and China and ASEAN's six advanced members agreed to reduce tariffs on these products to zero within three years, while CLMV should eliminate their tariffs no later than 2010 (Hao 2008). China also initiated special preferential tariff programs under the EHP and exempted 133 products from Myanmar from January 2004 and 87 items from January 2006. The benefits of such programs for Myanmar are, however, not yet obvious, as shown in Figure 6.1.

Imports: China as a major supply source

Soon after the opening up of border trade in 1988, China appeared in trade statistics as a major supplier of commodities and goods to the Myanmar economy. Myanmar's imports from China have increased since then, although imports have experienced ups and downs, as shown in Figure 6.1.

Imports experienced rapid growth on three occasions: once in the first half of the 1990s, again at the beginning of the twenty-first century and in 2006. Accordingly, Myanmar has become more and more dependent on imports from China. The share of Chinese goods in Myanmar's total imports rose from about one-fifth in 1990 to about one-third in 2006.

The first rapid growth of Chinese imports resulted from the unleashing of pent-up demand from the Myanmar population after the open-door policy begun in 1988. Myanmar people had long been cut off from daily consumer goods and durables during the socialist period. Once they achieved access, the demand for such goods shot up (Kudo 2005a). While consumer goods made up 6 per cent and 12 per cent of total imports in the fiscal years[8] 1980/81 and 1985/86 respectively, the corresponding figures shot up to 35 per cent in fiscal year 1990/91 and to 42 per cent in 1995/96 (Central Statistical Organisation 2003). China provided the main source of supply and Chinese products poured into the emerging consumer-goods markets in Myanmar.

Just after the opening up of border trade with China, textiles (mostly yarn and fabrics) flooded onto Myanmar markets (Table 6.4). Textiles occupied nearly 40 per cent of total imports from China for the period 1988–91. Tobacco then increased its share, up to 14 per cent for the subsequent period 1992–95. Road vehicles, power generators, electrical machinery and apparatus, and manufactures of metal, each accounted for about 5 per cent in the first half of the 1990s.

Entering the second half of the 1990s, however, the inflow of Chinese imports stagnated. The Myanmar Government became annoyed with the country's expanding trade deficits by the mid-1990s and resorted to stricter import controls, particularly on luxury and non-essential goods. Accordingly, the influx of Chinese consumer goods and durables declined. Textiles and tobacco provide two examples: the former decreased its share of total imports from China from 38 per cent for the period 1988–91 to 16 per cent for the period 1996–99; the latter declined from 14 per cent for the period 1992–95 to 6 per cent for the period 1996–99.

Table 6.4 Myanmar's major imports from China (per cent)

Rank	Items	1988–91	1992–95	1996–99	2000–03
1	65[a] Textile yarn, fabrics, made-up articles	37.7	19.8	16.2	18.1
2	71 Power-generating machinery and equipment	3.6	4.5	5.7	8.5
3	78 Road vehicles (including air-cushion vehicles)	3.7	6.1	4.0	7.5
4	72 Machinery specialised for particular industries	1.0	2.6	7.2	6.3
5	77 Electrical machinery, apparatus and appliances	5.1	4.6	5.1	5.8
6	74 General industrial machinery and equipment	0.6	0.9	3.2	5.6
7	33 Petroleum, petroleum products and related articles	4.5	4.3	2.8	5.2
8	69 Manufactures of metal, n.e.s.	5.4	4.1	6.5	5.1
9	67 Iron and steel	3.6	4.5	3.8	4.5
10	76 Telecommunications and sound-recording equipment	2.0	1.4	1.0	2.7

[a] Standard International Trade Classification (SITC) numbers
Source: UN Comtrade Database.

In contrast, imports of capital and intermediate goods steadily increased throughout the 1990s. These goods were supplied to the emerging manufacturing sector for import substitution in Myanmar. For example, machinery and transport equipment (SITC 7)[9] increased its share from 12 per cent for the period 1988–91 to 40 per cent for the period 1996–99. Imported textiles (SITC 65) had been used not only for domestic consumption but as raw materials for the growing export-oriented garment industry since the mid-1990s. A garment industry 'boom' occurred in Yangon in the late 1990s and at the beginning of the twenty-first century. The rapid growth of the garment industry in Myanmar was supported partly by raw-material supplies from China.

Myanmar's imports from China showed rapid growth for the second time at the beginning of the twenty-first century. Imports grew at the average annual rate of 22.7 per cent for the period 2000–03. Textiles, road vehicles, power generators, electrical machinery and apparatus and general industrial machinery increased their shares of total imports from China.

Such an increase could reflect the huge inflow of Chinese economic cooperation and commercial loans. As will be discussed later in this chapter, Chinese economic cooperation expanded, in particular towards the end of the 1990s, when successive economic and technical cooperation programs were signed between the two countries. Most of these were tied, whether legally or de facto, to supply from Chinese companies, and state-owned enterprises in particular, and thus stimulated imports from China.

Border trade: the main artery of the Myanmar economy

Trade between Myanmar and China is heavily dependent on cross-border trade. According to the district-specific export and import figures from China Customs,[10] coastal areas such as Shanghai, Shenzhen, Huangpu and Nanjing naturally occupy the major share of China's external trade. In contrast, Kunming, capital of Yunnan Province, accounts for less than 1 per cent of China's external trade.

Since Yunnan is a landlocked province, commodities exported to or imported from Myanmar through the Kunming Customs Office are most likely transported by land through border gates such as Muse, Lwejel and Laiza.[11] We therefore regard the commodities that are cleared and recorded at the Kunming Customs Office as 'border trade' in this chapter.[12] This means that the border trade between the two countries makes up less than 1 per cent of China's external trade.

Even though the volume of border trade between the two countries is insignificant compared with China's total external trade, it represents the lion's share of China's trade with Myanmar. Border trade made up about 50 per cent of China's exports to Myanmar and about 70 per cent of its imports from Myanmar during the period 2000–07 (Table 6.5). Moreover, Yunnan Province's share of Myanmar's total border trade was 73 per cent, whereas that of Thailand was 14 per cent in the fiscal year 2003/04 (Than 2005). Border trade is important for Myanmar and for Yunnan Province.

Table 6.5 China's border trade with Myanmar ($US million)

	2000	2001	2002	2003	2004	2005	2006	2007
Exports via border	293.5	261.2	358.3	446.3	500.6	540.6	656.0	800.4
(Percentage of total exports)	59.1	52.5	49.4	49.1	53.3	57.8	54.3	47.3
Imports via border	66.9	93.7	105.4	134.5	164.5	223.5	166.8	231.6
(Percentage of total imports)	53.6	69.8	77.0	79.3	79.5	81.5	66.0	62.5

Note: China's border trade is defined as commodities cleared and recorded by the Kunming Customs Office.
Source: China Customs.

The main route of border trade on Myanmar soil is the 460-kilometre-long road connecting Muse on the Chinese border (opposite Ruili in Yunnan Province) and Mandalay, Myanmar's second-largest city, in central Myanmar. This road constituted a part of the old 'Burma Road' that opened in 1936 to supply the

KMT government in Chungking. The road was paved and expanded for truck transportation in 1998 on a build–operate–transfer (BOT) basis by Asia World, one of the biggest private business conglomerates, headed by a son of the former drug lord Lo Hsing-Han.[13] Before the completion of the new road, travel from Mandalay to Muse took a couple of days and sometimes even a week during the rainy season; it now takes only 12–16 hours by motor vehicle.

Border trade between the two countries has experienced ups and downs, reflecting not only market situations but political, security and macroeconomic conditions in a broader sense. It also sometimes falls prey to illegitimate business, corruption and power struggles. It is well known that the ouster of former Prime Minister General Khin Nyunt in October 2004 originated from a clash between intelligence and army units in Muse (Hlaing 2005). Nevertheless, in spite of these ups and downs, border trade between the two countries has been legitimised, regularised and institutionalised.

The first border-trade agreement was signed in August 1988 by Myanmar Export and Import Services (MEIS) and Yunnan Machinery Import Export Corporation to use bank transactions between the Myanmar Foreign Trade Bank and the Kunming Branch of China Bank. MEIS established border-trade offices in Lashio, Muse, Kyugok, Namkhan and Koonlon. According to notification from the Ministry of Commerce (no. 7/91), MEIS implemented the so-called new border-trade system in October 1991.[14] The Myanmar and Chinese Governments signed a formal border-trade agreement in August 1994. A border-trade office was established in Muse in August 1995 and introduced 'one-stop services' on a trial basis. The office was extended to the fully fledged Border Trade Department of the Ministry of Commerce in August 1996. In July 1997, the Export First Policy was applied to border trade as well as to seaborne trade, and imports were allowed only against export earnings thereafter. From November 1997, all border trade had to use US dollars to settle transactions, not local currencies such as the Myanmar kyat and the Chinese yuan. In January 1998, the Muse office was expanded and started to function as a one-stop-service border gate.

Further policy changes occurred towards the end of 2000. From November 2000, local currencies—namely, the Myanmar kyat and the Chinese yuan—could again be used for payments in border trade. From January 2001, the Border Control Force (Na Sa Kha) started to supervise and implement border-trade activities. This force was led by a military intelligence officer and comprised all related organisations, including immigration, customs, the internal-revenue department, police, drug-control offices, the Myanmar Economic Bank, and so on. The ostensible purpose of the force was to promote border trade in a systematic manner. In reality, however, military intelligence monopolised the most lucrative route for border trade, which eventually led to a major clash within the regime's leadership in 2004.

The regularisation and institutionalisation of cross-border transactions and further road development contributed to boosting border trade between the two countries at the beginning of the twenty-first century. China's exports to Myanmar through border posts increased by 3.1 times, from $US261.2 million in 2001 to $US800.4 million in 2007, whereas China's imports from Myanmar via border trade expanded by 2.5 times, from $US93.7 million in 2001 to $US231.6 million in 2007. The Myanmar Government also promoted all border trade not only with China but with Thailand, India and Bangladesh, to compensate for the economic sanctions imposed by the West, and the Chinese border recorded the most meaningful success. Myanmar's border trade with China has therefore become a main artery of its economy.

Economic and business cooperation

China and Chinese enterprises are heavily involved in Myanmar's industrial, infrastructure and energy development through economic cooperation. China is not a member country of the Development Assistance Committee (DAC) of the Organisation for Economic Cooperation and Development (OECD) and it does not disclose its economic cooperation programs. The Myanmar Government also does not disclose details of its receipt of economic assistance from abroad. We can only estimate the facts from reports appearing sporadically in the press. China's economic cooperation programs are often nothing more than commercial-based business. Even though Chinese enterprises offer suppliers credits at no or low interest, in reality they add the cost to the plants and commodities they export to Myanmar (Ebashi 2006). On the other hand, most Chinese economic cooperation programs are tied to Chinese firms, and state-owned enterprises in particular. It is difficult to distinguish genuine economic cooperation projects from commercial ones without detailed information. This section includes both cases.

Gathering information from such scattered sources shows that China's provision of economic cooperation to Myanmar seems to have expanded from about 1997 when the United States imposed economic sanctions that banned new foreign investments. Appendix 1 shows the list of agreements on economic and technical cooperation signed between the two countries after 1996. Moreover, Senior-General Than Shwe's state visit to Beijing in January 2003 seemingly marked another epoch, when China offered Myanmar a preferential loan amounting to $US200 million and a grant of $US6.25 million. Just after China's commitment, the so-called 'Black Friday' of 30 May 2003 occurred (when Daw Aung San Suu Kyi was attacked by pro-regime elements), an event that prompted the United States to impose stricter sanctions in July 2003, which included an import ban on all Myanmar-made products. China stepped into the vacuum created by the Western sanctions and compensated for Myanmar's needs for trade and economic cooperation.

It is said that China's foreign aid, or economic cooperation, is motivated by two main objectives: to secure a favourable environment in its neighbours and to secure natural resources—energy in particular (Kobayashi 2007). Both of these factors are critically important for the Chinese economy to grow and for China to become a global economic power. Myanmar is a suitable partner under both criteria. Accordingly, Myanmar is one of the major recipients of Chinese economic cooperation (Table 6.6). It was the third-largest recipient of Chinese economic cooperation in 2000, receiving $US186.7 million, and ninth largest in 2005, receiving $US289.8 million—which was about three times more than the total amount of assistance provided by the DAC member countries in the same year.

Table 6.6 China's economic cooperation, 2000 and 2005 ($US million)

	2000			2005		
	Country	Turnover	Resources	Country	Turnover	Resources
1	Pakistan	329.4	Coal, gas	Sudan	1342.8	Oil, gas
2	Bangladesh	231.2	Coal, gas	Nigeria	799.9	Oil, gas
3	**Myanmar**	**186.7**	**Oil, gas**	Pakistan	751.4	Coal, gas
4	Sudan	118.8	Oil, gas	Bangladesh	614.0	Coal, gas
5	Mali	105.1	Gold	Indonesia	534.6	Oil, gas
6	Yemen	97.9	Oil, gas	India	412.9	Coal, iron ore
7	Laos	93.7	Potassium	Angola	305.7	Oil, diamonds
8	Zimbabwe	87.6	-	Vietnam	299.2	Bauxite, coal
9	Vietnam	87.5	Bauxite, coal	**Myanmar**	**289.8**	**Oil, gas**
10	Sri Lanka	63.6	-	Egypt	276.5	Oil, gas

Source: Adapted from Kobayashi (2007:130).

China's economic cooperation and business dealings with Myanmar were directed to three main fields: infrastructure development, support for SEEs and energy exploitation.

Infrastructure

Among the many infrastructure projects financed and constructed by the Chinese Government and Chinese enterprises, attention is immediately directed to those of electric-power generation. Myanmar has suffered a severe shortage of electricity since the end of the 1990s and the government has initiated massive dam-building programs for hydro-power generation.[15] According to a foreign businessman in Yangon, Chinese companies constructed six hydro-power plants and one thermal power station in the period between 1996 and 2005, the installed capacity of which constituted about one-third of the entire national capacity (Ebashi 2006).

Among these, the Paunglaung Hydro-Power Project in central Myanmar clearly showed the financial, managerial and technical capabilities of Chinese companies in this field. It was completed by the Yunnan Machinery Import and Export

Corporation (YMIEC) in March 2005. Its installed capacity of power generation (280 MW) surpasses that of Baluchaung (168 MW), which had long been the biggest power source and which was constructed by Japanese companies with Japanese war reparations and economic cooperation after World War II. The Paunglaung Dam Project was the YMIEC's biggest undertaking. Indeed, it was the largest hydro-power plant China had exported to South-East Asia and Yunnan's largest foreign-trade project. The total cost of the project was estimated at $US160 million, which was financed by the Export-Import Bank of China (China Exim Bank).

As of March 2006, Myanmar had 11 major continuing hydro-power projects, with a total generating capacity of 1734 MW. Contracts were signed for seven projects and all were with Chinese enterprises. The largest project is the Yeywa hydro-power plant south of Mandalay, with a capacity of 790 MW. Yeywa will cost $US700 million. In August 2003, the China Exim Bank approved a $US200 million loan at preferential interest rates for the project (Bosshard 2004). The China Water Resources and Hydropower Construction Group (Sinohydro) and the China International Trust and Investment Corporation (CITIC) won contracts to provide generators and other equipment for the project. In addition to low-priced machinery and equipment and services, long-term and low-interest loans and export credits offered by public financial institutions made it possible for Chinese enterprises to become major players in this field.

Another example of significant Chinese economic cooperation in infrastructure development is the Ayeyarwady Transportation Project, which provides a transport line from Yunnan Province to Thaliana Port near Yangon. This project apparently started in October 1999, when a high-level Chinese delegation accompanied by Khin Nyunt visited Bam, the navigation head on the Ayeyarwady River. This project includes three infrastructure developments: constructing a container port near Bhamo, upgrading the road from the new container port to Muse/Lwejel on the Chinese border and dredging the river to ensure a safe shipping lane. The Myanmar Port Authority plans to transport two million containers a year in the future.[16] It also plans to construct a container yard, office buildings, residences and other amenities in the hinterland.[17]

Yunnan Province obviously seeks a direct route through Myanmar to a seaport from which it can export products to South Asia, the Middle East and Europe. Such an outlet would reduce transport costs and time and would bypass the Malacca Strait in the event of a conflict in the South China Sea (Malik 1998). With the completion of the project, the Ayeyarwady will link China's south-western frontier with the Bay of Bengal and the Andaman Sea.

State-owned economic enterprises

Since the beginning of the twenty-first century, the Myanmar Government has accelerated the construction of new state-owned factories (Kudo 2005a). The number of such factories increased by only 19 for the five years between fiscal years 1985/86 and 1990/91, but by 92 for the next five fiscal years, 1990/91–95/96, and by about 20–30 a year up to 2000. Thereafter there was impressive growth, with 53 public industrial enterprises set up in the fiscal year 2001/02 and 231 in 2002/03. Most of the new factories are for import-substitution industries that target domestic markets. Such a policy shift probably reflects the Myanmar Government's drive towards self-sufficiency in the agricultural and industrial sectors.[18]

China's economic cooperation programs strongly supported the massive construction of state-owned factories such as textile mills, plywood plants, rice mills, pulp and paper mills, sugar mills, agricultural equipment factories and other light manufacturing facilities. Table 6.7 shows examples of the Ministry of Industry Number One's factories that were constructed with the provision of Chinese financial and technical support and their machinery and equipment. Without Chinese support, these factories would never have materialised.

Myanmar's SEEs, however, have a long history of inefficiency, poor management and vulnerability to all the ills that plague public enterprises, including rent-seeking activities and corruption (Kudo 2005a). The SEEs are highly controlled by the central government in financial and managerial terms. With the lack of financial and managerial autonomy, newly built state-owned factories would not operate efficiently. For example, Japan was the top donor country to Myanmar, with its contributions accounting for 66.7 per cent of the total bilateral overseas development assistance (ODA) received by Myanmar between 1976 and 1990 (Kudo 1998:Table 1). Myanmar consistently ranked within the top-10 recipients and often ranked within the top five. A large portion of Japanese ODA was directed to the so-called Four-Industries Project through Myanmar Heavy Industries, a SEE under the Ministry of Industry Number Two. This project was to become self-reliant once ODA was suspended. In the end, most Japanese ODA provided to Myanmar turned into bad loans. This time around, proliferating state-owned factories could become a burden on the government budget, and eventually become bad loans for the Chinese stakeholders.

Table 6.7 New Myanmar Ministry of Industry Number One factories built with Chinese cooperation

Factory type	Location	Completion date	Contractor
Textile industry			
Garment factory	Kyaukse	January 2003	China World Best Group Co. Ltd
Textile factory	Pwintphyu	March 2005	Tianjin Machinery Import and Export Corporation
Textile factory	Pakkoku	October 2005	Tianjin Machinery Import and Export Corporation
Textile factory	Salingyi	November 2005	China National Construction and Agricultural Machinery Import and Export Corporation
Garment factory	Taungtha	January 2006	China World Best Group Co. Ltd
200 looms extension plant	Myintgyan	December 2004	n.a.
400 looms extension plant	Yamethin	January 2005	n.a.
Paper and chemical industries			
Paper factory (3)	Palate	January 2001	Tianjin Machinery Import and Export Corporation
Bleached bamboo-pulp factory	Thabasung	May 2005	China Metallurgical Construction Group Corporation
Ceramics industry			
Refractory brick factory	Kyaukse	December 2005	China National Building Machinery and Equipment Corporation
Cement factory	Kyaukse	January 2003	China National Construction and Agricultural Machinery Import and Export Corporation
Kiln production line (300 TPD)	Kyaukse	August 2005	n.a.
Foodstuff industries			
Instant-noodle factory	Sagaing	July 2001	Karehua Noodle Line Machinery Co. Ltd

Note: List includes factories completed after 2001 only. This list might not cover some factories that were not reported in the media.
Source: *New Light of Myanmar, Myanmar Times* and other press. Compiled by JETRO Yangon Office.

Energy development

As its economy grows rapidly, China's quest for energy sources abroad has expanded. Myanmar's oil and gas reserves have naturally attracted China's attention. China's presence in Myanmar's oil and gas fields has, however, been observed only recently. The China National Offshore Oil Corporation (CONIC) signed six contracts for production sharing with the Myanmar Oil and Gas Enterprise (MOGEN) of the Ministry of Energy from October 2004 to January 2005.[19] The China Petroleum and Chemical Corporation (SINOPEC) and its subsidiary Dian Quantum Petroleum Exploration also work the inland fields. Moreover, CONIC and its subsidiary Chimney Assets also won contracts to upgrade the four old oilfields in central Myanmar.

These companies are now at various stages of exploration and they have already made financial commitments of $US163 million. The Chinese investment is rather small compared with the total amount of foreign investment in Myanmar's oil and gas sector of $US2.635 billion—the largest recipient of foreign investment accounting for 34 per cent of the total outstanding up to March 2006.[20] It is only recently, however, that Chinese companies have started to invest vigorously in Myanmar. Of 26 Chinese foreign investments in Myanmar overall, 16 projects were made either in the fiscal year 2004/05 or 2005/06, representing nearly 70 per cent in terms of investment value. Most of those were invested in the energy and mining sectors.

Another big project is Petro China's plan to build a gas pipeline from the Shwe gas field off the coast of Rakhine State to Yunnan Province. The Shwe field comprises several large blocks, containing about 200 billion cubic metres of gas. Petro China signed a memorandum of understanding with Myanmar Oil and Gas Enterprise (MOGE) to buy gas from the Shwe fields for 30 years starting from 2009.

Myanmar already exports natural gas to Thailand via a pipeline, and gas exports reached $US2.25 billion in 2007, becoming by far Myanmar's biggest foreign exchange earner. Myanmar will have another big source of foreign earnings from gas exports to China in the near future. Moreover, oil and gas exports offer the Myanmar Government a diplomatic advantage over its neighbouring countries; indeed, India also made great efforts to secure Myanmar's gas from the same field. India eventually reached an agreement with Myanmar to purchase the gas with more favourable conditions based on a 'take-or-pay' arrangement, by which India gives Myanmar guaranteed earnings every year even if it is not able to access the gas. Myanmar has come out the winner in the Sino–India rivalry for energy.

Conclusion: who benefits and who pays?

Against the background of closer diplomatic, political and security ties between Myanmar and China since 1988, their economic relations have also grown stronger throughout the 1990s and up to the present. China is now a major supplier of consumer goods, durables, machinery and equipment and intermediate products to Myanmar. China also offers markets for Myanmar's exports such as timber, agricultural produce, marine products, minerals and, recently, natural gas. Border trade provides a direct route connecting central Upper Myanmar to Yunnan Province in China. Physical infrastructure developments such as roads and bridges and institutionalisation of cross-border transactions, including one-stop services, promote border trade. Without the massive influx of Chinese products, the Myanmar economy could have suffered more severe shortages of commodities.

China also provides a large amount of economic cooperation and commercial-based financing in the areas of infrastructure, SEEs and oil and gas exploitation. Without Chinese long-term loans with low interest rates, the Myanmar Government could not have implemented its massive construction of new state-owned factories such as textile and sugar mills. Although China's official foreign investment is rather small, it is not insignificant. It has recently poured money into oil and gas exploration and Chinese enterprises could soon be major players in this booming field in Myanmar. There can be no doubt that Myanmar's economy is now heavily dependent on economic ties with China.

The lop-sided trade with China has, however, failed to have a substantial impact on Myanmar's broad-based economic and industrial development. About 70 per cent of Myanmar's exports to China is timber in the form of logs or roughly sawn timber. Wood extraction and its export are quite different from other major export items such as beans and pulses and garments, as the latter has induced the improved utilisation of existing factors of production such as land and labour in the whole economy. In contrast, timber exports are no more than exploitation of a limited natural resource that happened to remain untapped during Myanmar's past as a closed economy.

Moreover, Chinese firms could exploit natural resources in Myanmar excessively without considering environmental sustainability. Myanmar ranked seventy-eighth for China's imports and its share constituted only 0.04 per cent in 2007. Even though China is the most important trading partner for Myanmar, Myanmar is not such a significant trading partner for China. China and Chinese firms have little incentive to pay much attention to the sustainability of Myanmar's export commodities or to the environmental impacts of such exports to China. Chinese firms can shift their import sources from Myanmar to another country. Myanmar benefits from trading with China in the short run, but it could lose from it in the long run.

China's economic cooperation and commercial loans also apparently support the present regime, but their effects on the whole economy will be limited under an unfavourable macroeconomic environment and a distorted incentives structure. In particular, the newly built state-owned factories could become a burden on the Myanmar Government's budget and eventually represent bad loans for the Chinese stakeholders. Myanmar's debt arrears accumulated to $US100 million by 2003 and, in 2005, the China Export and Credit Insurance Corporation (SINOSURE)[21] rated Myanmar eighth of nine in country-risk ratings (in which the first rank indicates the safest countries and the ninth indicates the most risky countries) (Bi 2008a). Moreover, Wilson (2007:87–90) argues, mentioning several examples, that China's 'embrace' of Myanmar is by no means open-ended and China has not always achieved its goals. Chinese stakeholders, including Chinese taxpayers, might have to pay the debts at the end of the day.

All in all, strengthened economic ties with China are instrumental for the survival of the Myanmar regime in the midst of economic sanctions by Western nations. They are not, however, a powerful force promoting the process of broad-based economic development in Myanmar. After all, Myanmar people could be the losers, since they have to live under a repressive regime that might not have survived this long without Chinese support.

References

Akimoto, Y. 2004, 'Hydro-powering the regime', *Irrawaddy*, Online edition, <http://www.irrawaddy.org/aviewer.asp?a=3757&print=yes&c=e>

Bi, Shihong 2008a, 'China's economic cooperation with Myanmar', in Toshihiro Kudo (ed.), *An Investigation into the Myanmar Economy: How the military government has survived*, (In Japanese), IDE Selection No. 12, Institute of Developing Economies, JETRO, Chiba.

Bi, Shihong 2008b, 'Border economic activities between Yunnan Province and Laos, Myanmar and Vietnam', in Masami Ishida (ed.), *A study on Mekong regional development: emerging border economic zones*, (In Japanese), Research Report No. 2007-IV-23, Institute of Developing Economies, METRO, Chiba.

Bosshard, P. 2004, *China Exim Bank and China Development Bank Case Studies*, International Rivers Network, <http://www.irn.org/programs/china/Exim_Bank.pdf>

Central Statistical Organisation 2003, *Statistical Yearbook, 2003*, Central Statistical Organisation, Yangon.

Department of the Myanmar Language Commission (DMLC) 1993, *Myanmar–English Dictionary*, Ministry of Education, Yangon.

Ebashi, Masahiko 2006, 'A note on Myanmar's situation after Khin Nyunt's ouster', *SPF Voices from the World*, On-Demand Publication Series, Sasakawa Peace Foundation.

Fujita, K. and Okamoto, I. 2006, *Agricultural policies and development of Myanmar's agricultural sector: an overview*, IDE Discussion Paper Series No. 63, Institute of Developing Economies, JETRO, <http://www.ide.go.jp/English/index4.html>

Global Witness, 2005, *A Choice for China: Ending the destruction of Burma's northern forests*, <http://www.globalwitness.org/reports/show.php/en.00080.html>

Hao, H. M. 2008, 'China's trade and economic relations with CLMV', in Sotharith Chap (ed.), *Development strategy for CLMV in the age of economic integration*, ERIA Research Project Report 2007, no. 4, Institute of Developing Economies, JETRO, Chiba.

Hlaing, K. Y. 2005, 'Myanmar in 2004: why military rule continues', *Southeast Asian Affairs 2005*, Institute of Southeast Asian Studies, Singapore.

International Monetary Fund various issues, *Direction of Trade*.

Jannuzi, Frank S. 1998, 'The new Burma Road (paved by polytechnologies?)', in Robert I. Rotberg (ed.), *Burma: Prospects for a democratic future*, Brookings Institution Press, the World Peace Foundation and Harvard Institute for International Development, Washington, DC.

Kobayashi, Takaaki 2007, 'China's foreign aid policy: development and reforms', *Journal of JBIC Institute*, no. 35, October, pp. 109–47.

Kudo, Toshihiro (ed.) 2008, *An Investigation into the Myanmar Economy: How the military government has survived*, (In Japanese), IDE Selection No. 12, Institute of Developing Economies, JETRO, Chiba.

Kudo, Toshihiro 1998, 'Political basis of economic policies under Burmese socialism', *Southeastern Asian Studies*, no. 4, Tokyo University of Foreign Studies, pp. 139–77.

Kudo, Toshihiro 2005a, *Stunted and distorted industrialization in Myanmar*, IDE Discussion Paper Series No. 38, Institute of Developing Economies, JETRO, <http://www.ide.go.jp/English/index4.html>

Kudo, Toshihiro 2005b, *The impact of United States sanctions on the Myanmar garment industry*, IDE Discussion Paper Series No. 42, Institute of Developing Economies, JETRO, <http://www.ide.go.jp/English/index4.html>

Lintner, B. 1990, *The Rise and Fall of the Communist Party of Burma (CPB)*, Southeast Asian Program, Cornell University, Ithaca.

Lintner, B. 1994, *Burma in Revolt: Opium and insurgency since 1948*, Westview Press and White Lotus, Boulder, San Francisco, Oxford and Bangkok.

Lintner, B. 1998, 'Drugs and economic growth: ethnicity and exports', in Robert I. Rotberg (ed.), *Burma: Prospects for a democratic future*, Brookings Institution Press, the World Peace Foundation and Harvard Institute for International Development, Washington, DC.

Malik, J. M. 1998, 'Burma's role in regional security—pawn or pivot?', in Robert I. Rotberg (ed.), *Burma: Prospects for a democratic future*, Brookings Institution Press, the World Peace Foundation and Harvard Institute for International Development, Washington, DC.

Myanmar Times various issues, (weekly English magazine).

Myint, H. 1959, 'The "classical theory" of international trade and the underdeveloped countries', *Economic Journal*, vol. 68, pp. 317–37.

New Light of Myanmar various issues, (state-run daily English newspaper).

Ott, M. C. 1998, 'From isolation to relevance: policy considerations', in Robert I. Rotberg (ed.), *Burma: Prospects for a democratic future*, Brookings Institution Press, the World Peace Foundation and Harvard Institute for International Development, Washington, DC.

Selth, A. 1996, *Transforming the Tatmadaw: the Burmese armed forces since 1988*, Canberra Papers on Strategy and Defence No. 113, Strategic and Defence Studies Centre, Research School of Pacific and Asian Studies, The Australian National University, Canberra.

Than, M. 2005, 'Myanmar's cross-border economic relations and cooperation with the People's Republic of China and Thailand in the Greater Mekong Subregion', *Journal of GMS Development Studies*, vol. 2, no. 1, October.

Than, T. M. M. 2003, 'Myanmar and China: a special relationship?', *Southeast Asian Affairs 2003*, Institute of Southeast Asian Studies, Singapore.

Wilson, T. 2007, 'Foreign policy as political tool: Myanmar 2003–2006', in M. Skidmore and T. Wilson (eds), *Myanmar: The State, community and the environment*, Asia Pacific Press, Canberra.

Appendix 1: Bilateral agreements between Myanmar and China since 1996

SPDC Chairman Than Shwe's visit to China (January 1996)
Agreement on Economic and Technical Cooperation
Protocol on Cultural Cooperation
Framework Agreement on Provisions of Interest for Subsidised Credit
State Councillor Luo Gan's visit to Myanmar (March 1997)
Agreement on Myanmar–China Border Area Management and Cooperation
Agreement on the Chinese Government Providing a Grant of RMB5 million to Myanmar
Agreement on Supply of Agricultural Machinery, Equipment and Spare Parts and Technical Cooperation
Vice-Premier of State Councillor Wu Bangguo's visit to Myanmar (October 1997)
Framework Agreement on a Preferential Loan with Interest Subsidised by the Chinese Government
Vice-Foreign Minister Tang Jiaxuan's visit to Myanmar (January–February 1998)
Agreement on Mutual Exemption on Visas for Holders of Diplomatic and Official (Service) Passports
SPDC Secretary-1 Khin Nyunt's visit to China (June 1999)
Agreement on Economic and Technical Cooperation
SPDC Vice-Chairman Maung Aye's visit to China (June 2000)
Joint Statement on the Framework for the Future of Bilateral Relations and Cooperation
Vice-President Hu Jintao's visit to Myanmar (July 2000)
Agreement on Economic and Technical Cooperation
Agreement on Tourism Cooperation
Agreement on Science and Technology Cooperation
SPDC Secretary-3 Win Myint's visit to China (October–November 2000)
Memorandum of Understanding between the Union Solidarity and Development Association (USDA) and the All China Youth Federation (ACYF)
Minister for Home Affairs Jia Chunwang's visit to Myanmar (January 2001)
Memorandum of Understanding on Narcotic Drugs Control
Minister for Land Resources Tian Fengshan's visit to Myanmar (July 2001)
Memorandum of Understanding on Cooperation in the Geological and Mineral Resources Sectors
Vice-Foreign Minister Wang Yi's visit to Myanmar (August 2001)
Agreement on Economic and Technical Cooperation
President Jiang Zemin's visit to Myanmar (December 2001)
Agreement on Phytosanitary Cooperation
Agreement on Cooperation in Fisheries
Contract for Improving Petroleum Recovery on IOR-4, Pyay Field
Protocol for Cooperation in Border Area
Agreement on Economic and Technical Cooperation
Agreement on the Promotion and Protection of Investment
Agreement on Cooperation in Animal Health and Quarantine
SPDC Chairman Than Shwe's visit to China (January 2003)
Agreement on Health Cooperation
Agreement on Economic and Technical Cooperation
Agreement on Cooperation in the Field of Sports
Vice-Premier Li Lanqing's visit to Myanmar (January 2003)
Agreement on Partial Debt Relief for Myanmar
Memorandum of Understanding on Extending a Grant for the Supply of Culture, Education and Sporting Goods by China to Myanmar
Memorandum of Understanding on the Program of Aerospace and Maritime Courses Provided by China to Myanmar
Vice-Premier Wu Yi's visit to Myanmar (March 2004)

Memorandum of Understanding on the Promotion of Trade, Investment and Economic Cooperation
Agreement on Economic and Technical Cooperation (Provision of a Grant of RMB50 million)
Framework on Cooperation for Promoting Trade and Investment between China Export and Credit Insurance Corporation and the Myanmar Ministry of Finance and Revenue
Government Concessional Loan Agreement for MPT Project Phase II between the Export-Import Bank of China and the Financial Institution Authorised by the Government of Myanmar
Memorandum of Understanding between UMFCCI and the China Council for Promotion of International Trade
Loan Agreement on Hydraulic Steel Structure (Lot HSS-1) of Yeywa Hydro-Power Project
Strategic Cooperation Agreement on Myanmar National Telecommunications Network Construction Project
Commercial Contract for the Supply of Hydraulic Steel Structure Works and Electrical and Mechanical Equipment for Kun Hydro-Power Project
Commercial Contract for Myaungtaka-Hlinethaya-Yekyi 230KV Transmission Lines and Substation Project
Memorandum of Understanding on the Supply and Installation of Complete Equipment for Float-Glass Production Line with Melting Capacity of 150 TPD and for Tempered Glass, Laminated Glass and Mirror Glass Production Lines
Contract for Construction of No. 4 Urea Fertiliser Factory at Taikkyi Township
Memorandum of Understanding on Hydraulic Steel Structure (Lot HSS-2) and Electromechanical Equipment (Lot EM-1) of Yeywa Hydro-Power Project
National Theatre Renovation Project
Rice-Milling Machine Installation Project
Combine Harvester Production Project
Three Small-Scale Hydro-Power Plants Project
Project for Propagation of Quality Sugarcane and Cotton Strains
Geological and Minerals Exploration in Myanmar–China Border Region
Lashio–Muse Railroad Project

Endnotes

[1] According to DMLC (1993:266), *paukphaw* means '1. sibling, 2. intimate, and is an affectionate term conferred upon the Chinese by the Myanmar people'.

[2] For further detail, see Lintner (1990 and 1994).

[3] Lintner (1990:45) reports that a major reason why the mutiny did not happen earlier was that the ordinary soldiers and local commanders were uncertain about China's reaction to such a move.

[4] Imports from Japan made up nearly 40 per cent of Myanmar's total imports before 1988, due mainly to supplies related to Japan's economic cooperation programs. Japan suspended most aid after the political unrest of 1988, except for a few continuing projects. Without full-fledged overseas development aid programs, its share declined remarkably to only 2.7 per cent in 2006.

[5] Statistics Canada constructs the *World Trade Database* based on the United Nations' Commodity Trade Statistics Database (UN Comtrade), and the database-retrieval services are used for Tables 6.3 and 6.4.

[6] Data from China Customs are classified by the Harmonised Commodity Description and Coding System (HS); HS 44 represents 'Wood'.

[7] See Kudo (2005b), who provides a detailed account of the growth and decline of Myanmar's garment industry in the 1990s and up to 2005.

[8] The fiscal year starts in April and ends in March of the next year.

[9] SITC stands for Standard International Trade Classification.

[10] District-wide figures have been available since 1999.

[11] There are five trade posts on the Myanmar side of the border with Yunnan Province: Muse (mile 105), Lwejel, Laiza, Kanpeiktee and Chinshwehaw. Among them, Muse is the most lucrative in terms of the volume of trade, accounting for 87 per cent of the total in 2002 (Than 2005:44).

[12] Mya Than (2005:40) provides five definitions of cross-border trade: formal or official border trade, informal border trade, illegal border trade (smuggling), transit trade and barter trade. He also points out that all statistics on border trade are usually underestimated.

[13] A small part of the road was constructed and owned by another private company, Diamond Palace. That company was said to have been owned by military intelligence headed by Khin Nyunt, then Secretary No. 1 of the SPDC. The Myanmar military saw the strategic importance of the road and intended to avoid full ownership and operation by one private company.

[14] Details of the new system, however, are not known to the author.

[15] For details, see Akimoto (2004).

[16] Interview with the Myanmar Port Authority in Bhamo, September 2002.

[17] The implementation of the project has apparently been delayed due to disputes between the two countries on levying customs duties (Wilson 2007:88) and national flags flying on vehicles. A Chinese specialist reports, however, that the project will be implemented between 2011 and 2015 (Bi 2008b).

[18] The agricultural policy of Myanmar has exhibited a strong inclination towards self-sufficiency; see Fujita and Okamoto (2006).

[19] Information is from *New Light of Myanmar*, *Myanmar Times* and other media.

[20] It is said that there is a large number of informal Chinese investments and businesses in Myanmar, most of which operate under the names of Myanmar citizens. Such cases do not appear in the Myanmar Investment Commission (MIC) statistics.

[21] SINOSURE is the only policy-oriented Chinese insurance company specialising in export credit insurance. It started operation on 18 December 2001. SINOSURE offers coverage against political and commercial risks (SINOSURE web site, viewed February 2008).

Education and Health Update

7: Myanmar education: challenges, prospects and options

Han Tin

The setting: the land and its people

Traditionally, five pillars make up Myanmar society: farmers, workers, students, monks and the military. All Myanmar children who have attended school are aware of these five pillars because of the pantheon of national heroes revered throughout the nation. Farmers are represented by Saya San, who led the Peasant Revolt;[1] workers by Thakin Po Hla Gyi, who led the oil-workers' strike;[2] students by Bo Aung Gyaw, an early student leader;[3] the monks by U Wisara, who was martyred in a British jail;[4] and the military (Tatmadaw) by Bogyoke Aung San, the founding father of the Tatmadaw and the architect of Myanmar's independence.[5] All of them struggled against the colonial power with the common goal of gaining freedom and independence. These five pillars are potent symbolic forces and together they achieved the creation of an independent nation. It is important now more than ever that these five pillars of Myanmar society again create an atmosphere of empathy and trust and work towards the common goal of developing the nation. Such a symbiotic relationship among these five groups is sorely needed in Myanmar at present.

Myanmar has, since independence, prided itself on its values of self-help and self-reliance. For many decades, it has been going its own way. For the country to evolve and take its place in the world as a modern developed nation, self-reliance alone is not enough. Greater efforts on Myanmar's part, together with empathy, cooperation and assistance from the world community, are most necessary. Myanmar has some means, but they are limited. It needs understanding and support from the international community. It needs encouragement to begin developing a system of good governance that will see the nation again take its place in the family of nations. The onus is, however, also on Myanmar to initiate changes to move away from a 'dominator'-type of society towards a more tolerant, liberal one.

During the previous century, many countries in Asia—such as South Korea, Indonesia, the Philippines and Japan—emerged from authoritarian and militaristic moulds of government and embraced a more liberal form of governance. Myanmar, which has had an extreme authoritarian government since the early 1960s, as well as suffering the indignity of colonial rule and the long legacy of rule by extreme authoritarian kings and feudal lords, is finding it extremely difficult to break out of the mould. As has been the case throughout Myanmar's history, its people, in spite of their hardship, distress and anguish, hope for a better life. To break the mould of authoritarianism, the very psyche of the population will have to evolve—but not at the expense of its culture, traditions, customs and values.

In this respect, education has much to offer, for it plays an important role in the personal and social development of the young, who represent the future. The International Commission on Education stresses this fact in its report to the UN Educational, Scientific and Cultural Organisation (UNESCO). It states: 'Getting the reform strategies right, by a broad-based dialogue, and by increasing responsibility and involvement of stakeholders at every level, will be a crucial element of educational renewal' (UNESCO 1996:26).

Myanmar education: the roles of the stakeholders

The major stakeholders in education are parents, teachers and students. The success or failure of the education process depends on the interaction of these three groups and the changing roles they play in, or are assigned by, the society in which they live. In addition, they are affected by government policies and the influences of religious institutions such as monasteries, churches and mosques. Most importantly, however, it is the interactions of the child with the teacher in the contexts of the school and the community and with the parents and the family in the contexts of the home and the community that determine the outcome of the child's education. Such relationships among the stakeholders are pivotal to creating the kind of cultural change necessary to sustain a post-authoritarian society. As such, the roles of teachers, parents and students will be discussed.

The role of teachers

Philosophies such as Buddhism and Confucianism advocate the enhancement and glorification of filial piety: the respect and devotion of an individual for their parents and teachers. In a predominantly Buddhist country such as Myanmar, teachers have traditionally been regarded as one of the 'five gems' and considered on the same plane as the Buddha (who himself was a teacher), the Scriptures, monks and parents. In such societies, teachers assume the role of substitute parents. This places a great amount of responsibility on them. The social roles of teachers and students are drawn so rigidly that expecting the latter to participate in dialogue and decision making is often deemed inappropriate (Han Tin 2004). Similarly, in other spheres of Myanmar life, especially where hierarchies exist, as in the military, in the monasteries and in instances in which superior–subordinate relationships occur, the divisions are rigidly drawn. The commands or orders of a superior are almost never questioned or challenged. It is, however, an experienced reality in education that teachers can, and do, have life-influencing effects on students. Many individuals who have succeeded in life invariably attribute their success to one or more of their teachers, who are remembered with much respect, affection and gratitude.

Teachers have great potential to act as agents of change. Teachers are, however, as a group, highly conservative and traditionalist, and tend to resist change. For instance, the two Departments of Basic Education[6] and the Myanmar Education Research Bureau have held training sessions on new methodologies and classroom strategies to counter rote learning but with little success. When the teachers returned to their classrooms, they reverted to their old methods after a time. This indicates the need to change the attitude of teachers by improving methods of teacher training—pre-service and in-service—and further increasing their professionalism. Teachers are crucial players in any endeavour to create a more enlightened population. Kennedy (1998) has pointed out that 'outcomes of education are affected by the quality of the teaching workforce. Well-qualified and committed teachers will make the difference between success and failure for many students.'

At a time in Myanmar's education system when the dedication, commitment, confidence and high social status of teachers are being eroded by malpractice and corruption, it is clear that corrective measures must be taken without delay to arrest this backslide. As Hattie (2004) remarked, 'it is what teachers know, do and care about which is very powerful to the teaching–learning equation'. Teachers have one of the most significant influences on the learning of students.

The function of teachers is essential, as they have to inculcate important values in future generations and ensure the holistic development of their students. The best teachers strive continuously to develop in their students respect for other races, other cultures, other religions, other conventions, other traditions and other points of view. They are aware of the moral or conventional nature of social values that are to be employed in character education and 'values lessons'. It follows that the training of teachers should also include the pursuit of moral, intellectual and aesthetic virtues and their acquisition. The major task of teachers would then be to impart these virtues to their students in addition to the main task of teaching the standard school subjects. Until the early 1960s, school activities included '*pyi thu ni ti*' (lessons on civics, ethics and good citizenship). This was very much in line with present-day 'affective education', 'values education' and 'character education'. To make headway in an attempt to reduce the corruption that exists in all work environments at all levels, lessons on ethics with emphasis on honesty and trust should be reintroduced in schools.

Teachers occupy a unique and influential role in Myanmar society and have the potential to act as agents of social change; imbuing their students with liberal and humanistic values and ideals so that when they become parents they will be less authoritarian and will bring about a movement away from the authoritarian model of social relations that exists in Myanmar. In addition to this, teachers have the potential to use their status in the community to try to interact with parents and influence them in such a way that they will be less authoritarian towards their children. By changing the mind-set of parents, teachers will be making it possible for future generations to move away from the dominator-type of society that exists today.

The role of parents/families

Children are born into the nation, the religion and the social class with which their family identifies. Few will dispute the power of the family as a socialising agent. Religion and moral codes tend to support traditional views, especially the dominant position of the father in the family and the special reverence accorded to motherhood in orthodox Burmese Buddhist families.

In Myanmar, financial constraints often discourage many poor parents from sending some or all of their children to school. Often these parents keep their children gainfully employed to supplement the family income, or keep them at home to look after their younger siblings while both parents are away at work in the fields or elsewhere. Such a scenario is true of many of the poor communities in rural areas.

A different picture emerges from the cities and towns. Most urban parents are aware that their children stand a better chance of succeeding in life with an education. Many parents strive (in many cases, beyond their means) to send their children to the best schools to obtain what they hope will be quality education. A worrying feature that is emerging is that some rural families have shifted towards urban areas because of the belief—real or imagined—that more job opportunities exist in the cities. This author has previously (Han Tin 1994) pointed out that most of the rural families who leave their villages often settle in peri-urban areas or satellite towns. Due to the high cost of living in cities, both parents invariably have to work to make ends meet and the children are left to their own devices. Also, the disruption from traditional village life deprives them of the support of the 'extended family' and the village monastery. The resulting disorientation often leads to antisocial behaviour and, ultimately, these children find themselves in the most vulnerable group of the population and their parents' expectations are seldom realised. Fortunately, migration from rural to urban areas in Myanmar has not been excessive. Urbanisation in Myanmar still appears to be slow. According to the latest UNESCO Institute of Statistics estimates (based on World Bank development indicators), the rural population for 2005 was still 69 per cent of the total.

The role of students

The largest and the most important stakeholders in education are the students. According to the UNESCO Institute of Statistics (2007), of a total population of

48 379 000, the group aged from birth to 14 years makes up 25 per cent. Since 1988, when Myanmar emerged from self-imposed isolation of 26 years, the young people of Myanmar have become increasingly aware of what life has to offer. At the post-school level in the cities, the expectations of these young people are more varied as well as being more focused than previous generations. Most feel that the schooling they have received has failed to prepare them for the world of work. With the support of their families, they are willing to invest in courses that provide them with learning and skills that will enable them to strive for upward mobility. This is attested to by the popularity and success of private, non-government educational establishments, which have sprung up throughout Myanmar (see chapters by Lorch and Lall in this volume). Though such institutions have taken up the 'slack' in educational provision, the motives of some of these privately run establishments are rather dubious. Quality control is a necessity in these circumstances. Accreditation and recognition must be given by a professional body, which should be non-governmental, but with Ministry of Education representation.

The education process

The process of education is concerned chiefly with the interaction between the teacher and the child together with the classroom practices that occur within the school environment. Peer pressure is also an important factor in shaping a child's behaviour. Parents within the context of the family and home provide the child with the security, support and guidance necessary for his or her proper intellectual and moral growth. Religion, in the form of monasteries, churches and mosques, also has a great influence on the socialisation of the young. There are close interconnections between the institution of family, the institution of religion and the institution of education. They act as partners in reinforcing the social education of the young. Teachers, parents and religious leaders have a moral responsibility to pass on values and principles to children. Most interventions in the provision of education occur at the policy, structural, school or home levels. More importantly, however, it is what the young people learn from the home and school environments that shapes their personality and character.

Issues in Myanmar education

The Education Sector Study (ESS), a collaborative effort of the Ministry of Education, UNESCO and the UN Development Program (UNDP), was a watershed in the development of education in Myanmar. The ESS was begun in 1990 and *Phase I—Final Report* (of the diagnostic phase) was completed in 1992. In 1993, *Phase II—Proposals for Education Sector Development* (volumes one and two) were published. The ESS identified a number of key issues for reform and presented them in terms of broad priority areas. The eight key issues identified for development of the education sector in Myanmar are:

- redefining the role of primary education
- strengthening curriculum development to meet changing needs
- creating a fair and efficient selection system
- making evaluation learning oriented
- linking education to life after school and the world of work
- improving the quality of teaching and training of teachers
- providing appropriate facilities and instructional materials
- improving sector management.

Although efforts have been made to address the issues identified by the ESS, they have mostly been inadequate. New methodologies and school textbooks have been introduced and tried, but rote learning is still the method preferred by teachers and students. The existing examination and assessment systems still encourage memorisation of facts, which has stifled attempts to instil analytical and creative thinking. The 11 years of primary and secondary education culminate in the matriculation examination, which is conducted on a nationwide scale. Due to attempts to control malpractice and corruption, things have improved; however, rote learning still exists, although to a lesser extent. It is detrimental to the integrity of the system when candidates still scramble to 'buy' sets of questions for approaching examinations.

Curriculum reform is an issue that also needs to be addressed urgently. The current curriculum is so overloaded with factual knowledge that it lends itself to rote learning. Classroom practices also do not allow for analytical, creative thinking or free discussion and expression of thought.

There has, however, been an important improvement to the school curriculum. With the support of the UN International Children's Emergency Fund (UNICEF) and the Myanmar National AIDS Program, a HIV/AIDS prevention and 'healthy living' curriculum has been introduced in primary and secondary schools nationwide, helping millions of children gain knowledge and develop skills that can help them stay healthy. As a result, thousands of lives that would otherwise have been lost will be saved.

Education in Myanmar still faces issues identified by the ESS and only massive investment by the government and international organisations will enable the education sector to contribute positively towards national development.

Prospects and options

Much has been said and written about how poorly Myanmar education is doing. There are, indeed, problems in all levels of education. At the preschool level, an atmosphere of benign neglect exists. There is only a rudimentary and limited teacher-training program for preschool teachers and care givers. The lack of control, standards and training of teachers is evident from the ad hoc system of schools in which three to four-year-olds are being taught the school curriculum of higher grades by rote learning. The joy of learning and the idea that school can be a place for socialising and fun as well as for learning are stifled from the very outset of a child's life. Most preschools are overcrowded and badly managed. Much will have to be done to ensure quality and acceptable standards.

At present, education in Myanmar is structured into five years of primary school, four years of middle school and two years of high school. In effect, a child receives 11 years of schooling (kindergarten and standards one to 10) before entering tertiary education. Kindergarten is taken to be part of the primary education cycle making it a de facto 'standard one'. A Myanmar child starts his or her schooling at five years of age and takes his or her matriculation examination at 16 years of age. This system needs to be reformed. The state school system should treat kindergarten as a nursery and school proper should start at standard one, and the cycle should run for 12 years.

Since 69 per cent (UIS 2007) of the population lives in rural areas and approximately 64.1 per cent are employed in the agricultural sector, provision of education to these rural communities should be geared towards their needs. The curriculum and programs used in rural schools should be flexible not rigid. The rigid, monolithic national curriculum, school terms and timetables that exist today will have to be reconsidered. For rural areas, a more flexible curriculum based on local needs should be devised and, where seasonal cropping occurs, school terms should be arranged so that rural family units can make full use of the manpower available to them without disrupting the schooling of their children. In such a way, the massive drop-out rate before completion of the primary cycle of education can be staunched in these disadvantaged areas. If rural schools are programmed as urban schools are and the plight of agrarian families is ignored, the pernicious effect of school drop-out rates on the already weakened education system will be increased further. It will no longer be state education for the masses, but for the elite. Furthermore, the Education Management Information System (EMIS), which has been set up by the Department of Basic Education, should carry out further school-mapping exercises and work out the needs of local communities in rural areas. An urban-school model does not usually work well in a rural setting. A realistic specification of needs for rural areas has to be undertaken and implemented urgently.

It is generally accepted that education, health, agricultural and rural development are the keys to social, economic and environmental reforms in Myanmar. Focus must also be placed on education with an agricultural bias. Kyaw Than (2006) says that Myanmar has 10 agricultural high schools, seven state agricultural institutes and one university of agriculture. It is sad to note, however, that, at present, some agricultural high schools have closed due to the paucity of student intake. This is a sorry state of affairs in an agricultural country such as Myanmar. It could be that the curriculum is too esoteric and is perceived as being of little intrinsic value by those for whom the schools are intended. The situation might improve if agricultural education is decentralised and local education councils are formed and given the room to fit courses to local needs. There should also be more 'hands-on' experience shared by agricultural extension personnel with local communities. Collaboration and participation by farmers are essential. They must be provided with practical solutions to their problems. The main thrust should be on improving the productivity of the crops that the poor consume. There is a need to target the areas where the largest numbers of poor people live (Win and Batten 2006). The Asian Development Bank (ADB 2007) supports this: 'In view of the importance of agriculture and its impact on poverty, strengthening the sector should be a key goal.'

Currently, agriculture is losing out as the nation's focus is directed towards exploring for natural gas, gemstones and minerals. This is unfortunate, as these resources are finite. On the other hand, agricultural productivity—like human resources—is a renewable factor. Much more should be done for the sons and daughters of rural folk engaged in agriculture. The farmers themselves should also be given an opportunity to gain literacy skills and therefore be able to participate more effectively in agricultural extension endeavours. The Community Learning Centre (CLC) initiative begun by the Myanmar Education Research Bureau (MERB) offers those with no literacy a chance to go from 'darkness into light'. So far, 71 CLCs have been established under the UNDP's Human Development Initiative (HDI) project. Other non-governmental organisations (NGOs), local and international, have joined the effort. According to MERB, there are now 480 CLCs.

Literacy-promotion programs are not new to Myanmar. In the late 1960s, a national campaign known as 'the three rs' was undertaken, involving university students and people from all walks of life—monks, workers, farmers and armed forces personnel. The campaign was deemed a success and lauded by UNESCO, which, in 1971 and 1983, awarded Myanmar its prize for literacy activities.

This important undertaking can be replicated with the cooperation of the five pillars of Myanmar society; however, the campaign model will have to be updated. Incentives must be provided for those illiterate people who join the programs. For example, a farmer who gains literacy through these programs must be rewarded. The reward should not be just a paper certificate, but micro-credit points towards his children's education. In this way, the father (who invariably is the dominant member of the family) will take pride in his own 'education' and feel satisfied that he is also contributing to his children's education. This will go a long way towards alleviating the problem of large numbers of drop-outs and the non-completion of even the primary cycle of education.

The importance of the professional training of teachers has been stressed repeatedly, but training alone is hardly the answer. Adequate remuneration and incentives must be provided to counter the dubious practices of some of teachers 'to earn a fast buck' by operating outside the formal state system. All this highlights the need for teachers to be better trained and to be more professional. There must be a substantial investment by the Ministry of Education in the training and retention of teachers. It is a major concern when the trust and high regard that parents and students once had for their teachers are being worn away by economic pressure, which is being felt at all levels of society. The status of teachers must also be reviewed in terms of increased salaries, allowances and fringe benefits. Their standing in terms of the hierarchy for public employees and the civil service must also be greatly improved. The teaching profession must be made to appear attractive so that a higher calibre of people will be inclined to enter it. Only by being helped to do the right thing will Myanmar teachers regain their rightful place as one of the 'five gems'.

As Myanmar slowly develops, in spite of its handicaps, it will need an increasingly larger workforce of mid-level technicians with hands-on experience and skills. The former Department of Technical, Agricultural and Vocational Education (DTAVE) was effective in the training of such manpower in the past. Many of its staff members were trained at the Colombo Plan Staff College in Singapore. The emphasis then was to produce mid-level technicians with usable and marketable skills. There is a need to return to a vocational system of education that serves the needs of the industrial and construction sectors.

Challenges for tertiary education: options

Many comments have been made about university education in Myanmar, most of them negative. Too much stress has been placed on a very rapid quantitative expansion with quality standards and control lagging behind. The number of higher-education institutes functioning under various ministries and the Civil Service Selection and Training Board increased from 32 in 1988 to 156 in 2008 (Table 7.1).

The rationale behind this expansion is to promote equitable educational development and access among the various regions in Myanmar. Today every state and division has a minimum of three higher-education institutes to cater to its needs. This is highly laudable, but the running costs of such institutes are extremely high and the budget allocation for most ministries is limited. There are inequities among the ministries resulting in institutes under the better-funded ones—such as defence, forestry and agriculture and irrigation—being better staffed, better equipped and better organised. As for the higher-education institutes under the Ministry of Education, the budget allocation is limited. Furthermore, this budget has to be distributed among the 10 departments under it. The reallocated budget for the two higher-education departments is then shared by the 64 universities, institutes and colleges under them.

Table 7.1 Number of higher-education institutions in Myanmar (2008)

	Ministry	Number
1	Education	64
2	Health	14
3	Science and technology	56
4	Defence	5
5	Culture	2
6	Forestry	1
7	Agriculture and irrigation	1
8	Livestock, breeding and fisheries	1
9	Cooperatives	5
10	Civil Service Selection and Training Board	1
11	Religious affairs	2
12	Progress of border areas and national races and development affairs	1
13	Transport	3
	Total	**156**

Source: Compiled by author.

Shortages of equipment and teaching materials, and more importantly the shortage of teaching as well as support staff, have adversely affected the standards of the new universities and higher-education institutes under the Ministry of Education. Much investment and effort will have to be made in order to regain the high standards achieved in the 1950s and 1960s by the two national universities of Yangon and Mandalay. Previously, degrees from these two universities were recognised internationally and their graduates were accepted for postgraduate studies by universities in the West and elsewhere. To achieve the high standards of these universities once again and to gain recognition and accreditation for their degrees would be beyond the present capabilities of the new universities. Recognition of some degrees has become problematic, even within the country itself. University of Distance Education graduates, for example, are finding it increasingly difficult to be competitive in the job market.

Research and development have also lagged behind due to inadequate funds. Although Myanmar's universities and tertiary education institutes have neither the time nor the money to engage in a 'theoretical treasure hunt', they should still try to recruit the best brains in the country.

The present trend towards computer literacy and the emphasis on information technology (IT) should be further strengthened. The establishment of Myanmar Information and Communication Technology Centres in Yangon and Mandalay is a progressive step. The proximity of Myanmar to India, and the extremely cordial relations that exist between the two countries, makes it attractive to tap the international 'outsourcing market', which has boosted the Indian economy. To do so, however, will require a steady and reliable source of energy. International assistance and loans would be essential to set up a national electricity grid. It is in the interest of the world community to strengthen the IT industry in Myanmar, as it will allow the country to make a quantum leap into the twenty-first century. As in its neighbour China, in Myanmar, free access to the Internet has yet to occur; however, 'cyber cafes' in the major cities have made email links with other countries possible for the general public.

According to Kyaw Than (2006), the Yezin Agricultural University is better staffed than most other institutions. Fifty-two per cent of its faculty have postgraduate degrees from various foreign countries. Furthermore, 180 of its new graduates are being sent annually to Arava Company Limited in Israel for 11 months' on-the-job training and to undertake a diploma course in agribusiness studies. Surely, such a program could be replicated for other universities and tertiary education institutes.

Sanctions and threats from some quarters of the international community are not working and should not be allowed to continue because the plight of the people of Myanmar is getting worse day by day. It is time to move forward. In this matter, could not the Association of South-East Nations (ASEAN) play a leading role? Cooperation and assistance from other nations should be increased. The main thrust should be in the sectors of health and education. The constructive engagement policies of Australia, Japan and ASEAN nations should be taken further.

Commonwealth countries initiated the 'Colombo Plan' after World War II to provide cooperation and assistance to South Asian nations. It was later enlarged to embrace other South-East Asian nations. The plan contributed much towards the development of member nations and Australia took an active and leading role in it. Myanmar was one of the Colombo Plan nations. If a similar plan could be initiated by the ASEAN states, with inputs from developed nations together with the two economic powers of Asia—China and India—much headway could be made.

Conclusion

Much remains to be done to restore Myanmar education to its former high standards. In order to achieve this, a holistic approach to education must be taken. The focus should be not only on formal education, but on informal education. Informal education via the mass media and popular literature is often forgotten when discussing education issues. It is highly effective in educating the general populace about social problems such as drug addiction, sexually transmitted diseases and the existence and spread of HIV/AIDS. In such a holistic approach, the needs and inputs of the major education stakeholders must be considered within the contexts of home and community and school and community. Religion and the policy environment will also influence the outcome of the education process.

Finally, Myanmar education will improve only when the education and training of its young improves. Their education should be carefully planned and mapped out. This chapter has identified the various stages in the education of a child and the development of its behaviour at which interventions could be made to establish habits of thoughtfulness, emotional discipline, self-management and conflict resolution. Only with such interventions will an evolutionary process begin in the mind-set of the population, making it possible for change to occur. Underpinning all this is a need for generational change, which will transform the psyche of the whole nation and enable its society to move away from a dominator type towards a more liberal and freer one.

References

Asian Development Bank (ADB) 2007, *Asian Development Outlook 2007*, Asian Development Bank, Hong Kong.

Akimoto, Y. 2006, *Opportunities and Pitfalls: Preparing for Burma's economic transition*, Open Society Institute, New York.

Asia Pacific Centre for Educational Innovation and Development 1999, *Secondary Education and Youths at the Crossroads*, UNESCO PROAP, Bangkok.

Asia Pacific Network for International Education and Values Education 2002, *Learning To Be: A holistic and integrated approach to values education for human development*, UNESCO PROAP, Bangkok.

Delors, J. et al. 1998, *Learning: The treasure within. Report of the International Commission on Education for the Twenty-First Century (The Delors Report)*, the Australian National Commission for UNESCO, Canberra.

Eisler, D. 2003, 'Foreword', in Marshall B. Rosenberg, *Life-Enriching Education*, Puddle Dancer Press, Encinitas, Calif.

Foster, L. E. 1981, *Australian Education: A sociological perspective*, Prentice-Hall, Sydney.

Han Tin 1994, *Education for All: Myanmar's country report submitted to EFA experts meeting, Jomtien*, the Myanmar National Commission for UNESCO, Yangon.

Han Tin 2000, 'Myanmar education: status, issues and challenges', *Challenges in the New Millennium, Journal of Southeast Asian Education/The Official Journal of SEAMEO*, vol. 1, no. 1, SEAMEO, Bangkok.

Han Tin 2004, The school, the teacher, the family and values education, Paper presented at the Conference on Education for Shared Values for Intercultural and Interfaith Understanding, the Australian National Commission for UNESCO, University of Adelaide.

Hattie, J. 2004, 'Teachers make a difference', in Steve Holden, *Teachers Matter, Professional Educator*, vol. 3, no. 1, March, Australian College of Educators, Deakin.

International Commission on Education for the Twenty-First Century 1996, *Learning: The treasure within: Report to UNESCO on Education* United Nations Educational, Scientific and Cultural Organization (UNESCO) Publishing, Paris.

James, H. 2005, *Governance and Civil Society in Myanmar*, Contemporary Southeast Asia Series, Routledge, United Kingdom.

Kennedy, K. 1998, 'Enhancing the status of teachers in the Asia-Pacific region: an exploration of the issues', *Asia-Pacific Journal of Teacher Education and Development*, vol. 1, no. 1, Institute of Education, Hong Kong.

Kennedy, K. 2004, 'Searching for values in a globalized world: can education provide an answer?', in S. Pascoe (ed.), *Values in Education: College Year Book 2002*, the Australian College of Educators, Deakin.

Ministry of Education 1992, *Education Sector Study—Phase I: Final report* [of the Diagnostic Phase], Ministry of Education–UNDP–UNESCO (MYA/90/004 Project), Myanmar Education Research Bureau, Yangon.

Ministry of Education 1993, *Education Sector Study—Phase II (Proposal for Education Sector Development. Volumes I and II)*, Ministry of Education–UNDP–UNESCO (MYA/91/010 Project), Myanmar Education Research Bureau, Yangon.

Ministry of Education 2003, 'Building a modern developed nation through education', *Myanmar Education Updates*, vol. 2, no. 1, Ministry of Education, Yangon.

Myanmar Education Research Bureau 2003, *Review on Adult Education in Myanmar*, <www.unesco.org/education/uic/pdf/country/Myanmar.pdf>

Singh, R. R. 1991, *Education for the Twenty-first Century: Asia-Pacific perspectives*, UNESCO PROAP (APEID), Bangkok.

Than, K. 2006, 'The status of the agricultural sector in Myanmar in 2004', in Trevor Wilson (ed.), *Myanmar's Long Road to National Reconciliation*, ISEAS–Asia Pacific Press, Singapore.

United Nations International Children's Emergency Fund (UNICEF) 2005, 'UNICEF says HIV/AIDS education in Myanmar can save thousands of lives', *UNICEF News Note*, <http://www.unicef.org/media/media_27322.html>

United Nations Educational, Scientific and Cultural Organisation (UNESCO) 2007, Education Survey, UNESCO Institute of Statistics, Montreal, <http://www.uis.unesco.org>

Win, M. and Batten, G. 2006, 'Sustainable agricultural and rural development: pathways to improving social, economic and environmental conditions in Myanmar', in Trevor Wilson (ed.), *Myanmar's Long Road to National Reconciliation*, ISEAS–Asia Pacific Press, Singapore.

Endnotes

[1] Saya San was the leader of the Burmese Peasant Revolt of 1930–31, which was the first concerted effort to resist British domination forcefully.

[2] Po Hla Gyi is renowned as the leader of an oil-workers' strike against the British in 1938, and is also the patron saint of traditional Myanmar boxing.

[3] Bo Aung Kyaw was a student leader in the All Burma Students Union, who was fatally wounded during a violent protest against the British authorities in December 1938.

[4] U Wisara was a prominent monk who led a resurgence of nationalist sentiment in 1929, was imprisoned by the British colonial authorities and died on a hunger strike in prison.

[5] General Aung San, Aung San Suu Kyi's father, was assassinated in 1947 before he could become independent Burma's first head of state.

[6] The Departments of Basic Education for Upper and Lower Myanmar.

8: Evolving Education in Myanmar: the interplay of state, business and the community

Marie Lall[1]

Introduction

Historically, education has been seen as a tool of human-capital creation, especially in developing countries. The development theorists' case for compulsory education is based primarily on the link between mass education and economic growth (rates of return from education) as well as on the link between female education, fertility rates and public health. In short, the better educated a population, the healthier the population will be and the better developed the country will become. The role of the State has always been central in delivering education and the prime role of the state education system is to underpin the fulfilment of broader societal development goals. These goals could predominantly be economic, political, social or cultural, determined by the national, regional and international contexts. There is, therefore, an obvious need to adjust the content of education in a given context to changing societal conditions and needs over time. Underpinning the role of the State in education is the acceptance, since the end of World War II, of education internationally as a public good and the idea that the State has a responsibility towards its citizens in providing at least a basic level of education for all.

In today's globalising world, however, there is a shift away from perceiving education as a public good, as the private sector is increasingly involved in delivering education services (Ball 2007). Education reform, often pushed by the International Monetary Fund (IMF) and World Bank-sponsored structural reform programs in developing countries, is not necessarily focused on poverty reduction and universal access, but on making education a business like any other. The key World Trade Organisation (WTO) agreement for this purpose is the General Agreement on Trade in Services (GATS), which incorporates the aim of unleashing progressive liberalisation of trade in services, including public services such as education. The WTO 'education agenda' is to facilitate the penetration of education services by corporate capital. Education services are to be progressively commercialised, privatised and capitalised (Rikowski 2002, 2008). The WTO's view is that trade and investment liberalisation leads to more competition, greater market efficiency and so, necessarily, to a higher standard of living. Development, it is often argued, can be achieved most efficiently and effectively through private-sector involvement. The trend therefore is for increased privatisation/commercialisation of education, reducing state responsibility vis-à-vis its citizens.

In practice, however, standards of living for many countries in the developing world (with the exception of China) have declined absolutely or relatively (compared with the richer developed nations) in recent years (Chen and Ravallion 2007). The education issues that have emerged in developing countries due to globalisation are access to education and the digital divide, the commodification of education through privatisation, 'brain drain' and the threat to the autonomy of nations for educational systems. While increasing private-sector involvement and privatisation is creating a two-track society within countries, it is increasingly also creating a greater divide between richer and poorer nations. Both these problematic trends weaken the State. Against this backdrop, how should we view private education and private-sector involvement in education in cases where the State is already weak and not capable of providing adequate education? This chapter tries to address the problematic issue of private education with regard to Myanmar, a country in which state education does not cover minimum societal needs and in which civil society (Lorch 2007) and private businesses have had to develop roles as alternatives.

The case of Myanmar is particularly interesting, as the standard of state education has declined markedly in the past few decades. At independence, Myanmar had the highest literacy rate in its own language across the former British Empire (Cheesman 2003). For many years, the level of education was one of the highest in Asia, prompting other Asian countries to see Myanmar as an example. Decades of under-investment and civil strife, however, resulted in the slow and steady decay of the state education system across the country. Despite the fact that school buildings continued to be built in cities and in villages during the socialist era, teacher education and teacher pay deteriorated markedly. The system has never recovered, and today Myanmar is facing an education crisis in its cities and in rural and tribal areas.

In many areas, monastic schools have increasingly come to underpin the state education system for the very poor. In tribal areas such as Kachin State, church organisations have played a similar, if slightly different role. With the advent of a small but increasingly affluent middle class, however, parents search for a third way to educate their children. Some of the very rich have sent their children to international/diplomatic schools or overseas, however, the middle classes do not have the means to follow suit. Consequently, in urban centres, a large number of unofficial schools in the private sector has sprung up teaching principally English and often other subjects as well. This is offered in addition to the state system, which remains compulsory. The cities, but Yangon in particular, are experiencing an increase in the development of edu-business. As a result, unlike in other developed and developing countries, the privatisation of education in Myanmar represents not so much a threat to the strengthening of a national education system, but an alternative for the small but growing middle class in the cities. This inevitably leads to a greater gulf between the urban elite and the wider, much poorer and often rural population. While the increased privatisation in most developing countries is to be deplored and increased marketisation is to be resisted by the government and parents, the case of Myanmar shows, however, that in this particular case private provision is one of civil society's responses to a state that no longer provides the minimum education needed by its citizens. This chapter will discuss how the private-sector schools are carving out a new space between state education and civil society/community organisations.

This chapter is based on a number of interviews and observations conducted during seven trips to Myanmar between 2005 and 2007. Most of the research was conducted in Yangon, but there was a field trip to Mitkyina (Kachin State) and the author also spent some time in Mandalay. A research assistant was employed to translate Burmese texts (newspapers and policy documents) and to collect data from the private schools in Yangon.[2] The chapter discusses the interplay of the state and the private sectors and how these are creating a new dynamic in the education world of Myanmar. It will do so in the general context of increased privatisation in developing countries, arguing, however, that in Myanmar the increased private-sector involvement is not 'used' by the State to reduce state education. The chapter will also discuss the effects of such private involvement, which, as elsewhere, is increasing the divide between the emerging middle class and the broader and poorer population, who have no alternative to the state system.

The issue of private-sector involvement—a global phenomenon

The debate about education for profit is a contentious one, and one that has led to a large amount of research (see, among many others, Ball 2007). The traditional, and largely Western, post-World War II view has been that education is a public good and should not be manipulated for private benefit. It is largely argued in the literature that private companies should not be able to profit from government investment in education and also that they should not be able to shape the education that children receive in order to make more profit.

More recent trends in the West and in developing countries, however, show a major shift in attitude—at the state/government level as well as among the middle classes, especially in developing countries. The trend of allowing for more private education and the increasing demand coming from certain sections of society are of course congruous and largely a part of an increasingly globalised world. Contrary to expectations, even the poorest sections of society sometimes turn to private provision, in the hope of giving their children a better future. An example of this is private slum schools in India, where parents can barely afford the few rupees a day for school fees (see Srivastava 2008). This often results in the State abrogating its responsibilities, as the private and the not-for-profit sectors offer alternatives for different sections of society.

As mentioned in the introduction, the WTO facilitates globalisation through the opening up of all spheres of social life—including public services—to international capital. In effect, the WTO's education agenda is to facilitate the penetration of education services by corporate capital. The key WTO agreement for this purpose is the GATS. This agreement incorporates the aim of unleashing progressive liberalisation of trade in services, including public services such as education. In the long term, no area of social life is exempt from these developments.

The UN Development Program (UNDP 1999), however, and others have warned that globalisation is increasing the gap between the rich and the poor, between connected and isolated cultural groups and that inequality within countries has increased dramatically in the past 20–30 years. Global forces are also leading to increasing population movement and thus to an exponential increase in intercultural interactions and exchanges. Whereas globalisation is opening doors for a highly mobile, highly skilled international elite, it seems to be closing them for many others, who will either seek to escape or remain locked in poverty.

Consequently, the issue of private education and increased privatisation of state education is problematic. The phenomenon is also different from country to country. Whereas in the United Kingdom, for example, it is more a case of 'commercialisation' because the assumption is that the quality of public services will be improved through the introduction of practices and the ethos typical of commercial practice, in India on the other hand, it is more about 'marketisation', because what is happening is the opening up of markets in areas where services were formerly under state monopoly control. It is not, however, always as simple as that; some of these markets are being quite carefully shaped with limited private-sector involvement and close state control, while in other cases there is no state regulation whatsoever.

The debate universally is, however, summed up best by Hatcher (2001:58):

> [T]he starting point has to be the recognition that there are two distinct logics at work. One is a logic of education, based on social and individual need, and notions of equity and democracy. The other is a logic of business, whose bottom line is profit. Not everything business wants to do is incompatible with education interests. But the logic of business is incompatible with the logic of education.

The question with regard to Myanmar is how far these two distinct logics really contradict each other or whether private education is one of the ways forward in the current difficult situation.

Education in Myanmar — past and present

The debate about the purpose of education goes beyond the economic/development argument as all education systems have a political objective: aside from human-capital creation, one of the primary aims of education systems in modern states is, and has always been, the political socialisation of the young. Education systems, especially in Asia, have their origins in processes of state formation aimed either at fostering resistance to the encroachments of Western and/or Asian imperialism, or at furthering post-colonial nation building. Definitions of national identity and visions of nationhood are often popularised by governing elites. One can argue that education has been used as a political tool throughout the ages and across the whole world to define national identity and underlie the political rationale of regimes (Lall and Vickers forthcoming). This has also been the case in Myanmar, where, throughout the socialist period, but also beyond that, education has been used for political purposes, largely to underpin the regime in power (Zarni 1998).

Since the end of the socialist era, however, and the opening up of the economy (and to a more limited extent the country) in the late 1980s, an interesting interplay of issues can be observed: governmental control, under-investment in the social sphere and a society searching for alternatives. As in most dictatorships, one of the reasons the military government has been keen to retain control of education is largely because of the belief that an 'independent' way of thinking poses a direct challenge to them. One could question whether the under-investment in the education system was motivated by the politics of control—the military elite perhaps hoping that a less-educated population would pose less of a challenge. Due to its deterioration, however, Myanmar's education system has also become highly ineffective as a political tool. The interesting nexus here is between a policy of under-investment and a society that is looking for alternatives that could in effect threaten the State even more.

This section will briefly describe the background of education in Myanmar before moving on to the private supplements and alternatives that have started to emerge in urban areas.

Background

The British colonial period established three types of schools of which the two upper-tier types were used to train people to fill the lower and middle ranks of the colonial administration, as they taught in English. The schools that taught entirely in Burmese were, however, by far the majority of schools. In 1945, the Department of Education was formed under the British Government to implement the Simla Scheme of Educational Rehabilitation. The scheme was financed out of the military budget. At that time, 42 post-primary schools and 2060 primary schools were opened. The Education Reconstruction Committee of 1947 decided that Myanmar needed a homogeneous system of schools and that the education system had to be state provided and state controlled (Lwin 2000:5).

At independence, Myanmar had the highest literacy rate in its own language across the former British Empire. This was due not only to the Burmese schools, but largely to the monastic schools that had always played, and continue to play, a major role in educating the poorer sections of society (Lorch 2007). Today, Myanmar retains a very high literacy rate, with 89.9 per cent of adults and 94.5 per cent of youth considered literate (UNESCO 2007). These statistics, although from a UN agency, are difficult to verify, but anecdotal evidence in urban areas shows most people reading on public transport and kerb-sides. The issue of literacy levels is therefore to be questioned largely in the rural areas.

For many years, other Asian countries saw Myanmar as an example in education. Decades of under-investment and civil strife have today resulted in the slow and steady decay of the state education system across the country. Despite the fact that during the socialist era school buildings continued to be built in the cities and in the villages,[3] teacher education and pay deteriorated markedly. It was also at this time that Burmese was made the medium for teaching at all schools, abolishing the colonial legacy of English schools for the elite. In higher education, however, this had repercussions as textbooks and other literature were not available in Burmese.

The state of education today: some different perspectives

During the State Law and Order Restoration Council (SLORC) period, all higher-education institutions were closed for years at a time. After the student protest of 1988, all universities were closed for two years. Another series of student strikes in 1996 and 1998 resulted in a further three years of closure. In Yangon, between 1988 and 2000, universities were closed for 10 out of 12 years. After the reopening of universities and colleges in 2000, the government relocated many universities to different sites and undergraduate programs were moved to campuses far away from any urban centre. Consequently, higher education by correspondence is taken up by those who cannot afford to live away from home. Keeping students away from cities is one of the ways the regime hopes to control any civil strife. Today, more than 700 000 students attend the 156 higher-education institutions and there are 10 000 teachers. A further 13 000 students are enrolled in one or two-year business-related courses (Zaw 2008a). Appendix 8.1 describes the structure of educational institutions in Myanmar.

Education, and especially higher education, is often criticised in the press in Myanmar and there is no doubt that it encounters problems. In a response to a critical *Burma Digest* article, however, Aung Kyaw Soe (2006) claimed:

> It may more correct to assess that [the] Education system is polarised, some students achieve more than others, either because of affordability of family, luck or hard work but I think we are seeing more Burmese graduates with undergraduate education from Burma are doing well in good graduate schools and work place[s]. I know more than 500 Burmese engineers with their first degree in Burma and second or third degrees from good overseas graduate schools.

According to a 2007 *Myanmar Times* special issue on education, the government established a 30-year education development plan in 2001–02 in order to develop a 'learned society' for the knowledge age, with the expansion of schools as a priority. The number of schools is said to have increased to more than 40 000, catering to eight million students (Zaw 2008b). Problems remain, however, especially with regard to access, quality and retention.

According to Khin Maung Kyi et al. (2000:145), the primary enrolment ratio is high. Nevertheless, primary education faces two main problems: there are not enough schools (the numbers range from one school for five villages to one school for 25 villages in the border regions); and there is a high drop-out rate, estimated to be about 34 per cent. The authors also point out the high repetition rate in rural and urban areas. UNESCO statistics are more positive: net enrolment rates at the primary level are 100 per cent for girls and 98 per cent for boys; at secondary level, the figures dropped to 43 per cent for both genders in 2005, with 91 per cent of all children completing primary education (UNESCO statistics web site 2005). This is in stark contrast with the report from the UN International Children's Emergency Fund (UNICEF) in 1995 that states that about only 27 per cent of all children completed five years of primary schooling and only 1.8 per cent of those who entered primary school completed secondary school (UNICEF 1995).

Another set of figures on Burmese education (Achilles 2005) cited net attendance in primary schools at 82 per cent for both genders (from 1998 to 2002) and the number of students who reached class five at 60 per cent officially and unofficially, based on surveys, at 78 per cent (for 1997–2003). Only 41 per cent of boys and 38 per cent of girls (from 1998–2002), however, made it into secondary school. Anonymous interviews in Yangon with an education charity confirmed the high drop-out rates, explaining that children showed up for the first school day and that statistics were based on this, but that as soon as a few days into the school year children, especially in rural areas, stopped attending. In part, such drop-out rates are the result of the high direct costs of sending children to school (such as buying books and uniforms). In rural areas, this is compounded by the high opportunity cost for parents who need their children's help working. Although schooling is free in principle, parents are expected to contribute to the financing of education, as state expenditure on education as a share of gross domestic product (GDP) is decreasing (Kyi et al. 2000:147). Those who cannot afford to attend state schools go to monastic schools or forgo their education altogether. Monastic schools were outlawed in 1962 during the socialist period and were allowed to return only in 1993. Today, however, 1500 monastic schools have been recognised by the government, catering for 93 000 children (Achilles 2005). In some cases, the building is provided by the State but parents have to pool their funds to pay for a teacher; this is especially the case in remote areas (Lorch 2007).

Jasmin Lorch has written about how community-based groups and especially monasteries have come to fill the void for poorer sections of society. She also focuses on the role played by non-governmental organisations (NGOs) in putting together informal education programs (Lorch 2007). Her paper, however, does not discuss the recent growing urban trend of private education, which caters to the middle and upper classes.

Private education in Myanmar

In the immediate post-independence period from 1948 to 1962, private and state education were accepted in basic and higher education. During the socialist era between 1962 and 1988, however, private institutions were eliminated and the State dominated. According to the Myanmar Government web site (<http://www.myanmar.gov.mm/Perspective/persp1998/9-98/edu.htm>):

> [T]hough the private sector has not yet formally been granted a status of setting up Universities with privileges to confer degrees, it has increasingly played an important role in the education market in consonance with the adoption of market mechanisms in the country's economy. The Private Tuition Law of 1964 permits setting up of private schools to teach single subjects per se. Permission is not granted to set up private schools to teach the full curriculum.

Private schools, which emerged since the 1990s, have developed as businesses and are not necessarily regulated by the Ministry of Education. The Ministry of Education in fact expects all Myanmar children to be registered in state schools. Private provision is accepted only over and above state education, with the exception of international schools. Policy as to what can or cannot be taught in private schools seems to have been developed in the past few years as such provision has increased. In fact, such policies seem to change quite arbitrarily and without much warning. The larger schools that operate as registered businesses are less affected than the smaller community-based outfits, which do not have the same kind of recognised business status.

Today, private schools have sprung up at pre-elementary, elementary, secondary and higher-education levels to cater to the popular demands of the market in English language, computing, accounting and business-related training. Some of them offer a wider curriculum, some focus on only a few subjects. Officially, private schools are not allowed to operate as an alternative to the state system—although there are a few that have a special status, such as the Yangon International School and the Diplomatic School in Yangon. These private organisations—sometimes calling themselves schools and sometimes education centres—are also engaged in preparing students for examinations held by overseas universities and professional institutes. Some schools are founded as a business company and some as a service company. Many insist on a low profile and many whom the research team wanted to interview refused to speak on the record. Only a few, such as the ones detailed in the Appendix (but not limited to these), will advertise widely and are accepted in some form and to some degree by the government. This is the case largely because children of government officials attend these schools.

The quality of the teaching and curriculum content varies from institution to institution and cannot be verified. The representative of the Summit International Centre, who was interviewed, said: 'Abroad they have organisations to control the private schools' quality. So private schools must try to meet the requirement of the standard of this organisation. We should also have an organisation like this here.'

There is also a distinction between private schools that act as supplementary schools at the primary and secondary levels and the post-secondary-level schools that prepare students for study abroad. A third category is international schools, such as the International, the Australian and the Diplomatic School in Yangon. Supplementary schools are the most common as children are expected to attend state schools. In fact, the State tries to regulate these schools by limiting the number of subjects they can teach.

Primary and secondary supplementary schools

On the author's first field trip to Yangon, for a conference in January 2005, I met a businessman who had set up a school that was teaching in English. The school was at the primary level only and was meant as a supplement to regular state-school attendance, teaching after official classes had ended. The school was located in the businessman's house in a residential area in central Yangon. It emerged during the next few meetings with other education specialists that such schools were common, but there were no official data about how many there were and what they taught. Interviews revealed that many taught only English, but an increasing number of schools offered a broader curriculum, some even employing English-speaking foreigners on an unofficial basis. A visit about six months later revealed that there had been a 'crackdown' on such schools and that they were now allowed to teach only English and computing/information technology (IT). The government was also trying to regulate this new market by dictating what fees the providers could charge, aligning them with the (very low) salaries teachers received in state schools. It emerged from interviews that, especially in secondary supplementary schools, under the heading 'English' a number of social sciences such as history was being taught, and that IT also meant maths and science. In this way, a fuller curriculum could be maintained. Official fees, of course, could be supplemented through black-market cash payments. A further closure of schools took place in May 2006, leaving only the elite schools that had direct support from the government (Burma Digest 2006). According to anecdotal evidence, however, between 2007 and 2008 large numbers of private schools seem to have reopened. Interviews across a number of schools with teachers, parents and principals revealed that the most important aspect of an expansion of the private-school system would be a change in government regulation, allowing for the full curriculum to be taught. Across the board, it was felt that what was needed most was clarification of the status of private education provision and clear directives on who was allowed to do what. The regulation was enforced mostly by school closures on an ad hoc basis. Apart from the elite schools operating as large businesses, there seems to be no dialogue between the stakeholders and any of the relevant ministries.

Despite the tight regulation on curriculum content, fees and teacher salaries, some larger consortiums have managed to set up private schools and education centres around the country. The International Language and Business Centre (ILBC) is such a venture and caters to a wide age group of students of English and other subjects. It is perceived as one of the most popular education institutions by the middle-class parents who were interviewed as a part of the research (Box 8.1).

Box 8.1

ILBC new class opens in Taunggyi and Lashio (Shan States)

According to the Managing Director, the International Language and Business Centre (ILBC), which has [the] most branches of private schools across the country and is based in Yangon, opened new branches in two cities Taunggyi and Lashio in the Shan States. They will accept pre school students up to GCE 'O' for summer course[s] and for regular classes. ILBC is the first one among the private schools in Yangon and has three branches in Yangon in Bahan, Tarmwe and Thingangyun with a total of 450 students.

Khit Myanmar Weekly, 17 March 2006, vol. 3, no. 25, p. 3.

Some private schools also operate with the help of volunteers. According to an article by Mara Khine (2006), a school named 'Growing Together' and teaching in English opened in Tharkayta Township, a suburban area of Yangon. It is run by Ma Khine Zar, who has a Masters degree in international relations, with the help of a Swedish ex-medical student and four volunteers. The school caters to pre-elementary children and all students are aged from three to five years. Khine Zar said the reason why they opened the school was so that children could learn English early. At the time the article was published, they had 30 students. It was not clear from the article if the school levied fees.

Beyond ILBC—a business venture—and pre-elementary schools staffed by volunteers, there are also summer schools that run like a business. An example is the Summit International Learning Centre in Yangon (Box 8.2). According to Ni Ni Myint (2008), it is schools like these that have encouraged parents to turn to education as a means of creating a brighter future for their children.

Box 8.2

English for skills priority summer school open

The Summit International Learning Centre in Yangon will open a summer school from March 6 to May 26, 2006 said the principal of this centre. The school will train English for skills using 50 per cent school time. Moreover, it will arrange mental maths, science & a social period. The summer courses are taken from International Courses which are specially made for summer class. The school will give original test books (not copied in Myanmar). There will be three separate classes for age groups between 4 to 12. There will be a school bus for the students. The school times are from 9 to 2:30. After the summer class, it will open for regular classes.

Khit Myanmar Weekly, 3 March 2006, vol. 3, no. 23, p. 2.

The Myanmar Marketing Research and Development (MMRD) publication called *The Edge* is a comprehensive listing of all educational institutions in Yangon, covering general education, language training, professional training and vocational training. Looking at the 2002 and 2007 versions, one can see a slight increase in institutional numbers (detailed in parenthesis in the following: 2002/2007). In the section entitled 'General education', the subheadings are 'Day care' (61/68), 'Kindergarten' (17/19), 'Pre-school' (89/100), 'Primary' (18/16), 'Secondary' (11—for 2007 only), 'International schools' (11/12) and 'GCE'O'/SAT' (22). The total number in 2007 is 216 in Yangon alone. Other subheadings are 'Basic education schools' and 'Universities' and 'colleges' (these last categories are the government institutions).

It is clear from the listings that most private institutions cater to the pre-primary age (which includes pre-school and kindergarten), nevertheless offering a variety of subjects such as Myanmar, English, maths and general knowledge as well as singing, playing and drawing. In certain cases, other languages such as Mandarin are also on offer. The day-care centres/kindergartens cater to those aged from three to five, but some offer their services from the age of one. The prices (for 2002) ranged from about 500–30 000 kyat a month. The older the children, the greater the variety of subjects taught (including IT, geography, history, science, arts, physical education, and so on) and the more expensive they are. The Montessori Children's House seemed at the time to be the most expensive pre-primary option, at 45 000 kyat a month. Today, the fees are much higher, with the Summit International Learning Centre's fee set at 75 000 kyat a month (Myint 2008). The parents, teacher and principals interviewed all accepted the fact that the private sector was available only to the upper echelons of society and some families in the middle classes who were prepared to spend between 25 and 50 per cent of their household income on fees. The representative of the Summit International Language Centre said in an interview that the school was offering its services at a reasonable price and tried to arrange lower fees for poorer parents ('Our school is sharing and caring'). The various interviews also revealed that parents chose schools on the basis of reputation and whether they employed foreign teachers. They saw the advantages for their children based mainly on the proficiency of English acquired in such schools as well as an education system more closely related to the exams needed to study abroad.

International schools, pre-collegiate programs and higher education

Aside from supplementary schools, there are other private education facilities. They are either international schools catering to the expatriate community and to some very rich Myanmar families or they are pre-collegiate and higher-education programs that help their students leave Myanmar to study abroad. The surge in the international education market started in Yangon in 1997, as middle-class parents wanted opportunities for their children to study abroad. Local entrepreneurs took risks by competing for contracts with overseas universities and colleges and by establishing private schools geared towards children who wanted to study overseas.

Winston Set Aung, a visiting lecturer in the Management Business Administration program at the Institute of Economics, quoted in a *Myanmar Times* article, said there were qualified schools affiliated with famous overseas universities and colleges and unqualified schools that had linked up with unknown foreign universities:

> It is very easy to make a profit this way, so that's why many private schools try to work as brokers with overseas schools. [However] let the

buyer beware. With more regulation for private schools, parents will see a better value for their money, and unqualified schools will surely lose out. (Zaw 2005)

There are also private schools in Myanmar that teach the American or the British curriculum and offer international qualifications. These schools start accepting students at pre-kindergarten level and those who follow the American curriculum usually need to study up to grade 12. As for the schools that follow the British curriculum, they prepare students to be able to sit for GCSE exams after the completion of matriculation, which is offered by the British Council Exams Unit. According to an article in *Khit Myanmar Weekly* (2006), more and more Myanmar students enter the Cambridge University exam every year. In 2006, there were 30 students aged between nine and 13 who passed the exam. According to the British Council (<http://www.britishcouncil.org/eumd-information-background-burma.htm>), however, which is keen to market British higher education, the Myanmar Government does not encourage international education promoted by the private-education sector:

> Education authorities assume that the [growth of the] private sector harms the image of state education and instead of improving their system they discourage the growth of the private sector. A few investors from the private education sector establish joint ventures with the Ministry of Education and only these ventures are free to promote their business under the umbrella of the education ministry.

The issue is particularly important in the higher-education sector, which used to be a beacon of excellence in Asia. Today, there are 156 higher-education institutions in Myanmar, of which 64 institutions are under the jurisdiction of the Ministry of Education (MoE) and 92 are under 11 other ministries and the Civil Service Selection and Training Board. All the higher-education institutions are state financed. After finishing their matriculation, most students will go to state universities or colleges for further studies. They do so at a comparatively young age, as they finish school at the age of 16.

Due to the declining quality of the state education system, students and parents crave better qualifications and study opportunities abroad. This is, however, an option only for the rich and upper classes, who can afford to send their children abroad.

> Although inflation in this country has been increasing year after year, wealthier parents have tried their best to enable their children to possess internationally recognised certificates. Middle class parents often make very considerable sacrifices to invest in their children's future. (<http://www.britishcouncil.org/eumd-information-background-burma.htm>)

The main market for international qualifications and preparation for these courses exists principally in Yangon. Quite a number of education agents there represent a range of study destinations in Singapore, Malaysia, the United States, Australia, New Zealand and Canada. There is, however, no official agent association to regulate these agencies. Increasingly, institutions from Singapore, Malaysia, Australia and New Zealand have become competitors for UK and US qualifications. Most of their customers are those who have their UK or US student visas rejected or those who cannot afford the high cost of study options in the United Kingdom or the United States.

Recently, the Myanmar press seems to be more prepared to report about Myanmar students who pursue their studies abroad. The March 2008 special edition of the *Myanmar Times* focusing on education had a number of articles about studying abroad and also featured interviews with students based in Singapore. In fact, according to Winston Set Aung, the research director at the Asia Development Research Institute, Singapore is now the preferred destination. He said that students going abroad to further their education should not be viewed as a brain drain on Myanmar:

> They will get international higher education experiences and good connections, which will be of benefit to our own country one day. Millions of Japanese and Chinese students have left their home countries to pursue higher education abroad. Today Japan and China are developing thanks to the combined strengths of their local graduates and those educated in the foreign countries. (Winston Set Aung cited in Kyaw 2008)

Australian universities also seem to be popular and the Yangon Institute for University Studies (YIUS) pre-university level studies centre has helped more than 30 students join Australian higher-education institutions (Thit 2008). They are not alone. Over the years, an increasing number of local professional training centres/institutions has come into the market, offering preparatory courses for UK/US exams and professional qualifications to thousands of students. The pre-collegiate program, based at the Diplomatic School in Yangon, is one such program. The program is organised by an American couple resident in Yangon cooperating with Myanmar teachers. The aims of the program as stated in the 2006–07 handbook are to help students develop their academic abilities so that they can gain acceptance to and possibly a scholarship from an American college or university or other English-speaking universities in the United Kingdom, Japan, New Zealand, Australia, Canada, Ireland, Singapore or the Philippines. The program promises to help with visa applications, prepare the student for life in a Western college environment and help with the planning of a career back in Myanmar. To this end, Teaching of English as a Foreign Language (TOEFL) training is included as well as a curriculum encompassing comparative philosophy and literature, modern world history, environmental biology, comparative life cycles and literature in the English language.

Others who might not be able to pay for such courses rely on private tuition. This, however, can be problematic, as the summary of an article from *Living Colour Magazine* describes (Box 8.3).

Box 8.3

Private subject tuition are [sic] investigated

Private subject tuition has been investigated in the 2006–2007 school year. This was announced on May 9, 2006 by No.3 Basic Education Department under [the] Ministry of Education. The township chief education officer is to instruct those who are providing tuition to apply to get permission to open the tuition class. The Township chief education officer has to report the tuition classes which are eligible within the rules and regulations of the above department. The officer also has to report the illegible tuition classes. If some problems occur and if he does not report them, he has to take responsible [sic] for all problems. The teachers from these tuition classes will be investigated too. If a school runs without permission, it will be terminated in accord with the law of 1984 Rules and Regulation of Private Subject Tuition.

Living Colour Magazine, vol. 132, July 2006, p. 18.

In hoping to give their children a better future with study options abroad, parents are also keen to send their children to formal institutions, although the quality of tuition is not verified or regulated. An article that appeared recently in the *Voice* weekly explains the situation (Box 8.4).

Box 8.4

Private schools ending with 'School' chosen over those that end with 'Centre'

If the name ends with 'school', private schools are more likely to be chosen than if it ends with 'centre' said a principal of the private international school which opens in Yangon, Myanmar. The parents choose this as it is related with the international private school field. In this field, more credible names end with 'school' rather than having a name ending with 'centre'.

According to the same principal over ninety per cent of parents did not check the credibility of the school. These parents send their children to what was perceived as popular schools [sic].

Until recently there were just two private schools (the most famous)—whose names end with 'school'—they are Yangon International School (Shwe Taung Gyar Street, Bahan Township, Yangon) and the Diplomatic School (Shin Saw Pu Street, Sanchaung Township, Yangon).

The Voice Weekly, vol. 3, no. 30, 7 May 2007, p. 8.

Outside Yangon in an ethnic minority area: the case in Mitkyina

The situation in Yangon is atypical of Myanmar in general. While there are similar trends to be observed in Mandalay, other state capitals have fewer alternatives to offer to the failing state system. On the Shan–China border, the author observed a number of Chinese schools. It was, however, not clear from interviews if the parents sent their children only to these schools instead of government schools, or if these were supplementary schools. What was clear was that parents had to pay for the schooling and for the books.

In Kachin State, various Christian churches supplement a large part of education. They see this as essential as the Myanmar system is based largely on Buddhist principles, while a large number of Kachin are Christian or animist. 'Private schools are not allowed, but when they [are] we will make it cheaper than going to state school,' one reverend said.

Some theology students and high-school teachers run a series of programs on a voluntary basis. They offer education and exam training to those who cannot afford the books and uniforms for the state-run schools. The program covers a maximum of four years and is offered in three centres across Kachin State. The students can then pass the matriculation exam that is offered in the tenth standard, which allows them to enrol at the higher-education level, mostly through the distance-learning programs.

Other supplementary schools operate on a more informal basis and are there primarily to help children understand and know their Kachin heritage. Kachin leaders who were interviewed differed in their views of how much of a threat the increasing Chinese influence was to their Kachin and Christian cultures. One interviewee in particular saw Chinese help as something that would counteract the Bamar influence, which was still perceived as the product of an occupying power. The fact that the Chinese language was becoming the choice par excellence for most parents was seen as a small price to pay. Another interviewee, however, viewed the Chinese influence with suspicion and said that unless a Kachin Christian school was allowed to operate instead of the state school, parents would start to choose Chinese alternatives. The people interviewed were interested particularly in raising funds to expand their Kachin cultural education. One of the members of the group wanted to cover a full and comprehensive curriculum so as to develop an alternative to the state system once such a thing was allowed.

Interestingly enough the one 'private' option that exists in Mitkyina is a Chinese school and college funded by the Taiwanese Government. So close to the Chinese border and with a number of trade routes linking Kachin State with Yunnan Province, one would have expected Chinese schools to have been set up, just as in Shan State. This was, however, not the case. As the Chinese language is becoming increasingly important for trade purposes and consequently more popular with parents, parents are sending their children to the Taiwan-funded school for their language training.

The connection between the Kachin and the Chinese is stronger than with their other neighbour, India. One church leader who was interviewed said that India's influence economically and in the education sector was negligible, but that higher education in India was still seen as higher quality than the Chinese alternative and that those who could do so would cross the border to study in India at a higher-education level.

Conclusion

The deterioration of Myanmar's education system underlies the low economic growth of the country. The economic side of Myanmar's education story is not one that is hard to tell. As Lorch has stated, civil society has jumped in where possible, but without managing to replace the State in any significant way. One particular section of civil society, the private sector, has used this business opportunity to turn education into a private and profitable good. The interesting fact is that the increased private schooling is fuelling the gap in Myanmar's authoritarian logic. The regime has let institutions decay and has not provided the resources needed to build a strong state education system. This is a short-sighted tactic, as it in effect loosens the regime's control over society. The private sector's education aims are profit, but they achieve this by encouraging an education system meant largely to help children leave Myanmar and study abroad. Currently, education in English is the most desirable education parents can acquire for their children. As this trend continues, the regime is allowing a condition that increases the absence of its legitimacy, because it equates good education with foreign education. This problem goes beyond civil society simply patching up an inadequate or insufficient social structure.

References

Achilles, J. 2005, 'Das Bildungswesen in Birma/Myanmar—Erfahrungen zum Engagement im Bildungsbereich', in U. Bey (ed.), *Armut Im Land der Pagoden*, Focus Asien nr. 26, <http://www.asienhaus.de/public/archiv/focus26-031.pdf>

Ball, S. 2007, *Education PLC*, Routledge, London.

Cheesman, N. 2003, 'School, state and Sangha in Burma', *Comparative Education*, vol. 39, no. 1, February, pp. 45–63.

Chen, S. and Ravallion, D. 2007, *Absolute poverty measures for the developing world 1981–2004*, World Bank Policy Research Working Paper 4211, <http://www-wds.worldbank.org/servlet/WDSContentServer/WDSP/IB/2007/04/16/000016406_20070416104010/Rendered/PDF/wps4211.pdf>

Crouch, C. 2003, *Commercialisation or Citizenship? Education policy and the future of public services*, Fabian Society, London.

Hatcher, R. 2001, 'Getting down to business: schooling in a globalised economy', *Education and Social Justice*, vol. 3, no. 2, pp. 45–59.

Khine, Mara 2006, 'Learning English young', *Ku Mu Dra Journal*, no. 208, 10 February 2006, p. 9.

Khit Myanmar Weekly 2006, vol. 3, no. 19, 3 February 2006, p. 5.

Kyaw, Htin 2008, 'Human capital to be developed, not copied', *Education—The Key to The Future, Myanmar Times Special Issue*, 2–9 March 2008.

Kyi, Khin Maung, Findlay, Ronald, Sundrum, R. M., Maung, Mya, Nyunt, Myo, Oo, Zaw et al. 2000, *Economic Development of Burma: A vision and a strategy*, Olof Palme International Centre, Stockholm.

Lall, M. and Vickers, E. (forthcoming), *Education as a Political Tool in Asia*, Routledge, London.

Lorch, Jasmin 2007, 'Myanmar's civil society—a patch for the national education system? The emergence of civil society in areas of state weakness', *SÜDOSTASIEN aktuell*, issue 3/2007, pp. 54–88.

Lwin, Thein 2000, *Education in Burma (1945–2000)*, chapter 3, <http://burmalibrary.org/docs/Education_in_Burma_(1945-2000).htm>

Myint, Ni Ni 2008, 'Summer schools first step on path to brighter future', *Education—The Key to The Future, Myanmar Times Special Issue*, 2–9 March 2008.

Rikowski, G. 2002, Globalisation and education, Paper prepared for the House of Lords Select Committee on Economic Affairs, Inquiry into the Global

Economy, 22 January,
<http://www.leeds.ac.uk/educol/documents/00001941.htm>

Rikowski, G. 2008, Globalisation and education revisited,
<http://journals.aol.co.uk/rikowskigr/Volumizer/entries/2008/03/02/
globalisation-and-education-revisited/1737>

Soe, Aung Kyaw 2006, 'A peep behind the curtain of Myanmar education system',
Burma Digest, 5 June, <http://burmadigest.wordpress.com/2006/06/05/
a-peep-behind-the-curtain-of-myanmar-education-system/>

Srivastava, P. 2008, 'School choice in India: disadvantaged groups and low-fee
private schools', in M. Forsey, S. Davies and G. Walford (eds), *The
Globalization of School Choice*, Symposium Books, Didcot, Oxon.

Thit, Aye Thawada 2008, 'Myanmar students choosing Australian and Singapore
unis', *Education—The Key to The Future, Myanmar Times Special Issue*,
2–9 March 2008.

United Nations Development Program (UNDP) 1999, *Human Development Report:
Globalization with a human face*, Oxford University Press, New York,
<http://hdr.undp.org/en/reports/global/hdr1999/>

United Nations Educational, Scientific and Cultural Organisation (UNESCO) 2007,
Statistics web site, <https://portal.ioe.ac.uk/http/stats.uis.unesco.org/
unesco/TableViewer/document.aspx?ReportId=121&IF_Language=eng
&BR_Country=1040>

United Nations International Children's Emergency Fund (UNICEF) 1995, *Children
and Women in Myanmar: A situation analysis*, United Nations
International Children's Emergency Fund, Yangon.

Zarni 1998, Knowledge, control, and power: the politics of education under
Burma's military dictatorship (1962–88), Unpublished thesis, University
of Wisconsin, Madison.

Zaw, Minh 2005, 'Interest in overseas education rises', *Myanmar Times*, 8–14
August 2005.

Zaw, Minh 2008a, 'HR key to development', *Education—The Key to The Future,
Myanmar Times Special Issue*, 2–9 March 2008.

Zaw, Minh 2008b, 'Education system set to create learned society',
Education—The Key to The Future, Myanmar Times Special Issue, 2–9
March 2008.

Translated articles from Myanmar newspapers and magazines such as:

Living Colour 2006–07.

The Voice 2006–07.

Ku Mu Dra Journal 2006–07.

Khit Myanmar 2006–07.

Appendix 8.1 Structure of educational institutions in Myanmar

The Myanmar education system is governed through five departments—the Department of Basic Education, the Department of Higher Education, the Myanmar Examination Board, the Myanmar Education Research Bureau and the Myanmar Language Commission—which are each led by a director-general or equivalent. There is also a Council of the Universities Academic Bodies and a Universities Central Administrative Council.

Basic education is divided into the normal mainstream as well as technical and vocational education. The time a child spends in the normal stream is five years in primary, four years in lower secondary and three years in upper-secondary levels. According to government data, there were 7.2 million students with 224 000 teachers and 38 800 schools in 1996–97. For technical and vocational education, there are seven state agricultural institutes, 17 technical high schools, 10 agricultural high schools, three commercial schools, two machinery repair and maintenance schools, 11 handicraft schools, six schools of home sciences and two schools of fishery—a total of 58 in 1996–97. There are five teacher-training colleges, 14 teacher-training schools and three correspondence courses for training various levels of basic education teachers. Today, there are 38 universities, one management college and five degree colleges (<http://www.myanmar-education.edu.mm/moe_main/index.php>).

Appendix 8.2 Examples of private schools in Yangon

1. Horizon International Education Centre

Level/grade: from Nursery GCE A level

Number of students: more than 100 in every year (local and international students)

Number of teachers (total): 24

Local teachers: 14

Foreign teachers: 10

Education system (British, US or other): combined US and British system

Medium of instruction (English or Myanmar): English

Aids, tools and activities: computer, arts, gym, swimming pool (at Hotel Nikko Royal Lake), school bus.

Foundation year (head office/main campus): 2000/Yangon

Address: No. 21, Pho Sein Street, Bahan T/S, Yangon

Telephone: 72 8016, 54 3926

Web site: www.horizon.com.mm

Email: contact@horizon.com.mm

Campuses: Horizon Main Campus (Yangon), Horizon (KG I) (Yangon), Horizon (KG II) (Yangon), Horizon (Mandalay).

2. International Language and Business Centre (ILBC)

Level/grade: pre-school to GCE 'O' level

Number of students: 450 (local and international students)

Total staff (teachers and others): 270

Founder: U Tin Maung Win, from Myanmar

Education system (British, US or other): using international system and own system written by local experienced teachers.

Examination system: Common Assessment Test (exam plus activities in class and school).

Aids, tools and activities: computer, arts, gym, library, canteen, swimming pool, school bus.

Foundation year (head office/main campus): 1995 March/Yangon

Email: info@ilbc.net.mm

Campuses: Bahan, Tarmawe, Thingangyun (Yangon), Mandalay, Taungoo, Myitkyina (Kachin State), Lashio, Taunggyi (Shan State).

3. Summit International Learning Centre

Level/grade: junior nursery to kindergarten (primary class to open in 2007–08 school year).

Student age: two to six for regular classes (from ages four to 14 for weekend English classes).

Number of teachers (total): 13 (local and foreign)

Founder: Daw Win May Than, from Myanmar

Principal: Daw Win May Than

Education system (British, US or other): British

Aids, tools and activities: arts, swimming pool (at Summit Park View Hotel), school bus, outdoor activities.

Foundation year (head office/main campus): August 2006/Yangon

Address: No. 248, Ah Lone Road, Dagon T/S, Yangon

Telephone: 72 2661, 72 5718

Web site: www.summit.bravehost.com

Email: summitilc@praize.com

4. Nelson International Education Centre

Level/grade: pre-school (primary school will open in 2008–09 school year).

Student age: three to five.

Number of students: 60

Number of teachers (total): 12

Principal: Daw Myat Thin Zar Htun

Foundation year (head office/main campus): September 2006

Address: No. 3, Tha Pyay Nyo Street, Sanchaung T/S, Yangon

Telephone: 51 0612

Web site: www.nelc-centre.com

5. Ayeyarwady Media Service

Level/grade: IELTS preparation courses and TOEFL (this school started offering English classes at basic, intermediate and premeditate levels. It also offers a Singapore polytechnic preparation course and sends students' applications to Singapore polytechnics. Cooperates with Temasak Polytechnic in Singapore, teaching Temasak's first-year business course. Qualified students from this school can receive a school grant from the Singapore Government.

Foundation year: July 2002

Consultant: retired professor of English Department of Yangon University

Course manager: retired associate professor (English Department of Yangon University)

Number of students: 17 last year; 36 this year (15 students now attending second-year course in Temasak, Singapore, among whom 10 receive grants and five pay their own expenses).

Target students: those from middle-class and higher-class families—especially students who want to study abroad but have not qualified with high enough scores, and whose parents can afford to pay for them.

Endnotes

[1] I would like to thank my Burmese research assistant, Thiri Zaw, who helped collect primary and secondary data in Yangon for this research project.

[2] There is very little material on education in Myanmar available and this chapter reflects the paucity of resources in that it cannot often cite other research. A lot of what has been documented here stems from the interviews conducted in the field and informal conversations with Myanmar citizens—some but not all of whom were education specialists.

[3] This was the time of education expansion in physical terms as many new schools were opened and the number of university students increased rapidly.

9: The (re)-emergence of civil society in areas of state weakness: the case of education in Burma/Myanmar[1]

Jasmin Lorch

Introduction

In September 2007, Burma/Myanmar experienced its largest popular uprising since 1988. The protests, which posed the first serious challenge to the military regime in nearly 20 years, were widely perceived as an outburst of popular frustration about the pervasive failure of the State to provide for the basic welfare of its citizens. From January on, the '88 Generation Students Group[2] led small-scale demonstrations that focused mainly on economic and social issues. Several signature campaigns tried to motivate people to write to the government describing their everyday problems, including rising food prices and the lack of access to education (Thawnghmung and Myoe 2008; see also the chapters by Horsey and Win Min in this publication). In the international media, the uprising was often described as the 'Saffron Revolution', because it was led by thousands of young Buddhist monks—a fact that took most Burma/Myanmar experts by surprise. In view of the economic hardships they faced and the multitude of social-welfare functions they performed, the Buddhist monks' leading role in the uprising is not incomprehensible. Most importantly, monastic education has long served as a stopgap function for the failure of the state-run education system. In the years before the uprising, the teaching load of the monks had increased tremendously as fewer and fewer parents could afford to send their children to a state-run school. At the same time, due to growing poverty, many ordinary people could donate less and less to the monks, who rely entirely on alms for their own funding. Shortly before the demonstrations, many monks allegedly could afford no more than one meal a day. As the example of the *Sangha*[3] suggests, the September uprising can therefore be seen as the outcome of an overstraining of community self-help networks trying to cope with the pervasive failure of the welfare state.

Civil-society development is a relatively new topic in Burma/Myanmar studies, as it has long been assumed that civil society cannot exist fully in such an authoritarian context (see, for example, Steinberg 1999). Contrary to such assumptions, some more recent studies have found that civil society has been (re)-emerging in the past few years (see, for example, Heidel 2006; ICG 2001;

South 2004). As this author has argued elsewhere, spaces for civil-society actors in authoritarian Burma/Myanmar exist in at least two areas in which the authoritarian state is weak or failing: first, in various sectors of the weak welfare state; and second, in some of the negotiated spaces of relative ethnic autonomy in the cease-fire areas (Lorch 2006, 2007).[4] Against this backdrop, the (re)-emergence of civil society-based self-help groups in the education sector is part of a larger trend that has been taking place in Burma/Myanmar in recent years: the military regime has started to tolerate welfare provision by civil-society actors in areas of tremendous welfare need that the State is unable or simply unwilling to deal with itself (Lorch 2007). Even though education is highly regarded in Burma/Myanmar, the state-run education system has been deteriorating continuously, in terms of accessibility and quality. In some rural areas, for instance, public schooling is not available at all, either because the government has never constructed a school building in the village or because teachers refuse to go to these remote areas (see also Marie Lall's chapter in this publication). Moreover, teachers and professors often lack basic qualifications, because the state-run teacher-training system has been steadily degrading. As a consequence, civil society-based organisations have begun to provide makeshift solutions to bridge the accessibility gap. At the same time, the commercial private sector has started to move into the quality gap and several private schools catering to the middle class have started operating in recent years (see Lall's chapter in this volume). In contrast with the non-profit-making civil society-based models, however, these schools usually charge quite high fees.

In principle, education should be a priority sector for international engagement, as it is a key to national development (Tin 2004), along with improvements in other important welfare sectors such as health. Moreover, if donors were able to engage with civil-society actors in the education sector, this could be a starting point for gradually changing Burma/Myanmar's authoritarian political culture (see Han Tin in this volume). The continuing engagement of the UN International Children's Emergency Fund (UNICEF) in Burma/Myanmar's education sector provides evidence that the donor community takes the importance of education for development seriously.[5] The role of the international aid community in the field of education has, however, so far been limited, as the government is highly suspicious of international involvement this sector, which—despite poor resource allocation—it considers an area of national interest. In particular, there is almost no institutionalised cooperation between donors and local civil-society actors in the field of education and information about the state of civil-society activities in this area remains scarce. Against this backdrop, this chapter focuses on an analysis of what spaces are available for civil-society actors in the education sector.[6] It argues mainly that even though civil-society groups have managed to bridge some of the gaps that exist in the formal education sector, they lack the capacity to provide a substitute for a functioning state-run education system.

Due to the lack of reliable data, the findings presented here should be regarded as preliminary results intended to inspire further research and discussion.

Civil society in the context of authoritarianism and state weakness: some theoretical reflections

Civil society under authoritarian rule

According to normative definitions, the sphere of civil society is characterised by its extensive autonomy from the State and the market, and by voluntary participation, tolerance, discursive procedures of decision making and horizontal networks. Correspondingly, it is assumed to generate trust and democratic values and to consequently promote democracy.[7] In order to identify and understand civil-society developments in authoritarian Burma/Myanmar, such normatively highly loaded concepts are not very useful. Compared with the theoretical ideal type, Burma/Myanmar's civil society is still embryonic in nature (Lorch 2006). This study therefore relies on a broad, empirical definition of the term:

> Civil society refers to the arena of uncoerced collective action around shared interests, purposes and values. In theory, its institutional forms are distinct from those of the state, family and market, though in practice, the boundaries between state, civil society, family and market are often complex, blurred and negotiated. Civil society commonly embraces a diversity of spaces, actors and institutional forms, varying in their degree of formality, autonomy and power. Civil societies are often populated by organisations such as registered charities, development non-governmental organisations, community groups, women's organisations, faith-based organisations, professional associations, trades unions, self-help groups, social movements, business associations, coalitions and advocacy groups. (LSE 2008)

As I have argued previously, civil society generally bears a relation to the state in which it operates.[8] A strong, democratic, constitutional state is the *sine qua non* for an autonomous and democratic civil society to flourish. In Burma/Myanmar, however, as one of the longest-enduring military regimes in the world, civil-society organisations usually mirror the 'dark sides' (Lauth 2003) of the authoritarian state in which they operate, such as hierarchies, exclusiveness and patterns of cooption. In order to be able to run their self-help programs, civil-society actors in authoritarian states frequently have to maintain functional ties with members of the ruling establishment—or even let themselves become partially coopted by the latter (Perinova 2005). Moreover, vertically structured relationships or religious and ethnic cleavages in society as a whole are usually found in civil society as well (Croissant 2000; Howell 1999). This general finding is especially relevant for religiously and ethnically segmented states such as Burma/Myanmar.

Spaces for civil society in areas of state weakness

Weak states are states that fail to deliver positive political goods—such as security, health, education, a reliable legal framework and functioning infrastructure—to their people (Rotberg 2002). Schneckener (2006) has attributed three core service-delivery functions to the State: first, the function of territorial control and the provision of public security; second, the function of welfare provision; and third, the function to establish a democratic constitutional state and a reliable legal system. In the service delivery view, strong authoritarian regime features and state weakness are not mutually exclusive (Schneckener 2004). As Rotberg (2004:5) puts it, 'There is a special category of the weak state...That is the seemingly strong case, always an autocracy, that rigidly controls dissent...but at the same time provides very few political goods.' Burma/Myanmar certainly falls under this category.[9]

More recent studies on the phenomenon of state weakness have shown that if the State fails to perform one of its core service-delivery functions, other actors can move into the gaps that exist. While Rotberg (2004) refers especially to warlords and other criminal non-state actors, Risse (2005) also identifies economic actors, non-governmental organisations (NGOs), family clans and other local groups that practise alternative forms of governance in areas of state weakness. Some of these groups account for civil-society actors in line with the definition that forms the theoretical basis of this chapter. As civil-society theories and the research on weak states have so far remained largely unrelated, theory does not tell us how precisely civil society constitutes itself in the context of state weakness. Ottaway (2004), however, has made the interesting point that in weak states 'modern civil society', which usually comprises secularised and formally organised groups such as NGOs, tends to be rather weak. At the same time, 'traditional civil society', which comprises mostly informal groups such as religious and ethnic organisations, can be quite strong as it provides coping mechanisms for state failure such as alternative, community-based schooling.

The State of Burma/Myanmar can be considered particularly weak with regard to the core function of providing for the welfare of its population. The failure of the state-run education system constitutes but a subcategory of this general failure of the welfare state. Furthermore, certain ethnic minority areas are not under the direct control of the central state, which limits its territorial power monopoly. Since 1989, the regime has concluded cease-fires with most of the armed ethnic resistance groups, thereby granting them some degree of autonomy. As a result, some room for manoeuvre exists for civil-society actors in the welfare-provision sector and in certain territories with a degree of ethnic autonomy.

The weakness of the state-run education system

Government expenditure on education is estimated to amount to only about 1 per cent of gross domestic product (GDP) (DFID 2008). In many rural areas, the government education system is non-existent. This includes frequent cases in which there is a school building but no teacher working in the village. Teachers are usually reluctant to go to the rural areas, particularly as they receive no adequate salaries to compensate them for this. If teachers are forcibly transferred to remote villages, they often do not stay there. As a consequence, rural schools in particular are mostly overcrowded and the student/teacher ratio is very high. Furthermore, schools are mostly poorly equipped and usually lack basic teaching materials such as benches, tables and textbooks. Moreover, schoolbooks and curricula tend to be outdated.

Teachers are mostly poorly trained and teaching methods tend to be repetitive, outdated, teacher centred and based on ex cathedra teaching. The state-run teacher-training system has been steadily deteriorating. Even the Ministry of Education (MOE 2006) itself admits that not all teachers have an academic qualification or have even 'attended certified courses'. Apart from the problems mentioned, there is also an obvious lack of vocational skills training as well as a dearth of capacity building in fields such as management, project-oriented work and even English, which international organisations and businessmen active in Burma/Myanmar recognise instantly as soon as they try to hire local staff. What is particularly worrying in this regard is that, according to several international aid workers, the education level is usually lower the younger the applicants are, which indicates a continuing erosion of the education system.

This erosion is characterised not only by a lack of access to, and the quality of, education, but by 'a system that suppresses critical thinking and...discourages creativity'. As a consequence, there is meanwhile, a 'pervasive cynicism about the process of education'.[10] In many instances, people seem to have given up on the State. As a consequence, several non-profit and self-help approaches to the provision of basic education, as well as professional and life skills, have (re)-emerged. In this regard, it is interesting that during a rare civil-society workshop conducted in Burma/Myanmar, most of the participants from civil society defined their opportunities in terms of unmet community needs for services—that is, in terms of gaps.[11] The current Myanmar local NGO directory (DLN 2005), which lists only registered organisations with an office in Yangon, mentions 57 NGOs, including monastic schools and church-based and Islamic organisations that engage in education. As many civil-society initiatives in Burma/Myanmar are informal in character and operate on a local level, the real number of self-help groups in the education sector can comfortably be estimated to be much higher.

Civil society-based education systems in government-controlled areas

Buddhist monastic education

Before British colonial rule, Buddhist monasteries were the main education institutions in Burma/Myanmar. Until today, monastic schools, or monastic education centres as they are often called, have been the most important civil-society institutions bridging the accessibility gap in the state-run education system in government-controlled areas. While public schooling is not available in many rural regions, there is a monastery in nearly every village (UNESCO 2002). Monastic schools cater particularly to poor children, are free of charges such as enrolment fees and usually provide teaching materials such as books for free. Moreover, many monasteries serve as schools and orphanages at the same time.

Traditionally, monastic education is characterised by non-formal and lifelong learning. In this sense, it can be said to represent the unity of life and religion, which still exists in many rural regions of Buddhist Burma/Myanmar. In its pure and traditional form, monastic education can thus be considered fundamentally different from the formal secular education system, which considers education as a preparation for life rather than a form of life itself (Tin 2004). In British colonial times, the fight for the right to a distinctively Buddhist education—as opposed to the secular education system imposed by the British—constituted a significant part of the anti-colonial struggle (Zoellner 2007a). Contrary to pre-colonial times, however, in present-day Burma/Myanmar, a secular national education system exists, but fails to provide adequate services. In this context, monastic schools often provide not only parallel but complementary education models, and the line between informal religious and formal secular education has become blurred to some extent. Besides non-formal and religious education, a growing number of monastic schools have started to also teach children basic skills needed for secular life; some of them have meanwhile even become (partly) incorporated into the formal education system.

Today, three main categories of monastic schools can be seen: the first confines itself to imparting Buddhist teachings; the second is made up of monastic schools that consider it their main task to impart Buddhist teachings but which, at the same time, also teach children basic literacy skills (although these second-category monastic schools are unable to hold exams or to award their pupils certificates that are recognised by the government); the third are those that adopt the government curriculum, which means that they engage in formal education. According to official government figures, 1183 of these third-category monastic schools are recognised by the government in a kind of coeducation system. They seem to be registered with the MOE and the Ministry of Religious Affairs (MRA). According to the same source, these 1183 schools reached 158 040 pupils in the

2003–04 academic year (MOE 2006). If monastic schools are recognised by the government, their pupils also have the possibility of acquiring an officially recognised degree. They can do their final exams either at a government school or at their respective monastic school, which then, however, has to send the exams to the ministry responsible for marking and issuing the certificates.[12] For officially recognised monastic schools, a kind of bridging system makes it possible for pupils to change from monastic to government schools. If, for example, pupils complete the primary level at an officially recognised monastic school, they are sometimes allowed to do a special test. If they pass this test, they can gain acceptance to a government middle school. According to other official statistics obtained from a UN agency active in the country and which are largely consistent with the official source (MOE 2006) cited above, the majority of all officially recognised monastic schools teach at the primary or post-primary levels. Some, but much fewer, teach at the middle level.[13] Furthermore, two to five officially recognised monastic schools were reported to teach at the high-school level.[14] Moreover, various monastic education centres also engage in vocational skills training such as computer training activities. The figures cited here are likely to be incomplete due to the lack of reliable data, but they point to a remarkable tend: by providing secular education and professional skills to poor children, some Buddhist monks seem to deliberately try to bridge the accessibility gap that exists in the state-run education system.

It should also be noted, however, that in terms of quality, monastic schools tend to show the same deficits as the state-run education system. For instance, learning is mostly by rote even though there are some important exceptions. Most monastic schools teach novices and lay children together and provide their educational services regardless of race and religion. Moreover, monasteries sometimes serve as protective umbrellas for more secular educational initiatives run by lay professional teachers or other lay volunteers (who may or may not have been trained). There are, however, also monastic schools whose main purpose is to counter similar efforts by the Christian churches and to prevent people converting from Buddhism to Christianity. This pattern is especially relevant with regard to those monastic schools that are also orphanages. Even though not all of the children they care for are Buddhist, some monastic orphanages require every child who wants to live in their compound to wear a Buddhist novice's robe. Even in orphanages where this is not the case, Christian or Muslim children are sometimes encouraged to convert to Buddhism. Asked about the religion of his students, one monastic schoolteacher said that after living in the monastery for a while the boys normally became Buddhist. Another more critical dimension of monastic education relates to gender. Monastic schools cater mainly to boys (UNESCO 2002), especially those that, at the same time, serve as orphanages.[15] The author also visited some monastic orphanages that were run by Buddhist nuns and catered to girls, but these did not provide secular education such as literacy and numeracy. Moreover, most of them faced even more economic hardship than those monastic orphanages visited that catered to boys.

Monastic education centres vary in size and in the degree to which they are coopted by the regime. While some have only a few dozen pupils, others have between 100 and 800 (some big monastic schools have even more pupils, but they are exceptions to the rule). As a basic principle, the bigger an institution is, the more coopted by the State it tends to be. Small and rural monastic schools often centre on one individual monk and are more or less independent from government interference. Their capacities, however, are also often limited and their teaching materials quite basic (South 2004). In constrast, large monastic schools often have quite reasonable facilities and offer a number of secular subjects, sometimes even including foreign languages, particularly English. Some of the big monastic education centres visited could even afford to hire university students or professional teachers to give courses and had their own professional skills training centres or income-generating facilities such as tailor or carpenter shops. Such relatively large-scale functions come, however, mostly with a certain degree of cooption. For example, a general pattern seems to be that government officials pay public visits to the monastery and give (largely symbolic) donations in order to take some of the credit for themselves. Another aspect of cooption is that many of the monks who run big monastic schools have received their own education at the state-run Theravada Buddhist University, which operates under the MRA and which the government considers a tool to promote but also to 'purify' and control the Buddhist faith.

According to one expert on Buddhism in Burma/Myanmar,[16] the young monks who led the 2007 uprising came predominantly from the private monk schools, a specific type of monastery. Monk schools are purely religious education institutions, which cater to adult monks and impart Buddhist teachings on a tertiary—that is, college or university—educational level. They thus constitute a subtype of the first category of monastic schools depicted above. State-run and private monk schools exist, and the young monks who played a leading role in the 2007 demonstrations came predominantly from the latter. Nevertheless, by protesting against the government's welfare policies and the fuel-price hike, these young monks certainly expressed the socioeconomic and political grievances of the whole *Sangha* and the population at large. (According to the same source, the demonstrations were so well organised because monks who belonged to the same monk school usually marched together in one block. Different monk schools could, in turn, coordinate their actions because young monks from different monk schools knew each other from their home villages and, before the demonstrations, called each other up.) In the aftermath of the uprising, the private monk schools have faced a harsh government crackdown and many of them have been abandoned or closed down.

Monastic schools, including orphanages, that cater to children are run mostly by a single monk or sometimes by a few (two to five) monks; they usually teach a certain number of young novices and an often larger number of lay children together. (In contrast, the monk schools usually host a fairly large number of already ordained monks.) To the author's limited knowledge, these monastic schools did not play a role in the 2007 uprising. Nevertheless, as some academics and a local aid consultant from within Burma/Myanmar suggested, some of them might have been affected by the subsequent government crackdown. This is particularly likely for monastic orphanages that cater to older boys and that resemble the monk schools in their organisational structures and beneficiaries, especially as they often require all boys in their compound to wear a Buddhist novice's robe.

So far, the role of the international donor community in promoting monastic education has been limited at best. While some monastic schools do receive funds and donations from international friends, such as travellers or small foreign NGOs, this happens largely on an individual basis. Except for a few notable exceptions, the cooperation is usually not institutionalised. The fact that hardly any Burma/Myanmar observers foresaw the 2007 uprising of the monks provides evidence that there is still a huge lack of information about the Buddhist monasteries and monastic schools and that further research is needed in order to assess their overall social and political impact.

Extra tuition, early childhood development, professional skills training and capacity building: the role of NGOs, community-based organisations and individuals

Commercial as well as non-profit 'learning centres' that provide extra tuition have become a common part of the urban landscape. A number of local NGOs and engaged individuals, often university students, run free or low-cost extra tuition programs in order to help children who have problems at government schools but are unable to pay for extra tuition. Many of these programs focus on English or help students prepare for their matriculation examination. While free or low-cost extra tuition often constitutes a valuable support for poor children, it should be noted that it can also be counterproductive. The quality of these programs is often quite inadequate and the volunteers who give lessons are often insufficiently qualified and have usually not been trained as teachers. As in the public schools, learning is mostly by rote. Moreover, classes tend to be large (up to 100 students) and quite often students from different grades—ranging from primary to high-school level—are taught together. What is more, with the state-run education system deteriorating, it has become common practice for parents to have their children take extra tuition. As a result, some 10-year-old children interviewed spent almost all of their day in class, going to the government school in the morning, to extra tuition with costs in the afternoon and to another, free extra tuition in the evening—sometimes as late as nine or ten o'clock. With the absorptive capacity of a 10-year-old child unquestionably limited and the quality of the tuition often inadequate, the educational impact of some of these programs becomes questionable. It is also noteworthy that in many instances of extra tuition, the line between civil society, the State and corruption has become blurred. As teachers usually cannot live on their meagre salaries, many have resorted to extra tuition as a way to supplement their income. Some of these extra-tuition programs run by professional teachers operate at low cost and might constitute a valuable complement to regular tuition where classes are usually too big for teachers to be able to respond to individual students. In some problematic cases, however, teachers have stopped teaching the subject matters most relevant for passing the final exams in regular class and have transferred these teaching units to the extra-tuition courses instead. Some teachers even provide the notes, or handouts, on which the exams are based through paid tuition classes only.[17]

Limited space also exists for community-based and NGO activities in the early childhood development (ECD) sector, which is aimed at children up to five. At the village level, these initiatives are often informal and conducted by local community leaders. Some of the registered local NGOs run more formally organised nursery or pre-primary schools, which operate on a larger scale. According to an NGO worker, pre-primary schoolteachers usually try to stimulate creative thinking in children, play and sing songs with them and start to teach them the Burmese/Myanmar and the English alphabets. Some foreign as well as local church-based NGOs also focus on capacity building for local, unregistered community-based organisations that already have their own ECD programs in place but lack knowledge in child-centred teaching methods. The fact that several international NGOs have also managed to engage in ECD indicates that this sector is generally a bit more open than the education sector as a whole. Interestingly, it is the Ministry of Social Welfare (MSW) and not the MOE that is in charge of ECD. This seems to provide a small window of opportunity for enhanced civil-society engagement. As a local staff member of an international NGO active in ECD stressed, on an individual level, cooperation between NGO members and MSW officials sometimes worked quite well. What is still lacking, however, is a bridging system between non-state ECD programs and the state-run primary school system. According to a local employee of an international NGO that works in the ECD sector, once children transfer from an ECD program into the rigid state-run education system, they are often confused by the contrast in approach.

Another field of local NGO engagement is vocational-skills training. The 'Myanmar Professional Skills Training Association' in Yangon,[18] for example, offers courses in different fields including nursing, gardening and financial accounting. It also has a few computers and offers training that focuses on basic office skills. Most of the courses charge a small attendance fee and are thus unlikely to reach the hard-core poor. This NGO, however—like others in this field—faces financial constraints itself. The computer classes, for instance, are often interrupted by electricity cuts as the organisation cannot afford a generator. Moreover, this association usually relies on the voluntary engagement of its teachers and trainers, who are often local pensioners.

Some unregistered community-based organisations have also set up 'training centres' that offer post-high school education and target ill-educated school leavers. Teachers, ex-teachers or non-professional volunteers from the local community often conduct courses. Some of these training centres have received financial support and capacity building from international NGOs. Nevertheless, in most cases, teacher training is still a major need.[19] As a rule, NGO vocational training programs cannot provide students with an officially recognised degree. Some NGOs, however, maintain contacts with local enterprises and also help their graduates by writing recommendation letters to possible future employers. As the government is wary of all initiatives that might contribute to empowerment, a number of local NGOs do not engage in education directly, but have opted instead to engage in less controversial education support activities. Some give grants to poor parents whose children are enrolled in government schools. Others have established free hostels for poor children or young adults who leave their remote rural areas in order to seek education and training in the cities.

Local NGOs and community-based organisations also make important contributions in the field of capacity building for development-oriented work. This includes training activities in project management, proposal writing, financial accounting, community organising, leadership skills, conflict management and English. Basically, these programs target three different groups of people: first, (future) staff members of local NGOs; second, local community leaders such as pastors, village elders or socially engaged local businessmen who can later pass their skills on to their respective local communities—or potentially even establish their own informal skills-training centres; and third, (future) local staff members of international aid organisations. The 'Local Capacity Mobilising Initiative' in Bagan,[20] for example, provides a self-study program that requires applied thinking and a high degree of discipline. The course has more than 10 modules, including socially relevant issues such as community organising and conflict management. Students basically work through the materials themselves but come together for regular group discussions. Starting from Bagan, the organisers have managed to extend the program to two other cities. In order to have a sustainable impact on local communities, the organisers are seeking ways to establish alumni groups of graduates, which they plan to link up with already existing community-based organisation and NGO welfare programs in different towns and villages. The certificates that students can acquire after completing NGO and community-based organisation capacity-building courses are not recognised by the government. At least one community-based organisation visited, however, had its certificates accredited by an international educational institution. Moreover, community-based organisation and NGO certificates are often recognised by the local and international aid organisations active in Burma/Myanmar for which community-based organisation and NGO capacity-building courses have come to serve as pools from which they recruit their staff.

Community-based schools in rural areas

In rural areas where there are no public schools, community-based schools (CBS) are often crucial as a means for providing village children with a primary education. Such CBS are established and organised in a variety of patterns. In cases where there is a public school building in the village, but the local government cannot pay for a teacher, local communities frequently establish informal groups and collect money to pay the village teacher themselves. If no professional teacher is prepared to work in the village, community-based organisations sometimes even choose a teacher from among themselves. Mostly, these makeshift teachers are community leaders who are respected people and who have a certain education as well as certain skills, but who have never been trained as teachers. If the next government school is too far away from the village—for example, in a neighbouring village or town—local community-based organisations sometimes even construct the school building on their own and then either share the teacher with a nearby government school or recruit and pay the teacher themselves. Officially, the government mostly declares CBS of this kind 'extensions' to the government schools nearest to them. In reality, however, the respective local communities themselves have made all the efforts and expenses to establish and run these schools. If the local government does not choose the strategy of cooption, but rather seeks to prevent the establishment of CBS, these schools often operate under religious umbrellas. In Christian communities, CBS are usually connected to the local church (see the Christian education section below), while in Buddhist communities they tend to take the form of Buddhist monasteries.[21]

CBS constitute a perfect example of how local civil-society groups try to bridge the accessibility gap that exists in the formal education system. The problem of the lack of educational quality usually persists, however, as the 'teachers' who volunteer at local CBS have often not been trained. Nevertheless, CBS also offer a wide range of advantages. As they are rooted in the local communities, they often provide work and life skills that are particularly needed in the respective locality, such as training in agricultural cultivation methods or basic veterinary skills. In some cases, such skills-training measures are even linked to income-generating activities. CBS also serve important communication purposes and can constitute forums in which environmental as well as health and preventive health issues—for example, in the field of HIV/AIDS—can be discussed. Often such health training is conducted by using various forms of traditional arts such as puppet shows (UNESCO 2002). The 'Community Learning Centre' project of the UN Development Program (UNDP) and the UN Educational, Scientific and Cultural Organisation (UNESCO), which started in 1994, has promoted CBS as centres for the provision of non-formal education. A report that summarised the experiences stressed that, due to poverty, insufficient enrolment and high drop-out rates, 'non-formal education will continue to be a necessity' in the future and models such as CBS will be needed 'to provide the population with complementary opportunities for basic education and life-long learning' (UNESCO 2002:30).

Civil society-based education systems in cease-fire areas

Because of the remoteness of many ethnic areas, the systematic neglect of the ethnic minorities by the central government and the legacy of armed conflict, the welfare system of the central state is particularly weak in Burma/Myanmar's ethnic minority regions. As for education in particular, the situation is often further aggravated by the regime's rigid and discriminatory language policies. For example, in several cases, the central government has established schools in ethnic areas but insisted that tuition be conducted in Burmese/Myanmar and it has hired teachers who do not even understand the local ethnic language. As a consequence, ethnic children who do not speak Burmese/Myanmar do not benefit, and some parents even refuse to send their children to school.

Since 1989, the regime has negotiated cease-fires with most of the armed ethnic resistance groups and granted them some degree of autonomy, which in some cases extends to language and education. As a consequence, various armed groups and their affiliated ethnic political parties, but particularly the Kachin Independence Organisation (KIO) and the New Mon State Party (NMSP), are running their own school systems. Even though these education systems often predate the cease-fires, they have extended considerably since the cease-fires.[22] In Special Region 4 in Eastern Shan State, schools run by the central government exist alongside Chinese schools and so-called 'self-reliance schools', which operate under the authority of the education department of the National Democratic Alliance Army–Eastern Shan State (NDAA–ESS). The KIO, which has wide-ranging administrative autonomy over its area, is also allowed to have its own department for education and runs a teacher-training school (ICG 2003:9). The Kachin education system has about 1000 teachers. Most Kachin schools operate at the primary level, but there are also some Kachin middle and high schools.[23] The NMSP also runs its own education department, which, since the 1995 cease-fire, has even managed to extend its programs to Mon communities in government-controlled areas (South 2007:164ff.). In 2003, the NMSP ran as many as 187 Mon national schools as well as 186 'mixed' schools—that is, schools shared with the public school system, in which minority languages are still banned (South 2007). Even the youngest of the cease-fire groups, the KNU/KNLA Peace Council (KPC),[24] has already set up its own department of education. Although these para-statal administrative bodies and school systems do not constitute civil society-based education models as such, they are noteworthy because the line between the education system run by the central government and the alternative education systems provided by ethnic actors is gradually becoming blurred. This tendency is also evident among civil-society groups that have established alternative education programs in ethnic areas. Despite the highly ambivalent political character of most of the cease-fires, in some ethnic regions the resulting increase in ethnic autonomy has led to the emergence or enlargement of spaces for civil-society activities in the welfare sector in general and in the education sector in particular (Smith 1999; Purcell 1999; South 2004).

Christian education

Christian missionaries first introduced Christian education and church-run schools to Burma/Myanmar (for example, Zoellner 2007b). Even before British colonial times, a number of missionary schools were active in the country, and the first high school was in fact established by missionaries in 1872 (Tin 2004). After independence in 1948, the influence of the Christian schools was gradually pushed back as the U Nu government started to establish a secular national education system as part of its project of nation building. As in many post-independence contexts, education was considered crucial for the construction of an independent national identity (see, for example, Zoellner 2007a). Nevertheless, various Christian denominations continued to run their own officially registered schools up to high-school level. After the military coup in 1962, however, these schools were either nationalised or closed down. The Christian churches have been prohibited from running officially recognised (primary and secondary) schools or registering any other formal education programs with the MOE ever since. Nevertheless, some big and well-established tertiary education institutions such as the Myanmar Institute of Theology (MIT) continue to run their programs up to the present day, even though they are recognised primarily not as educational but as religious institutions (see later in this section). Moreover, various community-based educational initiatives that are highly informal but are tolerated by the government still exist under the umbrella of the churches today, particularly in the ethnic cease-fire areas where the majority of the Christian population lives. In cease-fire areas and ethnic areas of continuing armed conflict, church-based education programs often go hand in hand with community-based initiatives such as the establishment of CBS, which is also taking place in government-controlled areas. As Daw May Oo (2004) puts it:

> There are several things the church organisations do. Certainly one is to address the social needs in society…for example, the schools in remote areas. Churches send teachers to volunteer in a community because the government does not have a system and any kind of infrastructure does not exist…Then communities will build the school on their own and the teachers most of the time will be provided by the churches, or even by the bible schools…So these fundamental needs like education…most of the time in remote areas, will be addressed by the church organisations, instead of the government having a program or a system.

Other church-based education support activities, for public and community-based schools alike, include the donation of schoolbooks and other teaching materials, teacher training and the provision of school-cost scholarships for poor children, which cover fees, books and uniforms. Some Christian churches also maintain hostels that are free of any charges. For many children from remote ethnic areas, this support is crucial, because poverty means they can afford to attend secondary school only if there is a free, church-run hostel in the town where the school is located. Most of the student hostels also offer homework supervision and extra-tuition programs, which are conducted either by staff members of local church organisations or by private volunteers for whose activities the local churches provide protective umbrellas.

Some Catholic dioceses use lay missionaries—'*zetamans*' in the local language—in order to reach remote ethnic communities. Usually, it is the pastor who recruits the prospective *zetamans* from the young people in the diocese. Before sending them to the remote target areas, he trains them not only in bible studies but in basic secular educational and professional skills. After completing a preparation course, two *zetamans* at a time are sent to one remote community, where they are supposed to teach children basic literacy and numeracy skills, conduct training in agricultural methods as well as health education classes, and provide basic healthcare services for one year. The purpose of these teaching activities is, of course, not only welfare oriented, but to evangelise local communities (Geiger 2007).

Furthermore, according to a leading church official, the Christian churches run about 1500 pre-primary schools all over the country and in ethnic minority areas specifically. Interestingly, up to now, church-based pre-primary schools have been relatively free to formulate their own curriculum as long as they refrain from criticising the regime. Around 2006, however, the government announced it was going to develop national guidelines for the curricula of the church-based pre-primary schools. As jurisdiction over this matter seem to be divided (or even disputed) between the MOE and the MSW, however, this plan still seems to exist on paper only. Moreover, according to a church official, the government has announced that, in the future, teachers working at church-based pre-primary schools need to be trained by the government. The same church worker also said, however, that his/her organisation did not really worry about this plan, since the government had the capacity necessary to train only 50 pre-primary schoolteachers a year. Given the 1500 church-run pre-primary schools already in existence, this is totally insufficient.

Moreover, various Christian denominations run colleges—or so-called seminaries—that offer Christian education at a tertiary level and can be attended after matriculation. All in all, there seem to be about 30 seminaries across the country, but particularly in ethnic minority areas. Their prime ostensible mission is to teach bible studies, but as most of the books they use are in English, they also impart good spoken and written English skills. Many seminaries are highly self-organised and students often live in a compound. The 'Saint Markus Baptist College' in Lashio[25] is one such example. In theory, all important decisions are supposed to be made by the principal. He/she, however, usually has to travel a lot and thus, in practice, a committee of teachers administers the college. Some of the younger teachers have international teaching experience and contacts with churches abroad. Moreover, there is a students' council, which organises community activities such as sports competitions. Asked whether and how the organisation was controlled by the government, a teacher said, 'They are watching us from a distance…We feel afraid. So this means, we are controlled.' The Myanmar Institute of Theology (MIT) in Yangon serves as a Christian university and issues bachelor and masters' degrees. Even though it provides tertiary education, it is registered as a religious and not an educational institution and operates under the MRA. Students at MIT can study not just theology, but a limited number of secular subjects including English and economics. The degrees that students can earn from the seminaries and from MIT are not recognised by the government. They are, however, mostly recognised within the national Christian community within which most of the students seek employment after completing their education.

In addition, several local churches as well as the Myanmar Council of Churches (MCC), a national umbrella association, have scholarship programs that enable gifted students and young church community leaders to attend university either in Burma/Myanmar or abroad. International partner churches provide financial support to some of these programs. Since in the past scholarship holders have often stayed abroad, some church organisations have now inserted clauses into their scholarship application guidelines that commit beneficiaries to return to Burma/Myanmar and work in their local communities for a certain period. Some scholarship programs have been quite successful. Recently, for example, a group of university graduates founded the 'Scholarship Alumni Association' in Myitkina,[26] after returning from abroad. The association runs a church-based boarding school that targets local high-school graduates as well as the coordinators of the surrounding local churches' youth groups. Courses last for two years and focus on English, computer training and various professional skills including trade, management, accounting and agriculture. All boarding-school students are obligated to take part in 'social outreach activities' such as education and training programs aimed at the broader local community. Moreover, they have to pay visits to orphanages, hospitals and neighbouring villages. In order to promote creative thinking, the curriculum encompasses sports activities, teamwork, brainstorming, discussions and role-plays. The guidelines of the association also provide for a 'seniority system', which is specified as meaning that the older members—who are assumed to have more education and experience—must be respected and followed by their younger fellows.

Unlike the *Sangha*, Burma/Myanmar's Christian civil society often has rudimentarily institutionalised contacts with churches and even with international NGOs abroad. Such cooperation is, however, rarely coordinated and happens mostly on the basis of one church or NGO from abroad supporting one specific project or church within Burma/Myanmar. As a consequence, even international churches and organisations who have been working with churches in Burma/Myanmar for years usually do not have a coherent picture of the state of Christian civil society on the ground.

NGO and community-based organisation education and education support activities

Non-religious education and education support initiatives in ethnic cease-fire areas range from registered NGOs to highly informal community-based organisations. What all of them seem to have in common, however, is that in one way or another they are linked to the structures of the respective local ethnic cease-fire party.

The 'Alternative Local Learning Centre' in Kachin State,[27] which started operating in 2005, provides a good example of a rather informal community-based organisation initiative in the education sector. It offers capacity building and informal training in the analysis of social problems, project management, proposal writing and accounting. The centre focuses on the training of trainers and its final goal is to promote the formation of new, self-reliant NGOs. (It started by training 20 participants in 2005.) Moreover, its founders have put enormous effort into the establishment of a library with literature on community development and other social issues. In order to reach an informal agreement with the local cease-fire party, the organisers had to prove that their project was apolitical and would provide capacities that were essential to economic development. According to one of the organisers, the centre is not registered but 'tolerated' by the local ethnic authorities.

Other NGOs and community-based organisations have linked their education and education support activities even more closely to the local ethnic-party structures. The Metta Development Foundation,[28] for example, has developed a strategic partnership with the Mon Women's Organisation and supported the latter's adult literacy and capacity-building programs (South 2007). One of the biggest Kachin NGOs provides planning support and child-centred teacher training to the KIO and its school system. Even in the Wa Special Region, where independent civil-society organisations are still rare, NGOs in partnership with local communities have established schools in areas in which schools have not existed before. In the Wa Special Region, such initiatives have often been supported by international NGOs as part of their drug-eradication programs. In most other ethnic areas, however, international support for ethnic NGO and community-based organisation activities often remains scarce and the lack of funding seems to pose the biggest obstacle to the further expansion of ethnic civil-society activities in the education sector.[29]

Culture and literature committees

Culture and Literature Committees (CLCs), which focus on the preservation and promotion of a specific ethnic language and culture, have a long tradition in Burma/Myanmar's ethnic minority areas. In the case of the Mon ethnic community, for example, South traces the emergence of cultural groups back to the 1930s and 1940s. The Mon Literature and Culture Committee (MLCC), which still exists today, started its ethnic literacy training in the 1950s (South 2007). In the same period, CLCs served as the backbone of ethnic nationalist movements in various ethnic states. Due to repression by the regime and civil war, ethnic activities in the fields of culture and literature were largely dormant from 1962 until the 1990s. Since the conclusion of cease-fires in the 1990s, however, the regime has allowed various ethnic parties to issue publications in their own ethnic tongues (ICG 2003). As a consequence, many traditional CLCs re-emerged and several new ones came into being. Moreover, in reaction to the failure of the state-run education system, many of them have started to go beyond their traditional task of cultural preservation. Today, most CLCs focus on basic literacy and teach children and illiterate adults important spoken and written language skills. Most CLCs teach the local ethnic language and rely on community education approaches such as informal education programs and summer schools. Some of them, however, already seem to have incorporated Burmese/Myanmar language and other non-culture-related subjects such as numeracy into their curriculum. According to a UN representative, some CLCs are even able to engage in formal education and have adopted the government curriculum, especially in Mon State. Most of these CLCs are active at the primary level; however, there also seem to be some that teach at a higher level and impart a number of skills. The role of the CLCs is particularly important in ethnic regions where children do not speak Burmese/Myanmar. Here, tuition in the local ethnic tongue might often constitute the only way children can acquire basic skills.

As CLCs are legal organisations that exist in almost every ethnic village, many different activities take place under their umbrella. For instance, some CLCs not only provide education, they conduct important community organisation and preventive health activities such as raising awareness about HIV/AIDS. For such specific purposes, CLCs seem to cooperate with other local and sometimes even international non-state actors. In Christian areas, for example, they sometimes cooperate with the local churches and in predominantly Buddhist regions they sometimes work with the *Sangha*. Mon monks, for instance, give language and literacy training courses at the MLCC (South 2007). According to a local staff member of an international aid organisation, his/her organisation sometimes relies on the local CLCs for the publication of its information materials on HIV/AIDS in remote ethnic areas. The head office of the aid organisation in Yangon usually publishes the information brochures in Burmese/Myanmar or English; subsequently, it is the local CLCs that translate them into the ethnic languages of the target regions, but they sometimes encounter problems when they seek censorship approval to publish such materials. On the whole, the international donor community does not seem to have a lot of contact with the CLCs, and detailed knowledge about their activities is still rather scarce. While CLCs impart highly valuable language skills and perform other important welfare functions, at least some of them tend to exclude members of other ethnic groups. Consequently, they also bear the risk of being culturally divisive, thereby reinforcing ethnic cleavages.

Conclusion

The picture of civil-society initiatives in the Burmese/Myanmar education sector is diverse and multifaceted. Nevertheless, it is possible to identify some general trends: first, there are quite a lot of community-based initiatives in the education sector in the broadest sense. Most of these community-based groups, however, cannot engage in education directly. Instead, they are confined to education support activities such as the construction of school buildings or the collection of donations to pay for village teachers' salaries. Second, there is a number—but definitely a small number—of civil-society groups that can engage in education more directly. Most of these apply informal, community-based approaches to teaching, whereas so far only a few groups have managed to become involved in formal education and been allowed to teach the government curriculum. Among the groups that are able to engage in formal education, monastic schools are undoubtedly the most prominent. Third, most educational initiatives that are aimed at children take place at the primary or even at the pre-primary level. While there are some at the middle-school level, only a handful exists at the high-school level. There are, however, also several educational initiatives for (young) adults in the sectors of vocational skills training and capacity building. Fourth, civil-society organisations active in the education sector often serve multiple social functions and, apart from education, many of them provide other welfare services as well. Education is often broadly understood to include (preventive) health education and general capacity building. Fifth, even though the number of civil-society initiatives in the education sector has been increasing during the past few years, the government is still extremely suspicious of all educational activities conducted by non-state actors. As a consequence, private education has not so far been legally provided for, and the majority of the civil-society groups that are active in the education sector cannot register with the MOE. As a makeshift solution, some of them have chosen to register with the MSW or the MRA.

This leads us to the last but perhaps the most important point: most civil society-based educational initiatives take place under religious or ethnic umbrellas, such as Buddhist monasteries, Christian churches and ethnic CLCs. This last point has broader implications: in present-day Burma/Myanmar, various secular, religious and ethnic (cultural) education systems—all of which promote different life models—coexist. In some cases, the boundaries between these various education and life models seem to be quite clear-cut. Some Buddhist monastic schools teach only the *Dhamma*,[30] some Christian missionaries preach only the Gospels and some CLCs focus solely on the preservation of their ethnic cultural heritage; and, above all, there is a highly authoritarian state, which is still largely reluctant to accept the existence of an independent civil society and the alternative education systems it provides. There are, however, also cases where the boundaries between religious and ethnic (cultural) education on the one hand, and secular/non-cultural education on the other, are rather blurred. Traditional religious and ethnic cultural groups that predate the modern national education system have re-emerged and increasingly engage in secular, non-cultural and, in some rare cases, even formal education as well. New actors such as NGOs have also entered the scene. The rigidity of the regime's educational policies certainly does not reflect the reality on the ground. Instead of providing an enabling legal framework for private education, however, the regime still seeks mostly to either suppress or coopt alternative civil society-based education systems. Cooption of formerly independent groups thus constitutes another, negative form of the blurring of the lines between civil society-based and state-run education.

What does all this suggest in terms of the overall contribution that civil society is able to make to the education sector? While civil-society actors do provide valuable makeshift solutions to specific local problems, they lack the scope of action and the capabilities necessary to act as a substitute for a functioning state-run education system. The task of the latter would normally be to provide equal opportunities for quality education for the whole population regardless of status, religion or ethnicity. As civil-society actors in Burma/Myanmar usually provide localised, and sometimes even selective, services that are confined to specific religious and ethnic groups, they too are unable to live up to this task. Moreover, while civil-society actors manage to bridge some accessibility gaps in the state-run education system, they cannot bridge the quality gap. Instead, civil society-based education models tend to mirror the deficits of the state-run education system. The quality of education provided by civil-society groups varies widely and is sometimes highly inadequate. Just like professional teachers at government schools, voluntary teachers who teach at CBS or run free extra-tuition programs are often poorly trained and frequently rely on outdated teaching methods. As a consequence , tuition is often conducted in a highly hierarchical and repetitive way and learning remains mostly by rote. This is far from surprising, because the inadequate qualification of private and voluntary teachers results directly from the weakness of the state-run education system under which they received their own education and training.

The dynamics of civil-society development in Burma/Myanmar—in the education sector and in general—have not been well understood by the international community. The fact that hardly any expert or aid worker foresaw the 2007 uprising of the monks provides clear evidence for this. Extremely few international actors have contacts with the monastic schools, although they are the most important non-state providers of educational services. In fact, donor engagement with civil-society actors in the education sector has generally been limited up to now. An important reason for this is that Burma/Myanmar's embryonic civil society is only rarely able to live up to donor guidelines. Religious and ethnic education systems often promote philosophies and life models that donors are unfamiliar with. Cooption often gives civil society a double identity that makes donors feel uneasy. In order to develop better strategies, however, experts, politicians and aid workers will have to broaden their perspective to encompass the social dynamics of competing, parallel, coexisting and overlapping social systems in Burma/Myanmar. The case of civil-society development in the education sector is but one specific example that provides evidence for this blind spot.

References

Croissant, Aurel 2000, 'Zivilgesellschaft und transformation in Ostasien', in Wolfgang Merkel (ed.), *Systemwechsel 5. Zivilgesellschaft und Transformation*, Leske and Budrich, Opladen, pp. 335–72.

Department for International Development (DFID) 2008, Burma/Myanmar: UK assistance, Unpublished document, 17 April 2008, London.

Directory of Local Non-Government Organizations in Myanmar (DLN) 2005.

Edwards, Michael 2004, *Civil Society*, Polity Press, Cambridge.

Englehart, Neil A. 2005, 'Is regime change enough for Burma? The problem of state capacity', *Asian Survey*, vol. 45, no. 4, July/August, pp. 622–44.

Foreign Policy Failed States Index 2007 2007, viewed 1 April 2008, <http://www.foreignpolicy.com/story/cms.php?story_id=3865&page=7>

Geiger, Heinrich (ed.) 2007, *Myanmar. Bildung und Entwicklung in einem multiethnischen Staat*, Köllen Druck and Verlag, KAAD, Bonn.

Gosewinkel, Dieter, Rucht, Dieter, van den Daele, Wolfgang and Kocka, Jürgen 2003, 'Introduction', in Dieter Gosewinkel, Dieter Rucht, Wolfgang van den Daele and Jürgen Kocka (eds), *Zivilgesellschaft National und Transnational*, Wissenschaftszentrum Berlin für Sozialforschung (WZB) Jahrbuch 2003, Edition Sigma, Berlin, pp. 11–26.

Heidel, Brian 2006, *The Growth of Civil Society in Myanmar*, viewed 25 April 2008, <http://him.civiblog.org/_attachments/1791034/Myanmarper cent20Civilper cent20Societyper cent20text.pdf>

Howell, Jude 1999, Manufacturing civil society from the outside: some dilemmas and challenges, Paper presented at the European Association of Development Research and Training Institutes Conference, September.

International Crisis Group (ICG) 2001, *Myanmar: the role of civil society*, ICG Asia Report No. 27, Bangkok/Brussels, viewed 10 March 2008, <http://www.crisisgroup.org/library/documents/report_archive/ A400503_06122001.pdf>

International Crisis Group (ICG) 2003, *Myanmar backgrounder: ethnic minority politics*, ICG Asia Report No. 52, Bangkok/Brussels, viewed 10 March 2008, <http://www.crisisgroup.org/library/documents/report_archive/ A400967_07052003.pdf>

Lauth, Hans-Joachim 2003, 'Zivilgesellschaft als Konzept und die Suche nach ihren Akteuren', in Arnd Bauerkämper (ed.), *Die Praxis der Zivilgesellschaft. Akteure, Handeln und Strukturen im internationalen Vergleich*, Campus Verlag, Frankfurt/New York, pp. 31–54.

London School of Economics (LSE) 2008, *What is Civil Society?*, viewed 28 February 2008, <http://www.lse.ac.uk/collections/CCS/what_is_civil_society.htm>

Lorch, Jasmin 2006, 'Civil society under authoritarian rule: the case of Myanmar', *SÜDOSTASIEN aktuell*, issue 2/2006, pp. 3–37.

Lorch, Jasmin 2007, 'Myanmar's civil society—a patch for the national education system? The emergence of civil society in areas of state weakness', *SÜDOSTASIEN aktuell*, issue 3/2007, pp. 54–88.

May Oo 2004, Director of Communication of the Free Burma Coalition, Interview, Washington D.C., 20 February.

Ministry of Education (MOE) 2006, *EFA Implementation in Myanmar*, Ministry of Education, Government of the Union of Myanmar.

Ministry of Education (MOE) 2007a, *Education for All in Myanmar*, Ministry of Education, Government of the Union of Myanmar.

Ministry of Education (MOE) 2007b, *Towards Realizing the Millennium Development Goals: Goal 2: Achieve universal primary education & Goal 3: Promote gender equality and empower women*, Ministry of Education, Government of the Union of Myanmar.

Ottaway, Marina 2004, 'Civil society', in Peter J. Burnell and Vicky Randall, *Politics in the Developing World*, Oxford University Press, Oxford, pp. 120–35.

Pedersen, Morten B., Rudland, Emily and May, Ronald J. (eds) 2000, *Burma Myanmar. Strong regime weak state?*, Crawford House Publishing, Adelaide.

Perinova, Marie 2005, Civil society in authoritarian regime. The analysis of China, Burma and Vietnam, Thesis, Department of Political Science, Lund University, viewed 30 September 2005, <http://theses.lub.lu.se/archive/2005/05/23/1116839547-15844-327/thesis_of_Marie_Perinova.PDF>

Purcell, Marc 1999, 'Ace-handles or willing minions?: international NGOs in Burma', in Burma Center Netherlands and Transnational Institute (eds), *Strengthening Civil Society in Burma. Possibilities and dilemmas for international NGOs*, Silkworm Books, Chiang Mai, pp. 69–109.

Risse, Thomas 2005, 'Governance in Räumen begrenzter Staatlichkeit. "Failed states" werden zum zentralen Problem derWeltpolitik', *Internationale Politik*, September, pp. 6–12.

Rotberg, Robert I. 2002, 'The new nature of nation state failure', *The Washington Quarterly*, vol. 25, no. 3, pp. 85–96.

Rotberg, Robert I. 2004, 'Failed states, collapsed states, weak states: causes and indicators', in Robert I. Rotberg (ed.), *When States Fail. Causes and consequences*, Princeton University Press, Princeton, pp. 1–25.

Schneckener, Ulrich 2004, 'States at risk. Zur analyse fragiler Staatlichkeit', in Ulrich Schneckener (ed.), *States at Risk. Fragile Staaten als Sicherheits- und Entwicklungsproblem*, SWP Studie S 43, SWP, Berlin, pp. 5–27.

Schneckener, Ulrich 2006, 'States at risk. Zur analyse fragiler Staatlichkeit', in Ulrich Schneckener (ed.), *'States at Risk' zwischen Stabilität und Scheitern*,

SWP Internationale Politik und Sicherheit 59, Nomos, Baden-Baden, pp. 9–40.

Selth, Andrew 2001, *Burma: a strategic perspective*, Asia Foundation Working Paper No. 13, May 2001.

Smith, Martin 1999, 'Ethnic conflict and the challenge of civil society in Burma', in Burma Center Netherlands and Transnational Institute (eds), *Strengthening Civil Society in Burma. Possibilities and dilemmas for international NGOs*, Silkworm Books, Chiang Mai, pp. 15–53.

South, Ashley 2004, 'Political transition in Myanmar: a new model for democratization', *Contemporary Southeast Asia. A Journal of International and Strategic Affairs*, vol. 26, no. 2, pp. 233–55.

South, Ashley 2006, Email conversation, 16 November 2006.

South, Ashley 2007, 'Ceasefires and civil society: the case of the Mon', in Mikael Grawers (ed.), *Exploring Ethnic Diversity in Burma*, Nias Press, Copenhagen, pp. 149–77.

Steinberg, David I. 1999, 'A void in Myanmar: civil society in Burma', in Burma Center Netherlands and Transnational Institute (eds), *Strengthening Civil Society in Burma. Possibilities and dilemmas for international NGOs*, Silkworm Books, Chiang Mai, pp. 1–14.

Thawnghmung, Ardeth Maung and Myoe, Maung Aung 2008, 'Myanmar in 2007. A turning point in the "roadmap"?', *Asian Survey*, vol. 48, no. 1, pp. 13–19.

Tin, U Han 2004, Seminar on education in Myanmar, Paper presented at The Australian National University, 31 March 2004, Canberra, viewed 25 April 2008, <http://www.anu.edu.au/unesco/Tin.pdf>

United Nations Educational, Scientific and Cultural Organisation (UNESCO) 2002, *Myanmar. The Community Learning Centre Experience*, MYA/99/004, Improving Access of Children, Women and Men of Poorest Communities to Primary Education for All, UNESCO Asia and Pacific Regional Bureau for Education, Bangkok, viewed 25 April 2008, <http://unesdoc.unesco.org/images/0012/001252/125290e.pdf>

United Nations International Children's Emergency Fund (UNICEF) 2008a, *Providing Children With a Quality Basic Education*, viewed 1 April 2008, <http://www.unicef.org/myanmar/education.html>

United Nations International Children's Emergency Fund (UNICEF) 2008b, *UNICEF Program Helps Educate Children About HIV and AIDS*, viewed 1 April 2008, <http://www.unicef.org/myanmar/education_1435.html>

Will, Gerhard 2006, 'Birma: Stablie Herrschaft in einem versagenden Staat', in Ulrich Schneckener (ed.), *'States at Risk' zwischen Stabilität und Scheitern*, SWP Internationale Politik und Sicherheit 59, Nomos, Baden-Baden, pp. 197–228.

Zoellner, Hans-Bernd 2007a, 'Zeitleiste. Daten zur Geschichte Mynamars/Birmas unter besonderer Berücksichtigung der Entwicklung des Bildungswesens', in Heinrich Geiger (ed.), *Myanmar. Bildung und Entwicklung in einem multiethnischen Staat*, KAAD, Köllen Druck and Verlag, Bonn, pp. 20–1.

Zoellner, Hans-Bernd 2007b, 'Erziehung und Bildung in Myanmar/Birma—Eine Collage', in Heinrich Geiger (ed.), *Myanmar. Bildung und Entwicklung in einem multiethnischen Staat*, KAAD, Köllen Druck and Verlag, Bonn, pp. 23–34.

Endnotes

[1] This a modified and updated version of an earlier article on the same topic (Lorch 2007).

[2] The '88 Generation Students Group comprises former student leaders of the 1988 uprising, who were released from jail in 2004. On 22 August 2007, several prominent '88 Group leaders were arrested again for their role in leading the demonstrations.

[3] Community of Buddhist monks and nuns in Burma/Myanmar.

[4] In 2001, an International Crisis Group (ICG 2001) report first referred to the existence of civil-society organisations in areas of welfare demands not met by the State, particularly in ethnic areas. Since the late 1990s, several experts have pointed to the enlargement of civil-society spaces in ethnic areas (for example, Purcell 1999:89ff.; Smith 1999:37–49; South 2004:233).

[5] UNICEF is active mainly in early childhood development, the establishment of child-friendly schools and education activities related to HIV/AIDS prevention (UNICEF 2008a, 2008b). Moreover, from 1994–2002, the Human Development Initiative (HDI) of the UN Development Program (UNDP) ran an education project in Burma/Myanmar. In 1994, a 'Community Learning Centre component' was introduced within the framework of this project. The Community Learning Centre subproject was funded by UNDP and conducted mainly by the UN Educational, Scientific and Cultural Organisation (UNESCO 2002: for a short description, see chapter 4.3).

[6] Most of the information presented here was gathered in field trips between 2004 and early 2007. Several interviews were also conducted after September 2007 in order to assess the effects of the latest government crackdown on the civil-society initiatives reported.

[7] For a good overview of normative conceptions of civil society, see Edwards (2004).

[8] In my previous studies on civil society in Burma/Myanmar (Lorch 2006, 2007), which have a more theoretical focus, I have outlined a relational approach to civil society. For this purpose, I have linked the empirical descriptive definition of civil society of the London School of Economics (LSE 2008) cited here with the civil-society definition of Gosewinkel et al. (2003), who define civil society as specific types of action and interaction. As the present chapter focuses on the case rather than the theory, the LSE definition is chosen for the sake of brevity.

[9] Regarding the categorisation of Burma/Myanmar as a weak or failing state, see, for example, Englehart (2005); Foreign Policy Failed States Index (2007); Pedersen (2000); and Will (2006).

[10] Confidential communication with Alan Smith, April 2008.

[11] Ibid.

[12] In the summer of 2006, several experts and monastic schoolteachers interviewed said that officially recognised monastic schools were registered with the MOE and that it was also the MOE to which all officially recognised monastic schools had to send their pupils' final exams for marking. During another research trip in 2007, officials from the MOE itself claimed that all monastic schools were under the

MRA. Contrary to that, a publication of the MOE itself claims the MOE and the MRA are in charge of the officially recognised monastic schools (MOE 2006:25).

[13] According to this second official source, there are 1158 officially recognised monastic schools, which altogether reach 161 492 children. According to the same source, 144 008 of these children are taught at the primary or post-primary level and only 17 484 are taught at the middle level.

[14] This information is based on various interviews conducted in Burma/Myanmar in the summer of 2006. While some of the people interviewed claimed that five monastic schools taught at the high-school level, others said there were only two. The author was able to visit one of them and read the funding proposal of a second one.

[15] There seem to be almost no mixed monastic orphanages in Burma/Myanmar. Of the ones I visited, only one catered to both boys and girls.

[16] The expert cited here specialises in Buddhism in Asia and is a lecturer at a European university, but has studied at a government university in Yangon for one year, still visits Burma/Myanmar frequently and maintains contacts with a number of monks and monastic education centres.

[17] Confidential communication with Alan Smith, April 2008.

[18] Organisation known to the author; name and place changed for safety reasons.

[19] Confidential communication with Alan Smith, April 2008.

[20] Organisation known to the author; name and place changed for safety reasons.

[21] Confidential communication with Alan Smith, April 2008.

[22] Email conversation with South, 16 November 2006. According to South, the Karen National Union (KNU), the best-known insurgent group, which is still fighting the central government, also runs its own education system, albeit on a smaller scale.

[23] Confidential communication with Alan Smith, April 2008.

[24] KNLA stands for Karen National Liberation Army; the KNLA is the armed wing of the KNU.

[25] Organisation known to the author; name and place changed for safety reasons.

[26] Organisation mentioned in Geiger (2007); name and place changed for safety reasons.

[27] Organisation known to the author; name and place changed for safety reasons.

[28] Established in 1998, Metta is the biggest registered independent NGO in Burma/Myanmar. It grew out of the Kachin cease-fire, but in recent years it has managed to extend its scope of action to other cease-fire areas as well.

[29] Confidential communication with Alan Smith, April 2008.

[30] Teachings of the Buddha.

10: Islamic education in Myanmar: a case study

Mohammed Mohiyuddin Mohammed Sulaiman

Introduction

'Islam', which literally means 'peace' in Arabic, has been transformed into a faith interpreted loosely by one group and understood conservatively by another, making it seem as if Islam itself is not well comprehended by its followers. Today, it is the faith of 1.2 billion people across the world; Asia is a home for 60 per cent of these adherents, with Muslims forming an absolute majority in 11 countries (Selth 2003:5). Since the terrorist attacks of 11 September 2001, international scholars have become increasingly interested in Islam and in Muslims in South-East Asia, where more than 230 million Muslims live (Mutalib 2005:50). These South-East Asian Muslims originally received Islam from Arab traders. History reveals the Arabs as sea-loving people who voyaged around the Indian Ocean (IIAS 2005), including to South-East Asia.

The arrival of Arabs has had different degrees of impact on different communities in the region. We find, however, that not much research has been done by today's Arabs on the Arab–South-East Asian connection, as they consider South-East Asia a part of the wider 'East', which includes Iran, Central Asia and the Indian subcontinent. Indeed, the term 'South-East Asia' is hardly used in modern Arab literature. For them, anything east of the Middle East and non-Arabic speaking world is considered to be 'Asia' (Abaza 2002).

According to Myanmar and non-Myanmar sources, Islam reached the shores of Myanmar's Arakan (Rakhine State) as early as 712 AD, via oceangoing merchants, and in the form of Sufism. The conversion of local inhabitants to Islam was more by choice than coercion, and the same phenomenon was also the trend for all South-East Asian nations, such as Malaysia and Indonesia (Jilani 1999:63). There were no Muslim attempts to invade Myanmar from outside or to proselytise within (Thiker 1959:338). At the same time, Myanmar, unlike Malaysia or Indonesia, did not present a religious vacuum (Hall 1959:131). What is more, the islands of South-East Asia are easily accessible by sea and presented a very lucrative business and commercial environment (Moshe 1972:105).

Different Myanmar Muslim groups

Muslims in Myanmar are mostly Sunni, of the Hanafi sect, with a small and ever decreasing number of Shi'ite sect followers. Today, Muslims could constitute as much as 13 per cent of the total population, although some experts on Myanmar assume them to constitute about 4 per cent or less, as stated in the official Myanmar census.[1] Although the census insists that Muslims represent no more than 3.8 per cent of the population (MOFA 2005), the US Central Intelligence Agency (CIA 2005) states that they represent 4 per cent. Myanmar Muslims themselves estimate that they number approximately eight million.[2] It is not unusual for Muslims residing in non-Muslim countries to feel that the real Muslim census figures are underestimated. Thai Muslims complained about the 1960 Thai national census that recorded 1.5 million Muslims, when their number could have been double that, if not more (see Suthasasna 1983–84).

Muslims in Myanmar can be categorised into four different groups, omitting some significant Muslim minority communities: Pantay (Selth 2003:5–6), the largest group, includes the Rohingya of Rakhine (Arakan) whose members number approximately one million throughout the country; Bamar who converted to Islam in the time of Bamar kings and who call themselves 'pure Bamar Muslims'; Indian Muslims born in Myanmar of two Indian Muslim parents; and the Zerbadees, who are the children of mixed marriages between Indian Muslim fathers and Burman mothers (Matthews 2001:5). Each group has very different relationships with the Buddhist majority and with the regime of Myanmar today (Selth 2003:5).

Madrasahs in Myanmar

Madrasahs (Islamic religious schools) remain the only alternative for educating Myanmar Muslims in Islamic education, since the national school system does not cater for any particular faith or belief with the exception of Buddhism, the faith that more than 70 per cent of people profess. Throughout Myanmar, hundreds of madrasahs are operating, financed by domestic and foreign donations. It is a recent phenomenon that Bamar Muslims have endeavoured to be in touch with their wealthy counterparts in the Arab world to balance the influence of the Indian subcontinent's Islamic ideology.

Madrasah students attend for about 10 or more years, from standards one to 10, after which they pursue further studies in India, Pakistan or Bangladesh. In some unusual cases, students are sent to the Arabian Peninsula. There is no specific age for enrolling in a madrasah, but students as young as seven years are commonly accepted. Some would choose to spend about two to four years to memorise the 30 chapters of the Holy Qur'an without understanding the Qur'anic texts or their interpretations. Once the student completes the whole of the Qur'an, he would be called 'Hafiz', which would later become a prefix of his name.

He could continue his studies in the field of *Mawlawi*, in which he learns *Fique* (Islamic jurisprudence) and Arabic language, its grammar and the interpretation of the Qur'an. Although every student would have to go through standards one to 10 to complete a *Mawlawi* education, a *Hafiz* could start from standard three, four or five depending on his capability and the teachers' assessment of his capability to cope with his studies. On completion of his studies to standard 10, he would be called '*Mawlawi*', which would later become a prefix of his name.

It is a tradition that a man has to be either a *Hafiz* or *Mawlawi* to lead the five daily prayers in a mosque. It is normal to find a *Hafiz* or *Mawlawi* in almost every Muslim family, as this is regarded as a great honour. As far as the hereafter is concerned, Muslims of Myanmar postulate a reported saying of the Prophet that one who memorises the Holy Qur'an can save 10 of his family members from hell-fire when the Day of Judgment comes. Therefore, one among every 10 family members must be a madrasah graduate to save himself and his family from hell-fire.

Most Myanmar madrasahs are boarding schools exclusively for male students from all over the country. A Muslim boy can enroll in any madrasah irrespective of his ethic background. In some cases, obtaining a recommendation from a reputable Muslim clergyman ('*Ulama*) or religious person is needed to smooth the enrolment process. At the same time, new madrasahs welcoming young adult female students in *Tahfiz* (memorising the Qur'an) and *Mawlawi* courses are being established in Yangon and throughout the Yangon division.

Madrasahs choose to adopt either Burmese or Urdu as their language of instruction and reading Arabic grammar is compulsory, along with reading the Qur'an and the traditions of the Prophet (*Hadiths*). Graduates of madrasahs can translate Arabic religious texts in either Myanmar or Urdu language, but none of them can communicate fluently in conversational Arabic. In some cases, these Islamic-school graduates are indoctrinated by their respective '*Ulama* and lose a sense of rationality. Neither mathematics nor science subjects are taught in those madrasahs, although attempts are made to introduce English-language courses in some schools.

Some schools actively support *Tabligh*, the movement that aims to revive Islam among Muslims through a spiritual/personal approach, but they are not interested in converting non-Muslims to Islam.[3] It is compulsory for a graduate to spend a *Chillah* (40 days) with *Tabligh* by travelling to different parts of Myanmar to regenerate Islam. The *Tabligh* movement postulates that the reason for the fall of Islam was Muslims' failure to uphold the true teaching of Islam in its true form. Today, this noble movement has also become an institution of 'rehabilitation' to which disappointed parents send their mischievous youth with the aim of their sons becoming better Muslims.

The Myanmar administration has never made any serious attempt either to reform madrasahs or to incorporate them into the mainstream of the national education system, as has been the case in Thailand and Malaysia. The absence of an authoritative body governing Islamic schools within Myanmar encourages the mushrooming of madrasahs based on certain thoughts and ideas that seem to be Islamic. At times, differences of opinion about certain ideas on Islamic thought become so prevalent among Muslims that sometimes the State has to intervene to defuse tension among various Muslim communities. In one case, the authorities closed one Myanmar-speaking madrasah boarding school outside Yangon when its Muslim supporters were unable to resolve their own internal conflict.

Curriculum of madrasahs in Myanmar

Most madrasahs' curriculum and teaching systems are similar if not identical to those of the Indian subcontinent. There is no difference of any kind in the teaching textbooks and curriculum until standard four, after which the texts begin to vary. For example, one madrasah might adopt *Sharah Wiqayah* as a text for *Fiqh* (Islamic jurisprudence) while another might choose *Kanzad Daqa 'iq* as its teaching text for the same subject.

There is 95 per cent consistency in the textbooks used for Arabic grammar in all madrasahs. The texts vary again, however, in standard 10, the last year of studies. Some madrasahs will adopt the *Mishqad* book *Sahih Bukhari* (the traditions of the holy prophets compiled by Imam Bukhari), *Sahih Muslim* (the traditions of the holy prophets compiled by Imam Muslim), *Abi Dawood* (the traditions of the holy prophets compiled by Imam Abu Dawood), *Ni Sa'i'* (the traditions of the holy prophets compiled by Imam Ni'sa'i'), *Tirmizi* (the traditions of the holy prophets compiled by Imam Tirmizi) or *Ibnu Majah* (the traditions of the holy prophets compiled by Imam Ibnu Majah). Some madrasahs teach *Tahawi* (purification according to Islam) while others use *Muwatta' Imam Malik* (the traditions of the holy prophets compiled by Imam Malik). The selection of texts will vary according to the instructors' different opinions of the significance and relevance of the questions in the various books.

Languages used in Myanmar madrasahs

Myanmar Muslims are divided not only over different ethnicity and race, they are divided over different languages used in madrasahs. Indeed, this gap has been significant since the 1930s. In some cases, local communities consider this to be an irreconcilable problem.

Myanmar-speaking Muslims always point to the story of how the first Arab Muslims arrived in Mottama (Martaban) in Lower Myanmar in 1055 AD. An Arab merchant's two sons were rescued by Buddhist monks after their ship capsized near the Mon Kingdom. Today, those two Arab brothers are Byattwi and Byatta, two of the 37 *nats* (spirits), as known by Burman Buddhists (Mohiyuddin 2005:68). Myanmar Muslims are proud that a Muslim teacher educated the son of King Anawratha, King Saw Lu (Naing 2000:6). They also recall the oppressive King Bayinnaung (1551–81 AD), who forced Muslims to convert to Buddhism and forbade the slaughtering of cattle on Islamic holidays. On the other hand, he appointed Muslim translators in his palace and had contacts with King Akhbar of India (Naing 2000:7). King Tar Lun (1629–48) sent Muslim prisoners captured in Pegu, Yangon and Arakan to Central Myanmar, who then settled there.

Bamar Muslims persistently argue that they served under numerous Bamar kings in various capacities, such as teachers, horse riders and soldiers. Some Bamar kings were very fond of them and King Mindon (1853–78) is known to have given religious freedom to his people throughout the country. He built Masjids for Muslims serving his army and residing in his kingdom and appointed Kabul Mawlawi as a religious authority on Islamic matters, allowing him a gold-coloured umbrella (*shwe htee*), gold bowl (*shwe yae tauk phalar*) and gold spittoon (*shwe htawe khan*) (Lay 1971:67). Bamar Muslims also served the last king of Myanmar, King Thibaw (1878–85) (Lay 1971:78).

Bamar Muslims were therefore of the opinion that the Myanmar language should be used in all madrasahs, whereas Indian Muslims, who dominated the management and financed madrasah maintenance, imposed Urdu, the language used in Indian madrasahs.

In fact, an official request was made to teach Myanmar as the major language in all Islamic schools at the Bamar Muslim Education Conference held in Bago (Pegu) in December 1929. Bamar Muslims were offended by the statements made by the then chairman of the Burmese Maulawi Association, Maulana Ismail Ibnu Mohammed Bismillah, who gave the following reasons for Urdu to be maintained as the medium of instruction in all Islamic schools:[4]

- if Urdu was replaced by Myanmar (a language forbidden by Allah), the Muslims of Myanmar would witness a possible stagnation of Islam in the country
- Urdu was the language of Islam in India
- there was a great possibility that Islamic religious knowledge would eventually become extinct if Myanmar replaced Urdu.

As a result, the Bamar Muslim Education Conference, attended by more than 200 delegates and held at Yamethin on 28–29 December 1930, decisively outlined the difficulties faced by the Bamar Muslims and their reasons for wanting to change the language:

- there were no *Mawlawi* (preachers of Islam) who spoke Myanmar fluently
- many people were unable to understand what the Indian *Mawlawis* preached
- the way the *Mawlawi* preached Islam was difficult to follow in practice—so much so that many wanted to convert to other religions

- Muslims learned no modern languages—that is, Myanmar and English—while they learned Urdu and Arabic from a young age with no comprehensive understanding, making them no use in later years.

The delegates of the conference also proposed that the Bamar (Burman) Muslims should have at least one *Mawlawi* who could preach in every Myanmar town and it selected young Bamar Muslims to be sponsored to study Islam in Myanmar and English, not in Urdu and Arabic (Lay 1971:172–6). At the national level, in February–March 1937, Bamars endeavoured to make Myanmar the language of the House of Parliament despite protests from European and Indian members (Chakravarti 1971:156). Soon afterwards, Bamar Muslims formed the Burma Muslim Independent Organisation, which adopted the following slogans:

- Bamar race: our race
- Bamar language: our language
- Bamar writings: our writings
- Bamar nation: our nation
- Independence: our religion
- Peace: our discipline
- Capitalism: we don't need
- *Mawlawi*-ism: we don't need.

Later, Bamar Muslims also formed Bamar (Burman) Muslims Noe Kyar Yae[5] Association (BMNKYA) and Bamar (Burman) Women Muslims Noe Kyar Yae Association (BWMNKYA), with several objectives such as forming a separate identity for Bamar (Burman) Muslims, including a separate register in the Myanmar census.

Today, madrasahs from Yangon, Mawlamyaing, Rakhine and Ayeyarwady—where the majority of non-indigenous and non-Bamar people live—use Urdu extensively in translating Arabic texts, with a few Myanmar words in unavoidable circumstances. It is interesting to recall that the differences about which language to use once caused serious division among the Muslims of Myanmar. Burmese-speaking Myanmar Muslims called for their Urdu-speaking counterparts to demonstrate their undivided loyalty to Myanmar by speaking Burmese and not Urdu, while Urdu-speaking Muslim *'Ulama* maintained that Urdu had been the religious language in India and those who spoke Burmese in Islamic matters were 'Muslim bodies with Buddhist souls'.

On the other hand, Pyaw Bwe, Yamethin, Meiktila, Lat Pan, Su Lay Kone, Mandalay, Bone Owe, Shwebo, Kanbalu and many other towns in Upper Burma translate all texts into Myanmar.

It is therefore a common assumption that madrasah graduates from Upper Burma are weak in Urdu and in some cases could not even converse well with their counterparts from Lower Burma. What is more, those madrasah graduates face numerous obstacles securing a job as a madrasah teacher in Lower Burma as they are unable to converse in the language that Muslims from Lower Burma consider the 'Islamic [religious] tongue'. In many instances, they have to undergo Urdu-language courses before being appointed as madrasah teachers. On the other hand, madrasah graduates from Lower Burma easily find jobs in madrasahs in Upper Burma, despite their limited Myanmar-language skills.

Ideologies

Bamar Muslims from Upper Burma do not have Arabic (Muslim) names, unlike their counterparts in Lower Burma. Some of the latter keep their Muslim names for private use and prefer to be addressed by their Myanmar name. Some have been fighting vigorously against the Indian style of Islam by adopting Myanmar names and wearing Myanmar national dress. Most writings of Bamar Muslims focus on Bamar Muslim activities and seek to disassociate their community from non-Bamar Muslims, especially those of Indian descent. Some have gone to extreme lengths to differentiate themselves from Indian Muslims by saying, for example, that there is no difference between Bamar Buddhists and Bamar Muslims, except that Bamar Muslims consume no pork (see Chaye 1986).

Myanmar Muslims from Upper Burma are considered to be more liberal in Islamic thoughts and more accommodating towards different ethnic groups and other faiths. Madrasahs in this area teach students to be more open-minded than those in other areas, and no particular form of dress is considered 'pious'. Madrasahs in Lower Myanmar, however, make it compulsory for their students to dress in Indian style, wearing '*kurta*' and '*fez*'. All madrasah teachers in Lower Burma wear pious *kurta* and *fez* dress.

Any madrasah student or teacher who is not in 'pious' dress is considered to be a 'follower of deviate teachings and the servant of Satan' or anti-*Hadith* (against the traditions of the Prophet and against accepting the Qur'an as the only revealed source of Islam). Whatever the case is, assumptions about pious dress are meant only for madrasah teachers, not for the general Muslim public.

No text written by any native Myanmar Muslim is used in any madrasah anywhere in the country. The textbooks used are the same as those used in Indian and Pakistani madrasahs, emphasising faith and cultural matters, and leaving out social relationships between Muslims and non-Muslims, politics, psychology, sociology and philosophy. There could be several reasons why Muslims are not welcome in the civil service and state-controlled government institutions, the police or the army, but no madrasah graduate ever thinks of working along with their fellows of the Buddhist faith. At the same time, their qualifications would not allow them to join the civil service domain, as madrasah certificates are not recognised by the regime.

The concept of jihad is loosely translated as striving for one's best to achieve something that God wishes—not declaring war on non-Muslims over various preconceived notions. Since the September 2001 attacks, Myanmar's authorities have been increasingly concerned about the nature and establishment of madrasahs and the sources of donations and textbooks used in them. During some critical periods, madrasahs in and around Yangon and other places have been instructed to shut down and order their students to return to their respective homes until tranquility is restored in the country. Similar instructions are sometimes given to other schools as well.

The regime imposes restrictions on importing Islamic religious books and other texts from the Indian subcontinent and the Middle East, although its media proclaims that no such restrictions apply. In two cases, books in Urdu sent by Myanmar Muslim students studying in Pakistan were confiscated at the Yangon International Airport[6] and some bundles of books in Arabic donated by Myanmar Muslims living in Saudi Arabia were stored at the Thai–Myanmar border to be smuggled into Myanmar, if circumstances allowed.

Famous and reputable madrasahs in Myanmar

Myanmar is home to 759 Islamic schools, according to the official records of the regime. Madrasahs can be placed in two categories: madrasah (school) and *jami'ah* (university)—although all began as the former before transforming themselves into the latter. Some institutions adopt *jami'ah* and madrasah in their title, with no apparent explanation. Of all these institutions, some are well known for their academic staff, curriculum and discipline and management (selected madrasahs are listed in Appendix Table 10.1). The story of the establishment of two famous mosques and madrasahs provides an example of the respect with which their founders are still held.

Darul 'Uloom (Tarmwe)

A Muslim named Ibrahim purchased 17.5 hectares of land in Tarmwe, Yangon, in 1919, of which 19 square metres were allocated on which to build a mosque and the rest became a Muslim cemetery. The headmaster of this madrasah was Maulana Mufi Mahmud Daud Yussuf, who was born in Yangon in 1916. At the age of five, he was entrusted to Maulana Abdul Majid of Shah Jahan Puri, India, to learn Islam. He was later sent to the school of Randeniah to study English. After 1929, he undertook further studies at the school of Mazahirul 'Uloom in Saharan Pur and obtained a Mufti's (expert on Islamic jurisprudence) degree in 1936, the year he married his cousin. He performed the *Haj* (pilgrimage to Mecca) along with his teacher, Maulana Abdul Rahman. On his return from Mecca, he reluctantly accepted the post of the chairman of Surti Mosque, Yangon. Later, he was assigned to take charge of the Muslim cemetery and became the headmaster of the madrasah until his death. Today, the authorities have closed this Muslim cemetery and no new burials are allowed. Maulawi Saleh from Mawlamyaing now heads this madrasah.

Sufia (Botahtaung)

In 1957–58, Hakim Abdul Aziz set up a *Yunani* medicine shop in Bohtataung, where he noticed many Muslim children had no knowledge of Islam. Offering them sweets and snacks, he invited them to his medicine house, where he taught them about Islam. During a journey to Bago, he met Adbullah in Waw and Muhammad Saleh, Ahmad, Wali Ahmad, Yusuf Ali, Muhammad Qasim and Muhammad Ali, all of whom headed to Madauk. Here, they met Habibul Rahman, Muhammad Ismail, Muhammed Yakob (big) and Muhammad Yakob (small). They all continued their journey to Nyaunglaybin, where they met the sons of Maulana Abdul Ghafur, Abdul Majid, Abdul Manar and Mu'min. All of them, including Yusuf from Pyun Ta Zar, drove to Yangon and began a small school with 15 students.

Challenges faced by madrasahs in Myanmar

There seem to be no clear-cut rules and regulations for what a madrasah can do or cannot do in Myanmar. All rules and laws change from time to time. Every Muslim is aware that madrasahs are being closely watched and monitored by the regime, and they behave in the safest way possible. The US *Religious Freedom Report* and Human Rights Watch have on numerous occasions reported incidents involving the arrest and jailing of some Muslim teachers in state schools, who were teaching students how to read the Qur'an at home.

According to the Myanmar Government's own publications, Islam and its related affairs are controlled, regulated and managed by the Ministry of Religious Affairs of Myanmar, working through five Islamic associations (ibid.:69):

1. Islamic Religious Affairs Council
2. Muslim 'Ulama Association
3. All Myanmar Mawlawi Association
4. All Myanmar Young Muslim Youth
5. Myanmar Muslim League.

The Islamic Religious Affairs Council (IRAC) is the most active Islamic association as it has the blessing of the regime. The Islamic Centre of Myanmar (ICM), set up by the Bamar Muslim U Ba Chit,[7] acts as a mouthpiece for the IRAC and is active in interfaith dialogue. All its executive members adopt only Myanmar names with the prefix '*Al haj*',[8] such as Al Haj U Khin Maung Myint, Al Haj U Tin Nyunt and Haji Ma Daw Hla Shawe. Likewise, none of its committee members, including the daughter of its founder, U Ba Chit, Haji Ma Dr Sandar Chit, has a Muslim (Arabic) name (see ICM 2003).

The government allows publication of Islamic books and numerous magazines, especially by the ICM, such as *Al Irshad* (*Guidance*), *Milardun Nabi* (*The Birth of the Holy Prophet*), *Al Noor* (*The Light*), *Al Balaq* (*Spreading*), *Al Hilal* (*The Crescent*), *Al Falah* (*The Success*), *Al Minar* (*Minaret*), *Nurul Islam* (*The Light of Islam*), *Lisanul Islam* (*Language of Islam*), *Islam Myet Won* (*The Eye of Islam*) and *Al Munadi* (*The Call*).

All magazines are informative in nature and highlight local and global news about Islam, including the lives of Muslims in the United States, the winners of the King Feisal Award and feature poems and short stories. Also included are articles about science and Islam, the history of early Bamar Muslims, Muslims in ancient Myanmar, the impact of the Internet on modern youth, the danger of homosexuality and HIV/AIDS. Advertising is accepted from Ahamdiah Muslim Jammat, the organisation termed by the traditional 'Ulama as an 'out-of Islam group'.[9] The ICM also conducts summer Islamic classes for Bamar Muslims.

Muslims in Myanmar usually believe that they are discriminated against and are treated badly by the regime compared with people of other faiths. Muslims are unhappy that there are only two public holidays for Muslims, Aidil Fitri and 'Idil Adha, of which only one is a gazetted a public holiday, while Buddhists celebrate numerous religious public holidays. At the same time, many Muslims complain that the regime refuses to grant land or *waqf* (donations of land or property by a Muslim) to set up either a madrasah or a mosque in newly established towns such as Hlaing Thayar and South and North Dagon in Yangon Division.

The lack of an authorised Islamic or neutral news agency in Myanmar has provided fertile ground for all types of Islamic organisations. *Ahmadiyah* (anti-*hadith* groups) are gaining more strength among less-educated Muslim urban youths. The traditional 'Ulama's attempt to prohibit quoting any Qur'anic verse or *hadith* is confronted by a handful of modern youths who spent a few months learning Arabic at Azhar University in Cairo. These youths argue that Islam is for everyone and proclaim that ''Ulama must not be allowed to monopolise it'.

At the same time, the traditional 'Ulama have failed to inculcate a sense of Islamic identity in Muslim youths. Many Myanmar Muslims tend to hide their identity and prefer to classify themselves as Buddhist in some situations. Madrasahs will, however, remain in Myanmar into the future as there is no other alternative to the state education system available for Myanmar Muslims.

Appendix

Appendix Table 10.1 Famous and reputable madrasahs in Myanmar

Name	City/town
Darul 'Uloom	Tarmwe, Yangon
Sufia	Botahtaung, Yangon
Jamiatul 'Ulama	Kanbalu
Jamiat Arabia Mazahirul 'Uloom	Pyaw Bwe
Madrasah Nu'maniah	Yangon
Jamiatul Arabia Islamiah Ta'leemul Qur'an	Thingangyun, Yangon
Isha' Atul 'Uloom	Mawlamyaing
Imdarul 'Uloom	Kyaikmayaw
Madrasah Husseiniah	Maung Gan, Mawlamyaing
Madrasah Mahmudiah	Thingangyun, Yangon
Madrasah Arabia Hidayatul 'Uloom	Yamethin
Madrasah Furqaniah Hafizul Qur'an	Thingangyun, Yangon
(Arabic University of) Madinatul 'Uloomul	Yin Daw, Pyaw Bwe
(Arabic University of) Madrasah Azziziah	Nan Daw Kone, Meiktila
(Arabic University of) Madrasah Khaliliyah	Letpan, Kyaukse
(Arabic University of) Miftahul 'Uloom	Bone Owe, Mandalay
Madrasah Zammiriah	Kywe Chan Kone Mawlamyaing
Madrasah Hakimiah	Laputtar
Jami'ah Qasimiah	Ma Kyar Nwe Zin, Mandalay
(Arabic University of) Jamia'h Furqaniah	Thathon
(Arabic University of) Jami'ah Arabiah Shamsul 'Uloom	Letpan
(Arabic University of) Bisthanul 'Uloom	Pyin Oo Lwin
(Arabic University of) Jami'ah Huseiniah	Aung Lan
Jami'ah Arabiah Imdadul 'Uloom	Myitkyina
Jami'ah Nurul Islam	Kaw Ka Rate, Kayin State
Jami'ah Ashraful 'Uloom	Kaw Ka Rate, Kayin State
Jami'ah Arabiah Madinatul 'Uloom	Su Lay Gone, Kyaukse
(Arabic University of) Muhamadiah	Taung Myint, Mandalay
Jami'ah Arabiah Nadwatul 'Uloom	Kan Tar Kone, Shwebo
Jai'ah Arabiah Nadwatul 'Uloom	Myint Nge, Mandalay

Appendix Table 10.2 Number of monasteries, churches, mosques and madrasahs in Myanmar

State/division	Monasteries	Churches	Mosques	Madrasahs
Kachin State	655	389	20	23
Kayar State	147	95	2	5
Karen State	1014	605	48	69
Chin State	100	898	1	3
Sagaing Division	7666	148	94	38
Tanintharyi Division	1189	53	76	47
Bago Division	5689	146	56	55
Magwe Division	5870	44	29	29
Mandalay Division	8640	62	200	107
Mon State	2457	37	94	68
Rakhine State	2716	51	1238	105
Yangon Division	4109	221	171	111
Shan State	4695	343	85	35
Ayeyarwady Division	6240	173	152	64
Total	**51 187**	**3265**	**2266**	**759**

Source: Ministry of Defence of Myanmar 1997, *Tha Tanar Yang War Htun Say Phoe* (*Shining the Bright Light of Religion*), March, Yangon, pp. 48–73.

Appendix Table 10.3 Location of mosques within Yangon Division

Township	No.
Lathar	1
Lanmadaw	4
Pabedan	11
Kyauktada	8
Botahtaung	10
Ahlone	2
Sanchaung	1
Pazundaung	2
Dawbon	2
Insein	6
Thingangyun	6
South Dagon	-
North Dagon	-
Thanlyin	10
Tone Kwa	1
Kayin	3
Kwan Chan Kone	3
Twantay	7
Seikgyi Khanaungto	2
Dala	6
Than Ta Pin	1
Mingaladon	5
Thaketa	9
North Okkalapa	2
Shwepyithar	1
Hlegu	5
Kaw Mu	1
Taikgyi	8
South Okkalapa	5
Hlaing	4
Tarmwe	6
Kyeemyindaing	1
Mayangone	3
Mingala Taungnyunt	18
Hmawbi	7
Kyauktan	2
Yankin	1
Kamaryut	2
Hlaing Thayar	-
Coco Island	-
Sate Kan	-
Total	171

Source: Ministry of Defence of Myanmar 1997, *Tha Tanar Yang War Htun Say Phoe* (*Shining the Bright Light of Religion*), March, Yangon, pp. 48–73.

References

Abaza, Mona 2002, *Newsletter*, no. 28, August, International Institute of Asian Studies, Netherlands.

Central Intelligence Agency (CIA) 2005, *Factbook*, viewed 10 November 2005, <http://www.odci.gov/cia/publications/factbook/geos/bm.html>

Chaye, Sayar 1986, *Some Things Good to Know About Myself*, (In Burmese), A Mar Chit Press, Rangoon.

Chakravarti, Nalini Ranjan 1971, *The Indian Minority in Burma: The rise and decline of an immigrant community*, Oxford University Press, London.

Hall, D. G. E. 1959, *A History of Southeast Asia*, London.

International Institute for Asian Studies (IIAS) 2005, University of Amsterdam, Leiden, viewed 5 November 2005, <http://iias.leidenuniv.nl/iiasn/16/regions/sea7.html>

Islamic Center of Myanmar (ICM) 2003, *Summer Islamic Course. Volume II*, April, Islamic Center of Myanmar, Yangon.

Jilani, A. F. K., 1999, *The Rohingyas of Arakan: Their quest for justice*, Ahmed Jilani, Dhaka.

Lay, Pathi U Ko Ko 1971, *The Union of Myanmar and the Religion of Islam 1404–1945*, Yangon.

Matthews, Bruce 2001, *Ethnic and Religious Diversity: Myanmar's unfolding nemesis*, Institute of South East Asian Studies, Singapore.

Ministry of Foreign Affairs (MOFA) 2005, Government of the Union of Myanmar, viewed 10 November 2005, <http://www.mofa.gov.mm/aboutmyanmar/religion.html>

Mohammed Mohiyuddin Mohammed Sulaiman, 2005, 'Excluding the Included: Bamar (Burman) Muslims' Quest for Bamar-but-Islamic Identity in Burma', paper presented at 10th anniversary SEASREP (Southeast Asian Studies Regional Exchange Program) conference, Chiang Mai, Thailand, 8-9 December 2005.

Moshe, Yegar 1972, *The Crescent in the East: Islam in Asia Major*, Curzon Press, Jerusalem.

Mutalib, Hussin 2005, 'Who should speak for Islam in Southeast Asia?', *Reader's Digest*, August.

Naing, Wa Khae Ma Maung Min 2000, *The Union of Myanmar and the Religion of Islam, Part I & II*, Yangon.

Selth, Andrew 2003, *Burma Muslims: Terrorists or terrorized?*, Strategic and Defence Studies Centre, The Australian National University, Canberra.

Suthasasna, Arong 1983–84, 'Occupational distribution of Muslims in Thailand: problems and prospects', *Journal of the Institute of Muslim Minorities Affairs*, vol. V.

Thiker, H. 1959, *The Union of Burma*, London.

Endnotes

[1] Andrew Selth (2003:5) also noted a few who believed that Muslims could constitute 16 per cent, or eight million, of the total population, although most statistics for Myanmar are unreliable and this matter is not an exception. It is said that representatives of faiths other than Buddhism often mistrust the official religious statistics; see Matthews (2001:5).

[2] Speech delivered by Maung Ko Ghaffari, 12–15 February 2005, Cheongpyeong, Korea, cited in *Lisanul—Islam Magazine*, May–June 2005, Yangon, p. 86.

[3] The movement was founded by Mawlana Ilyas from India in the early 1940s with the noble intention of bringing the Muslims of India back to Islam. Today, the movement is widely accepted by the people of the Indian subcontinent. It does not publish any books and does not involve itself in any business activities. It shuns politics and refuses to join any activities that bring men to power, which is often misused to subjugate others.

[4] Speech by Mawlana Ismail Ibnu Mohammed Bismillah delivered at the Bamar Muslim Education Conference held in Pegu in December 1929.

[5] This literally means 'to be quick to hear while asleep, to awake easily, to be on alert, to be vigilant and watchful'. See Judson's *Burmese–English Dictionary* 1988, p. 586.

[6] An interview with one of the students in Pakistan, who requested his name not be revealed for security reasons.

[7] *Heartiest Acknowledgement to U Ba Chit*, published by the Islamic Centre of Myanmar, Yangon.

[8] Islamic term referring to someone who has performed the *Haj* pilgrimage to Saudi Arabia.

[9] An advertisement for Ahamdiah Bookstore in *Pyi Ar Man* magazine, October 1998, Yangon, p. 154.

11: Contemporary medical pluralism in Burma

Monique Skidmore

Introduction

Every day in Central Burma, Burmese people engage with their pluralistic medical system. As with medical systems all over the world, in Central Burma, confusing, competing and contradictory logics govern the use of this medical system by Burmese people. Central Burma can be defined as the deltas and valleys of the Ayeyarwady River, where the population is divided between the large population centres of Yangon, Mandalay, Pathein and Mawlamyaing and the many villages that surround the river and its tributaries. The aim in this chapter is to present a cultural understanding of the ways in which Burma's pluralistic medical system has been transformed through the past century or so. It examines the relationship between private and public healthcare systems and controversy about the use and provision of humanitarian and in-country aid, before examining transnational and cross-border forms of health provision accessed by Burmese people in their search for affordable and curative medicines. It seeks to make more complex analysis of the provision of health care by considering how users encounter and negotiate their way through the Burmese medical system. Finally, it considers some of the longer-term consequences that a lack of the right to health is bringing about in Burma.

Overview of the healthcare system

Burma ranks 190 out of 191 countries in terms of 'overall health system performance' (WHO 2000).[1] With one psychiatric hospital in the country and one doctor for 2772 people, health care is difficult to come by (WHO 2006). It is also inordinately expensive: of all the South-East Asian nations, Burma ranks first in terms of the amount that individuals spend on health care (80.6 per cent of the total expenditure on health in Burma in 2006) and last in terms of government health expenditure (2.8 per cent of gross domestic product or GDP). The *Human Security Report* (Human Security Center 2005) defines Burma as the world's most conflict-prone country and the twelfth-least secure in terms of core human rights abuses. Currently, 160 000 refugees from Burma reside in seven refugee camps in Thailand, with a further 400 000 working as illegal migrants in manufacturing, agricultural and sex industries. Many have become political refugees in countries such as the United States and Australia. Medical doctors continue to leave the country in significant numbers and important international healthcare providers, such as Médecins sans Frontières and the Global Fund to Fight Malaria, Tuberculosis, and HIV/AIDS, have recently pulled out of Burma (McGeown 2005), although the Three Diseases Fund is replacing some of their planned activities. The World Health Organisation (WHO 2007) expects HIV/AIDS to become a major cause of death among young adults in Burma in the next decade.

Transparency International (2007) regards Burma as the most corrupt nation on the planet[2] and, while its Corruption Perceptions Index presents a stark picture of Burma as a whole, it is less revealing of the necessity for hospital workers to steal medicines and supplies and sell them on the black market. The WHO's picture of the Burmese health system is also blunt as it is unable to capture the broad and diffuse effects of corruption and poverty on Burmese health needs and outcomes. These include the existence of up to tens of thousands of child soldiers (CSI 2004), 5000–10 000 female sex workers (Talikowski and Gillieatt 2004:193), human trafficking, food insecurity and extreme poverty (FOWFP 2008), one-third of Burmese children being malnourished (Zeller 2007) and illicit drug production and use (UNODC 2007a:3, 2007b).[3]

A national health committee or council was formed by the new military regime in 1988, and continues to operate with the Prime Minister as its chair. It has responsibility for implementing national health programs, such as the Health Vision 2030 Plan and the current five-year National Health Plan (2006–11). The committee has devised three major changes to health policy since the Ne Win era:

1. a policy of partnering with international, local and para-statal non-governmental organisations (NGOs) to jointly provide healthcare delivery
2. beginning in 1993, a cost-sharing mechanism in which patients pay for medical services and diagnostic and laboratory tests
3. fostering a dual public and private healthcare system. In the public sector, this involves the creation of biomedical and traditional medicine training, licensing, regulation and the provision of hospital, clinic and research facilities. In addition, ministries such as those of defence, railways, mines and industry provide some level of healthcare for their employees. The enabling of a private medical system has recently seen the development of private hospitals such as Pun Hlaing International Hospital and cancer, cardiac and dental clinics.

In terms of national public health, prevention and the regulation of medicines, a major response of the regime has been to enact a series of medical and public health laws in the past decade. These include the Law Relating to Public Health Care Services 2007, the Control of Smoking and Consumption of Tobacco Law 2006, the Body Organ Donation Law 2004, the Blood and Blood Products Law

2003 and the National Food Law 1997. A Department of Medical Research investigates issues such as malaria, snake bites and viral hepatitis. As of 2001, there were 742 hospitals (six hospital beds per 10 000 people), 1412 rural health centres[4] and 348 maternal and child welfare centres, in addition to health interventions provided by international NGOs (WHO 2005). The public health system also bears the brunt of casualties of the country's significant production and consumption of opium, heroin and methamphetamines. There are 26 major drug treatment centres and 40 minor ones throughout the country.[5]

Traditional medicine has been and remains a priority area for the previous and current military council and the healthcare system is designed to integrate traditional medicine through all levels of community health care, including education, training, registration, licensing and research. Fourteen traditional-medicine hospitals[6] exist in all divisions except for Chin State, and there are 43 district clinics and 213 township medical clinics. The Traditional Medicine Council Law of 2000 requires licensing for traditional-medicine practitioners, and that they hold either a Diploma or Bachelor of Myanmar Traditional Medicine.[7] Such qualifications are obtainable from the University of Traditional Medicine in Mandalay, which opened in 2001.[8] In addition, there is a national herbal park at Naypyitaw, a traditional medicine museum and indigenous medicine pharmaceutical factories.[9] In line with medical training in several other Asian countries, since 2003, the Bachelor of Medicine degree incorporates 36 hours of traditional-medicine teaching in the third year of the curriculum.

This official creation of a two-tier medical system of public and private health care rarely acknowledges a shadow two-tier system that has come to exist: that of the military and civilian divisions of health care. This divide has emerged in the contrast between free or low-cost health care of a reasonable standard in the high-tech military hospitals and the poorly funded public health system.

Military hospitals feature prominently in the state media in terms of receiving donations of biomedical equipment and showcasing the health system to international visitors. This is in contrast with the small amount of information available about the public health system. Recent reports about the general hospital in the capital of northern Kachin State, Myitkyina Government Hospital, offer a rare glimpse of working conditions. A lack of electricity has meant that delivery rooms have operated via torchlight except for two hours each evening. The Kachin News Group (2007) recently reported that patients requiring surgery needed to pay 7500 kyat ($US6) an hour for the use of the hospital-owned generator. This contrasts with the medical health infrastructure that has been created in the new capital of Naypyitaw, including a 1000-bed general hospital and numerous private clinics.

Patterns of health seeking

Beyond the division of the Burmese medical system into government versus private and military versus civilian sectors, the medical system can be broken down into the categories shown in Table 11.1.

Table 11.1 Myanmar medical system

Government			Private	
Military	Biomedicine		Private Companies	Hospitals, Cardiac, Cancer, Dental, Diagnostic, Pathology
Civilian	Biomedicine	Para-statal groups (USDA, MRC MMCWA), ministries	UN, INGOs, Local NGOs	Foreign doctors and volunteers
	Traditional Medicine		Trans-National Health Providers	Emergency health, Reproductive health, Trauma services
			Ayurvedic/Humoral Medicine	
			Traditional Medicine Practitioners	*Lethe* (midwives)
			Buddhist Sects (gaing)	*Bodaws, Weikza*, Occult practices
			Astrology	
			Magical Healers	Alchemy, *Inn Saya, Dat Saya, Medaws, Payawga Saya*
			Other Healing Systems	Wa, Karen, Naga healers, etc.

From the starting point of the user, given this complexity and unevenness of coverage, quality and cost, it is not surprising that competing and contradictory logics govern the use of this medical system. Some families bypass this system altogether. These are the high-ranking military officers and their families who are able to use the military's clinics, hospitals and diagnostic services, and hospitals in Singapore and Bangkok for complicated interventions and surgery. This is a trend also followed by the very small Burmese middle class. In border areas, it is common to cross into neighbouring countries to seek treatment.

Most Burmese, however, cannot leave the country and, for the majority rural population, the combination of poverty and the scarcity of trained medical personnel mean that local remedies and practitioners are the only options. As a general rule, decisions about illness are made within co-located families. In the first instance, Burmese most often seek symptomatic relief through dietary changes, pharmaceuticals and traditional medicines. In villages, the level of knowledge of traditional medicine is dependent on the personal interests of individual villagers. This knowledge has become very unevenly distributed with neighbouring villages having very different patterns of resort to health care. In some villages, elders pass traditional-medicine recipes to their children and they become unofficial consultants when illnesses occur.[10] In other villages, lacking such knowledge, the village shop stocks common pharmaceuticals that provide symptomatic relief, such as pain and anti-inflammatory medication.

When initial symptomatic relief fails, a gradual change through dietary modification is employed (this is often practised concurrently with other remedies). This homeopathic system is similar to Indian Ayurvedic[11] practices, but is a more gentle and altogether less systematic practice in Burma. The comprehensive nature of the Ayurvedic system has been largely lost in Burma with the decline of indigenous medical practitioners after British colonisation. Complicating this approach to health care is the simple fact that most Burmese are well aware of the need to include, for example, more protein and a greater variety of vegetables in their diet, but they are prevented from doing so due to food scarcity and poverty.

Biomedicine is increasingly the first medical system that Burmese turn to for disease treatment—with two provisos. The first is that the cost of biomedicine puts all but the simplest consultations and treatment regimes out of the range of most of the population. The second is the great fear of surgery in Burma, whereas other forms of bodily penetration such as the insertion of gold needles under the skin as a form of alchemical treatment, tattooing and, more recently, biomedical injections, are readily tolerated. The great appeal of biomedicine,[12] especially in the form of pharmaceutical injections, is the rapidity of symptomatic relief, which is often equated with magic, as the response can be so dramatic. This sensation is further enhanced by the comparison with the more gradual changes that occur through dietary and homeopathic healing systems. This logic has been extended by many Burmese to include the use of multivitamin and B-vitamin injections to counter some of the effects of malnourishment.

Most Burmese do not have such options. A great deal of illnesses fit into a range of 'bad fortune' that can include a spate of bad luck or a belief in being cursed, bewitched or under the power of various malevolent spirits. These illnesses are the domain of a veritable smorgasbord of occult healers, a significant number of whom are Buddhist monks. A common healing forum is the Burmese *gain*. A *gain* is a 'term referring to a group of people organised around a founder' (Tosa 2005:155). The *gain* founder is most often believed to be a wizard (*weikza*) possessing supernatural powers obtained through mastery of occult law and practices (Skidmore 2004:183–4). *Gain* membership and the proliferation of *gain* decreased after a law was issued during the Ne Win era banning monks from practising medicine and a separate law banning *gain* (Tosa 2002). The leadership (and revolutionary) potential of charismatic *gain* leaders and other individuals claiming occult mastery is a common theme in Burmese history (Houtman 2005:136). In fact, bronze statues of Saya San, a healer who led a rebellion against the British in the Ayeyarwady Delta in the 1930s, have been commissioned by the Department of Traditional Medicine and stand proudly outside traditional-medicine clinics and buildings. Such charismatic *gain* and other occult practitioners sit on the right of Table 11.1. Not everyone utilises these practitioners and urban dwellers rarely, if ever, move any further to the right of the table than consulting an astrologer, except for life-threatening illnesses.[13]

Life-threatening diseases such as cancer or HIV/AIDS provide clear evidence of the patterns of resort to healers used by Burmese people. A great many of the hundreds of patients the author has interviewed in Yangon in the past decade or so begin in the folk and traditional medicine traditions then start spending large amounts of money in the biomedical sector once their disease progresses to a debilitating stage. This includes, for example, bowel cancer that has necessitated surgery and then the use of a colostomy bag. Another example is HIV-positive patients whose disease has progressed to the stage of almost no immune function. These patients run out of money very quickly and that is the stage when they exit the biomedical sector.

This leaves dying patients with the options of faith, religion, miraculous cure or supernatural intervention. It also leaves these patients open to practices such as the drinking of mercury-infused juices, in the case of HIV/AIDS patients being treated by alchemists, which can cause a faster decline and further compromise a failing immune system. Palliative care then becomes necessary and families, religious institutions and a very small number of government services provide end-of-life care for patients (many of whom are dying from diseases that could have been cured or slowed if they had been treated adequately at a much earlier stage).

The use of, or engagement with, the health system then depends on a host of variables, the foremost of which are money and military or civilian status; but ethnicity, previous health experiences, exposure to biomedicine, fear of surgery, belief in magical and religious healers, belief in spiritism, the location of the patient and the severity and stage of illness or disease all play determining roles.

So far this chapter has described the outward composition of the medical system and the factors that govern access to and use of the system by Burmese patients. It has done so within the framework of national health policies and the complexity of providers. The other aspects of the healthcare system that are covered next are rarely considered core business by healthcare providers, but they are essential to an integrated understanding of Burmese healthcare needs.

Humanitarian and medical aid

The first of these broader factors are the forms of emergency medical, humanitarian and health-development programs provided by international and national NGOs and UN agencies in-country. The first NGOs to begin work in Burma, Médecins sans Frontières and World Vision International, began operations in 1992. Aid provision within Burma has been scaled up significantly in the past five years, despite international economic sanctions against the regime and the limited mandates of organisations such as the International Labour Organisation (ILO), the UN Development Program (UNDP) and the UN Office on Drugs and Crime (UNODC). The politicised nature of aid and the restrictions on international aid workers have meant that community-based and local NGOs have become channels for aid. It also means that many aid agencies have aligned themselves with government organisations in quasi-partnerships that have significant ethical dimensions. Transparency and impartiality have thus been key to the continuing effort to expand aid and monitoring by UN agencies in recent years.

A recent rapid appraisal of the humanitarian situation in Burma has noted that the humanitarian situation needs to be reconceptualised from one of human security to one of social security, emphasising the need for and partial success in recent years of the UN agencies and other organisations in pushing back or at least containing the Burmese state's continuing attempt to penetrate all aspects of the civil sphere (Duffield 2008). Duffield (2008:41) argues for a rationalisation of international aid architecture in Burma to 'increase the range and depth of social welfare support'. This suggestion is all the more cogent given the State Peace and Development Council's (SPDC) increasing view of many forms of international humanitarian aid as either potentially or actively subversive of the military's continuing rule.

Duffield's report highlights the fragile, broken and often non-existent public welfare and health system in Burma and the significant role that international aid is playing in propping up, extending and establishing basic health services in the absence of a public welfare system.

Human rights abuses

The second of these broader factors are the serious core human rights abuses cited by the *Human Security Report* (Human Security Center 2005). A great number of aid and activist organisations have documented the political and economic context of human rights violations as part of establishing the parameters of the humanitarian crises in Burma.[14] There is also an international public health and epidemiological perspective on human rights issues in Burma, particularly on Thai–Burma border populations (Beyrer and Stover et al. 2007; Beyrer 1998; Belton and Whittaker 2007). Reading the countless reports from these organisations about the death, torture and lack of access to health of forcibly displaced and refugee populations, there can be no doubt that Burma is a country currently in the midst of a medical and humanitarian crisis. The current health system is unable to deal with let alone reduce human rights abuses. It is not just a case of too few facilities, resources and trained personnel. It is also the pervasive fear of retribution for health personnel who knowingly treat and give aid to activists, opposition politicians and all those who agitate for democracy.

Transnational and cross-border health care

Sufferers of human rights abuses, such as tortured political prisoners or land-mine victims, pour illegally across the nation's borders, most often into Thailand. The third of these broader issues, then, concerns the dual nature of aid provision to Burma: a recent significant increase in in-country aid as well as competing funding regimes for the provision of cross-border and transnational health care.

In the civil war areas of eastern Burma, Neumann and Bodeker (2008) describe a revitalisation of traditional Karen medical knowledge and practices, in part because of acute shortages of pharmaceuticals and biomedicine. Their work has documented how Buddhist monks provide spiritual and mental health care and explores the ways in which traditional healers are working to fill healthcare gaps in the region. The Wa also depend in large part on traditional health practices and Magnus Fiskesjö (2008) has written of how this corpus of knowledge and practice has fared in its encounter with modern medicine, as well as how it has been disrupted significantly by forced relocations and the detrimental impact on the capacity of the Wa to build on their own traditions and to access adequate health care. These studies are significant because of the difficulty of conducting scholarship on health issues outside central Burma.

The provision of emergency health care and infectious-disease prevention programs exists outside Burma's formal healthcare system. Cynthia Maung and the Back Pack Health Worker Team (BPHWT) and researchers such as Naing (2008) and Suzanne Belton (2008) cover the provision of aid within war zones, the HIV/AIDS epidemic in Burma and Thailand and emergency care for reproductive health issues in refugee populations. Maung and the BPHWT have described a dire healthcare situation in eastern Burma, where long-term, low-intensity conflict has given rise to a state of 'chronic emergency' (see Mahn Mahn's chapter in this volume). Their work shows how, in some parts of Burma, major public health issues arise as a direct result of civil conflict and widespread human rights abuses perpetrated by armed groups. Forced displacement, forced labour and the destruction of food supplies are only a few of the human rights violations that have a significant impact on health in this region. Belton's work has been located around the Thai–Burma border refugee camps, where Karen and other Burmese refugees encounter particular reproductive-health needs and challenges. The Mae Tao Clinic in Mae Sot works to identify and address these, providing important treatment, education and supplies to thousands of Burmese patients. Naing has analysed the HIV/AIDS epidemic affecting many Burmese migrant fishermen in Thailand, with an interest in developing effective prevention programs among those at risk. Other programs exist in neighbouring countries to aid Burmese working in the sex industry, victims of human trafficking and those who are affected by the 2004 tsunami—most particularly illegal migrants in and around Phuket in Thailand.

The failure of the State to provide accessible health care means that the roles of globalisation and transnationalism cannot be understated in the provision of emergency and preventive health care as well as the availability of medicines. The flow of illegal, unregulated medicines, some requiring cold-chain facilities and injectable vaccines containing attenuated viruses, is directed into Burma from all of its neighbours. In the modern pharmacies of Mongla in Wa State, for example, medical products from multinational companies such as Johnson and Johnson with Chinese script are available (Skidmore and Nordstom forthcoming). In the markets of Yangon, skin-whitening creams from India are sold beside heart medication from Thailand and psychiatric medications such as chlorpromazine and lithium manufactured in China (Skidmore 1998).[15]

Mongla is only one border town on the centuries-old southern Silk Route with significant numbers of Burmese people crossing the border on a daily basis. Burmese people similarly cross into the Indian state of Manipur through the Burmese border town of Tamu, and into Thailand via a series of busy border crossings. Medicines and illegal drugs and pharmaceuticals are carried across the region through these old trading routes (Skidmore and Nordstrom forthcoming). The help-seeking patterns of Burmese who live in proximity to border crossings thus contain more options than those living in the nation's central river valleys.

Conclusion: human rights and the right to health

As in other developing nations, particularly in Africa, in Burma, a substantial proportion of government medications and preventive-health materials are sold on the black market. The theft of medical equipment, medicines and other products from international and UN organisations means these products can be purchased easily in Yangon's main markets.

The transparency of aid delivery and the provision of materials from international donors are issues that continually confront in-country aid providers. The Australian medical practitioners currently working in Burma (Myanmar/Burma Update 2007) attest to the latent capacity and talent still evident among the Burmese medical fraternity, but the cost of health care, the continuing exodus of qualified medical personnel, the loss of much traditional knowledge since the colonial period and the existence of conflict zones within the country are all factors contributing to limit Burmese people's access to health care. Taken as a whole, the possibility of affordable, accessible and evidence-based health care is extremely limited for the majority of Burma's 54 million inhabitants. In this context, it is not surprising that Burmese people turn to folk and magical forms of medical practices, such as exorcists, alchemists and wizardry, when they have exhausted their financial resources and cannot find relief.

In the wake of the suppression of the so-called 'Saffron Revolution' in September–October 2007, it is perhaps timely to conclude with some thoughts about the long-term consequences of the lack of a right to health. There is indisputable photographic evidence of shootings and beatings administered to protestors during the attempted Saffron Revolution[16] and the former UN Special Rapporteur on Human Rights in Myanmar, Sergio Pinheiro, put the death toll at 31 with up to 4000 arrested and 1000 still detained as of 11 December 2007 (UNHRC 2008:4). In earlier work (Skidmore 2005, 2003), I described the long-term consequences of inculcating a state of fear and of perpetual vulnerability in the urban populace. Since September 2007, there has been a demonstrable increase in the efficiency by which terror, as distinct from fear, can be created among the population. In other countries in which violence has been perpetrated and witnessed, there are well-documented harvests of suicide, trauma and mental health problems. It is not possible to gather such health data in Burma, yet psychological health must surely be considered when describing Burma's humanitarian and health crises. Paranoia, nightmares, confused and impaired thinking and psychological defences such as denial are also prevalent among the Burmese I have interviewed in the wake of the violence in Yangon (Skidmore 1998). Jail terms for monks and civilians who took part in the demonstrations, as well as reports of torture within prisons and harsh sentences to prison and labour camps, have together created a pathological psychological climate. In Yangon, the anger that Burmese Buddhists feel at the continuing barricading and closure of monasteries and the continuing arrests of monks is palpable. To seek health care for trauma and fear, however, is to risk charges of subversion and treason.

In making these comments about the mental health of the urban populace, the purpose is not to detract from the serious human rights issues that occur among forcibly displaced civilian populations in Burma's civil war zone. In addition to the significant volume of core human rights abuses occurring in Burma, however, is a virtually undocumented and untreated epidemic of psychological trauma. This psychological trauma is a crucial aspect of a lack of a right to health and it is in part related to the subversion of medical ethics that is required of Burmese people who train and practice medicine in Burma today. There are precious few provisions for psychological, psychiatric or counselling help for those suffering from the long-term effects of living in a state of fear. At times of crisis such as during the September 2007 street protests against cost-of-living increases and military rule, anxiety, fear and paranoia can become acute, but medical personnel also live in fear of giving aid to people branded as enemies of the State or criminals during these moments of resistance.

The latter part of this chapter documents forms of health care offered by non-state providers, but also the forms of illness and disease that are not permitted to exist and therefore to be treated. It does so to emphasise not just the patent inadequacy of the current regime's expenditure on health care, but to draw attention to the continuing denial of the fundamental right to health for the majority of the population.

Epilogue

On 2 May 2008, as this volume was being finalised, severe tropical Cyclone Nargis made landfall in Ayeyarwady Division at near peak intensity. Winds were measured at the height of the cyclone at 215 kilometres an hour. The cyclone passed just to the north of Yangon. Within the Ayeyarwady Delta, the storm caused a tidal surge of up to four metres, inundating paddy fields with sea water.

The death toll from the cyclone is staggering, with official figures of 130 000 dead and 2.4 million people affected. The United Nations believes it left 900 000 people homeless.[17] It seems clear that a large number of children and elderly Burmese are among the dead. The cyclone caused extensive damage to towns and villages in the delta as well as in Yangon and its peri-urban townships.

The cyclone developed on 27 April and Sri Lankan, Bangladesh and Burmese authorities issued warnings. The Bangladesh Government, for example, urged farmers to finish bringing in their rice harvest (*Voice of America News*, 29 April 2008). In Burma, the military regime issued warnings on 2 May that a severe cyclonic storm was over the Bay of Bengal. It concluded with the comment that '[w]eather is partly cloudy to cloudy in the Andaman Sea and elsewhere in the Bay of Bengal' (*New Light of Myanmar*, 2 May 2008).

While the inadequacy of the government warnings became patently obvious when approximately 95 per cent of all structures within the delta were destroyed by Nargis, the regime's response to the disaster received strong international condemnation. The British Prime Minister labelled the aftermath of the cyclone a 'man-made catastrophe' (*The Irrawaddy*, 21 May 2008) because of the regime's refusal to allow international disaster-relief teams to provide emergency aid. The military regime blocked the access of crucial supplies, which probably caused the death and suffering of numerous people. The number of people who died in the aftermath of the cyclone because of the regime's refusal of aid and its inability to reach survivors in time might never be known. It is clear, however, that the SPDC does not have disaster-relief planning capability or emergency supplies and that it deliberately withheld international aid to Cyclone Nargis survivors.

This chapter describes a withholding of the right to health from the Burmese people as a human rights abuse on an enormous scale. The charge of crimes against humanity must be proven over a sustained period as a deliberate policy.

This chapter has sketched the outline of a comprehensive failure to provide for the health needs of the Burmese population and of 46 years of continuing human rights abuses perpetrated by the military regime and its paramilitary, militia and security forces and organisations. The military regime's response to the loss of life and emergency humanitarian needs generated by Cyclone Nargis raises the spectre of a lack of a right to health in contemporary Burma as a continuing, sustained and often systematic form of a crime against humanity.

References

Belton, S. 2008, 'The Reproductive Health Crisis Among Burmese Refugees' in Monique Skidmore (ed.), *Medicine in Myanmar: Past and present*, Nordic Institute for Asian Studies Press, Copenhagen.

Belton, S. and Whittaker, Andrea 2007, 'Kathy Pan, sticks and pummelling: techniques used to induce abortion by Burmese women on the Thai border', *Social Science and Medicine*, vol. 65, no. 7, pp. 1512–23.

Beyrer, C. 1998, *War in the Blood: Sex, politics, and AIDS in Southeast Asia*, White Lotus, Bangkok.

Beyrer, C. and Stover, E. et al. 2007, *The Gathering Storm: Infectious diseases and human rights in Burma*, Human Rights Center, University of California, Berkeley, and Center for Public Health and Human Rights, Johns Hopkins Bloomburg School of Public Health.

Child Soldiers International (CSI) 2004, *Global Report 2004: Myanmar*, viewed 22 May 2008, <http://www.child-soldiers.org/library/global-reports?root_id=159&directory_id=165>

Duffield, M. 2008, *On the edge of 'no man's land: chronic emergency in Myanmar*, Working Paper No. 01-08, Centre for Governance and International Affairs, University of Bristol.

Fiskesjö, M. 2008, in Monique Skidmore (ed.), *Medicine in Myanmar: Past and present*, Nordic Institute for Asian Studies Press, Copenhagen.

Friends of the World Food Program (FOWFP) 2008, Q&A with World Food Program Country Director for Myanmar, Chris Kaye, January 2008, <www.friendsofwfp.org/site/pp.asp?c =7oIJLS Os G pF&b=3594603>

Houtman, G. 2005, 'Sacralizing or demonizing democracy? Aung San Suu Kyi's "personality cult"', in Monique Skidmore (ed.), *Burma at the Turn of the Twenty-First Century*, University of Hawai'i Press, Honolulu, pp. 133–53.

Human Security Center 2005, *Human Security Report 2005: War and peace in the twenty-first century*, Human Security Centre, University of British Columbia, Canada.

Kachin News Group 2007.

McGeown, K. 2005, 'Aid in Burma: when it's time to give up', *BBC News*, 25 September, <http://news.bbc.co.uk/2/hi/asia-pacific/4268618.stm>

Naing 2008, 'Burmese fishermen and HIV prevention programs', in Monique Skidmore (ed.), *Medicine in Myanmar: Past and present*, Nordic Institute for Asian Studies Press, Copenhagen.

Neumann, C. and Bodeker, G. 2008, 'Karen healing beliefs and practices', in Monique Skidmore (ed.), *Medicine in Myanmar: Past and present*, Nordic Institute for Asian Studies Press, Copenhagen.

New Light of Myanmar 2005.

New Light of Myanmar, 2 May 2008, viewed 2 June 2008, <http://www.wunderground.com/hurricane /2008/nargisnews.jpg>

Skidmore, M. (ed.) 2005, *Burma at the Turn of the Twenty-First Century*, University of Hawai'i Press, Honolulu.

Skidmore, M. 1998, Flying through a skyful of lies: survival strategies and the politics of fear in urban Burma (Myanmar), PhD Dissertation, McGill University.

Skidmore, M. 2002, 'Menstrual madness: women's health and well-being in urban Burma', in A. Whittaker (ed.), *Women's Health in Mainland Southeast Asia*, Haworth Medical Press, New York, pp. 81–99.

Skidmore, M. 2003, 'Darker than midnight: fear, vulnerability and terror making in urban Burma (Myanmar)', *American Ethnologist*, vol. 30, no. 1, February, pp. 5–21.

Skidmore, M. 2004, *Karaoke Fascism: Burma and the politics of fear*, University of Pennsylvania Press, Philadelphia.

Skidmore, M. and Nordstrom, Carolyn (forthcoming), Public culture.

Talikowski, Luke and Gillieatt, Sue 2004, 'Female sex work in Yangon, Myanmar', *Sexual Health*, vol. 2, no. 3, pp. 193–202.

The Irrawaddy, 21 May 2008, viewed 2 June 2008, <http://www.irrawaddy.org/opinion_story.php?art_id=12166>

Tosa, K. 2002, Weikza: the case of Thamanya Taung Hsayadaw, Essay presented at Burma Studies Conference Burma–Myanmar Research and its Future, 21–25 September, Gothenburg, Sweden.

Tosa, K. 2005, 'The chicken and the scorpion: rumor, counternarratives, and the political uses of Buddhism', in Monique Skidmore (ed.), *Burma at the Turn of the Twenty-First Century*, University of Hawai'i Press, Honolulu, pp. 154–74.

Transparency International 2007, Persistent corruption in low-income countries requires global action, Press release, 26 September, Transparency International, London/Berlin, pp. 1–3.

United Nations Human Rights Council (UNHRC) 2008, *Report of the Special Rapporteur on the Situation of Human Rights in Myanmar, Paulo Sérgio Pinheiro, Mandated by Resolution 6/33 of the Human Rights Council*, viewed 3 June 2008, <http://burmalibrary.org/docs4/SRM-HRC-7-24-en.pdf>

United Nations Office on Drugs and Crime (UNODC) 2007a, *Opium Poppy Cultivation in Southeast Asia: Lao PDR, Myanmar, Thailand*, United Nations Office on Drugs and Crime, New York.

United Nations Office on Drugs and Crime (UNODC) 2007b, *World Drug Report*, United Nations Office on Drugs and Crime, New York.

Voice of America News, 29 April 2008, viewed 2 June 2008, <http://voanews.com/english/archive/2008-04/2008-04-29-voa19.cfm?CFID=59893764&CFTOKEN=32487379>

World Health Organisation (WHO) 2000, *World Health Report 2000: Health systems—improving performance*, World Health Organisation, Geneva.

World Health Organisation (WHO) 2005, *World Health Report 2005: Make every mother and child count*, World Health Organisation, Geneva, viewed 22 May 2008, <http://www.who.int/whr/2005/whr2005en.pdf>

World Health Organisation (WHO) 2006, *World Health Report 2006: Working together for health*, World Health Organisation, Geneva.

World Health Organisation (WHO) 2007, *World Health Report 2007: A safer future, global public health security in the 21st century*, World Health Organisation, Geneva.

Zeller, F. 2007, 'Food shortfall looms in crisis-hit Myanmar, UN warns', *Agence France-Presse*, 3 October.

Endnotes

[1] The World Health Organisation (WHO) has not conducted overall health performance rankings since 2000 as the ranking system proved controversial among member states.

[2] The 2007 Corruption Perceptions Index ranks 180 countries in terms of perceived levels of corruption. Burma ranks equal last with Somalia out of the 180 countries assessed.

[3] Opium poppy cultivation has decreased by 83 per cent in nine years, from 130 300 hectares in 1988 to 21 500ha in 2006. Poppy cultivation is, however, again on the rise, with a 29 per cent increase in cultivation in 2007 to 27 700ha and a 46 per cent increase in production due to higher yields. Methamphetamine production appears to be continuing to increase rapidly with 19.1 million pills seized in the country in 2006 compared with 3.6 million in 2005 (UNODC 2007b).

[4] There were also 350 dispensaries, 86 secondary health centres and nine medical institutes.

[5] In addition, there are six Regional Drug Abuse Rehabilitation Centres and two Youth Rehabilitation Centres (New Light of Myanmar 2005).

[6] Two of these hospitals have 50 beds; the remainder have 16 beds.

[7] Related laws are intended to regulate the quality and sale of indigenous medicines.

[8] Before this there was an Institute of Traditional Medicine in Mandalay, which opened in 1976, and later a similar institution in Yangon.

[9] There are an estimated 9000 herbal and medicinal plants now being grown throughout the country.

[10] An exception to this rule appears to be knowledge of emmenagogues—medications taken to induce miscarriage or as a method of fertility regulation (Skidmore 2002).

[11] Ayurvedic medicine is an ancient philosophy of health care native to the Indian subcontinent, sometimes considered as a Hindu system of health care because it derives from the oral advice on living in the Hindu *Vedas*. It is used by millions of people in India, Nepal, Sri Lanka and increasingly in the West and is known widely as the world's oldest continuously practised system of medicine. '*Ayurveda*' translates roughly as 'wisdom for living' or 'knowledge of long life'.

[12] Biomedicine, or 'Western' medicine, is called *Ingleik* medicine in Burma as it was most widely introduced by British colonisers.

[13] I have interviewed a very broad cross-section of Burmese people, including retired senior government ministers and opposition political party members and followers, who have been suffering terminal illnesses and have sought treatment from magical healers.

[14] These organisations include the United Nations, the Thai–Burma Border Consortium, the Karen Human Rights Group, Human Rights Watch Asia, Amnesty International, Médecins sans Frontières and the Back Pack Health Medical Team.

[15] A survey of family-run businesses in Thein-byu Ze, one of Yangon's main markets, shows that importers of raw materials for indigenous Burmese medicines source their products from more than 20 different countries (Skidmore 2003, unpublished field notes). Iran, for example, is only one of the many countries with which Burmese merchants have long-established trading relationships. Indigenous Burmese medicine is sent to what is commonly called the 'border line', meaning the official land exit points from Burma. These are mainly on the Chinese and Thai borders. Traders in border towns such as Tachilek then send the indigenous medicines around the world. In these efforts, Burmese traditional-medicine manufacturers and exporters are eagerly supported by the military regime. The pinnacle of such support occurred during the ascendency of the former Prime Minister, General Khin Nyunt, who was the patron and chair of the Traditional Medicine Council and who realised the multimillion-dollar industries in traditional medicine that existed in neighbouring China and India.

[16] See, for example, the web pages of activist news organisations such as the Democratic Voice of Burma and the *Irrawaddy Magazine*.

[17] See UN Office for the Coordination of Humanitarian Affairs (OCHA) web site for *Situation Reports*.

12: Health security among internally displaced and vulnerable populations in eastern Burma

Mahn Mahn, Katherine C. Teela, Catherine I. Lee and Cara O'Connor

Introduction

Since 1962, Burma has been ruled by a military junta, currently known as the State Peace and Development Council (SPDC), which has brutally suppressed the population, particularly ethnic minority groups. Burma is one of the most ethnically and linguistically diverse countries in the world and ethnic minorities make up a large part of its population, inhabiting approximately half of the land area of the country, especially along the country's mountainous border frontiers. Since 2005, the military regime has greatly intensified its violent campaigns against a number of groups including the Karen, Karenni, Mon and Shan communities in eastern Burma, while maintaining strict rule in central regions as well.

More than 50 years of civil war in Burma have displaced hundreds of thousands of ethnic people. They have fled their homes, hidden for safety and/or faced forced relocation. Compounding their loss of home and security, conflict and human rights violations have stolen their basic human right to health—with those living along the border and in the remote interior of Burma most severely affected. The military junta has consistently blocked efforts by community-based and international organisations to deliver humanitarian aid to these restricted border regions. Alternative approaches to the provision of basic and essential public health programs in these areas that utilise the existing ethnic health organisations are urgently needed.

The current security situation in eastern Burma

In addition to continuing human rights violations by the SPDC during the construction of roads and other development projects—in particular, the widespread use of forced labour—pervasive offensives continue to be waged in the areas in which cross-border health organisations provide services. Both forms of military presence are known to increase human rights violations (Burma Human Rights Yearbook 2006). As these rights violations and fighting continue, so does the displacement of villagers as families flee to the jungle and yet-to-be attacked villages.

One example of a military-led development project that is increasing rights violations and having direct implications on access to health care is the continued construction of a road meant to link SPDC camps in the north and south of Toungoo District in northern Karen State. The construction of this road means that increased numbers of military personnel occupy the area and whole villages have been forced to move. Villagers are forced to work on the construction of the road and many flee to avoid direct attack and conscription at the hands of the SPDC. In addition, the new road creates a formidable barrier that blocks attempts by villagers to escape attacks. It also puts those who do attempt to cross the road at increased risk of attack and landmine injury as it is common practice for the Tatmadaw to shoot on sight as well as to place landmines on either side of the road.

The risk is the same for health workers. This is just one of the many examples of how development and rights violations by the SPDC decrease villagers' access to health by cordoning off the path by which they can access health facilities and blockading the way by which mobile medical units can reach those in hiding. This road, like others constructed by the junta, will inevitably lead to an increased military presence and attempts to control the area, as well as efforts by the Burmese Government to increase access to these ethnic areas in order to create more projects such as the development of goldmining operations and access for the construction of dams—all of which, as has been shown by several groups, creates and increases the number of human rights violations perpetrated by the Burmese armed forces (Burma Human Rights Yearbook 2006; Karen Human Rights Group 2006). In turn, as shown in *Chronic Emergency* (2006), associations exist between these rights violations and health outcomes. Not only are villagers faced with direct threats from rights violations, they face detrimental outcomes to household-level health such as high malnutrition rates among children and high malaria prevalence.

In addition to militarisation for the purpose of development projects, there are continuing attempts by the SPDC and some cease-fire groups to control a greater amount of territory. This leads inevitably to an increase in fighting between armed combatants. The SPDC continues to commit human rights violations against civilians as a strategy to weaken these resistance groups. In recent years, the frequency of these attacks has increased. Since February 2006, 370 people have been killed and more than 30 000 villagers have been displaced as a direct result of attacks from the Burmese army (*Chronic Emergency* 2006). The Burmese army has increased its presence in almost all border areas, typically in the post-rainy season military offensives, which have increased in frequency and intensity in recent years.

In addition, the military presence in the border regions, including the area controlled by Burma's main cease-fire group, the Kachin Independence Organisation (KIO), is increasing (see Naing 2007). In part, this is due to normal seasonal advances by the Burmese military, but it is also linked to fallout from the brutal crackdown after the 'Saffron Revolution' protests that occurred in September 2007. For the KIO area, the increase in military tensions was brought on by its refusal to issue a statement in opposition to that released by UN Special Envoy for Burma, Ibrahim Gambari, on behalf of detained democracy leader Aung San Suu Kyi. This is not the only area to witness an increase in military presence since the protests and across the country tensions have risen. In all areas where the military presence and activity are increasing, villagers will be the ones to bear the brunt of human rights violations, forced labour, active fighting, the placement of landmines and the levying of taxes.

These factors, the lack of adequate and appropriate community and facility-based health care and the results shown in *Chronic Emergency* (2006) clearly indicate the need for interventions for these vulnerable populations in internally displaced person (IDP) communities. The action, however, must come from border-based programs, developed and implemented by health workers and individuals from the communities in which the programs take place. These organisations have a unique knowledge of the situation and thus access to IDP populations not otherwise accessed by organisations, particularly international non-governmental organisations (NGOs). The need for border-based healthcare programs is apparent and utilising the existing infrastructure of ethnic health organisations is the only way these vulnerable populations will receive basic primary health care and public health interventions. In the remainder of this chapter, we document precisely the forms of cross-border health intervention that can reach and sustain the vulnerable and internally displaced populations living in Burma's eastern conflict zones.

The health status of internally displaced persons

According to official figures, Burma's health indicators are currently among the worst in the region. Information collected by the Back Pack Health Worker Team (BPHWT) from the eastern frontiers of the country, where communities have faced decades of civil war and widespread human rights abuses, indicates an even greater public health catastrophe in areas where official figures are not collected.

A survey conducted in 2004 by the BPHWT showed malaria to be the most common cause of death, with more than 12 per cent of the population at any given time infected with *Plasmodium falciparum*, the most dangerous form of malaria (Fox and Kumchum 1996). Malnutrition is unacceptably common, with more than 15 per cent of children at any time showing evidence of at least mild malnutrition—rates far higher than their counterparts who have fled to refugee camps in Thailand. The World Food Program, which includes more than mild malnutrition in its calculations, estimates that 32 per cent of children under five years of age in Burma are malnourished.

Human rights violations are very common in this population. In the year before the survey was conducted, almost one-third of households had suffered from forced labour, almost 10 per cent experienced forced displacement at least once and one-quarter reported that their food had been confiscated or destroyed. Approximately one in 50 households had suffered violence at the hands of soldiers and one in 140 households had a member injured by a landmine within the past year alone.

The report, *Chronic Emergency*, was the first to measure basic public health indicators and to quantify the extent of human rights abuses among IDP communities in the eastern conflict zones of Burma. These results indicated that the poor health status of these communities was intricately and inexorably linked to the human rights context in which health outcomes were observed. Without addressing the widespread human rights abuses and inability to access healthcare services, a long-term, sustainable improvement in the public health of these areas cannot occur.

Border-based health programs

Life under the junta and the consistent armed conflict that plagues Burma have resulted in the flight of more than one million indigenous Burmese, who have sought asylum in camps across the border, and in 600 000 to one million IDPs (Mullaney et al 2008; Skidmore 2003). Health care within Burma is grossly deficient in terms of coverage, utilisation and technical quality (Fox and Kumchum 1996), with the government spending only 2.2 per cent of total gross domestic product (GDP) on health care (Sullivan et al. 2004). In addition, the junta's 'four-cuts' policy—a broad effort to cut off food, funding, information and recruits for opposition groups, mainly in the border regions, through extensive and collective human rights violations such as forced displacement, forced labour and destruction of food supplies—worsens the health of IDPs. This imposed 'burden of ill health' weakens the IDP community and helps the junta keep this population subjugated.

Finding ways to provide health care to IDPs is a particular priority for indigenous and international groups that are consistently restricted by the junta (Beyer et al. 2006; Stover et al. 2007). The withdrawal of the Global Fund to Fight AIDS, Tuberculosis and Malaria from Burma in 2005, because of the increasingly restrictive parameters placed on its work, highlights the need for alternative strategies to reach IDPs in the border regions.

One method of providing health care to IDPs is through border-based work: programs administered and managed from locations in neighbouring countries that carry out their activities inside Burma. By basing themselves in neighbouring countries, these organisations are able to support and develop a system of mobile clinics and teams of indigenous mobile medics, who have unique access to the vulnerable populations within Burma.[1]

Cross-border work is becoming increasingly credible as a way to get health care to populations in conflict zones, as illustrated by the increased support from organisations funding border-based work. In addition, the local capacity of border-based health organisations has increased to allow for the receipt of funds to work along Burma's borders with Thailand, India and China and, to a lesser extent, with Bangladesh. Financial support for border-based work, however, is still lacking and deserves more attention and funds, as this is the only way in which these populations can be accessed. Here we will focus on organisations working from Thailand. Below are brief descriptions of a select group of border-based organisations working along the Thai–Burma border, many of which collaborate to develop programs and health policies.

Back Pack Health Worker Team

In an attempt to address the healthcare crisis in eastern Burma by establishing a consistent primary healthcare provision program for IDPs, medics and leaders from Karen, Karenni and Mon States formed the Back Pack Health Worker Team (BPHWT) on 19 August 1998. The BPHWT aims to equip people with skills and knowledge in order to manage and solve their own health problems, while working towards sustainable development in Burma. All BPHWT activities take place inside Burma, but the organisation's headquarters is in Thailand, where a team of medics, doctors, coordinators and administrators runs the program.

The BPHWT works by sending groups of mobile medics and supervisors, arranged in teams of three to five individuals, into eastern Burma to provide primary healthcare services as well as medical care for injuries (from landmines, gunshot wounds) and reproductive health care (safe births and family planning). As well, the BPHWT coordinates with other networks such as schools and women's groups to disseminate health education to local communities; it provides medical and other necessary supplies for community health workers, organises seminars and workshops to increase the knowledge and skills of health workers and collects and analyses health data.

Each BPHWT team is responsible for a specific catchment area, with an average population of 2000 people. A select group of these medics goes to Thailand to receive biannual training, to restock supplies and return health data from the field before returning to train the rest of the medics in their teams at field sites in IDP areas. In addition, these workers train traditional birth attendants (TBAs), village health volunteers and various other individuals whose work is health related.

In 2000, the BPHWT launched its TBA program, with a goal of addressing the high maternal and neonatal mortality among IDPs in this conflict zone. In these areas, community-based provision of reproductive health care through highly mobile TBAs enables a degree of access that is not feasible via the more traditional facility-based approaches. The BPHWT provides training, supplies and overall coordination for the TBA program from Thailand.

Mae Tao Clinic

The Mae Tao Clinic was started in 1989 by Dr Cynthia Maung, a Burmese refugee, in response to the need for healthcare provision for those fleeing to the Thai–Burma border to escape the brutal crackdown in central Burma and offensives by the Burmese military in the border region. The Mae Tao Clinic has grown into a comprehensive healthcare provision centre that includes an inpatient and outpatient department (IPD/OPD), reproductive health (which includes basic emergency obstetric care), a laboratory, prosthetics department and an HIV/AIDS prevention centre (Mae Tao Clinic 2006).

As well as providing services on the Thai side of the border, the Mae Tao Clinic is significantly involved in border-based work. The Mae Tao Clinic supports three clinics inside Burma and serves as a training hub for clinical skills as well as human rights awareness training, computer literacy and community management for medics working on either side of the border.

Burma Medical Association

The Burma Medical Association (BMA), a health professional-based organisation, was founded in 1991. The association conducts extensive border-based programs in communicable disease control and maternal and child health, as well as focusing on health curriculum development, health policy development, coordination of health worker training and offering technical support to public health programs on the border. The BMA also serves as a networking entity and a communications hub for border-based health work on the Thai–Burma border.

National Health and Education Committee

The National Health and Education Committee (NHEC) is an ethnic organisation-based entity that focuses on health and education policies/programs for ethnic nationalities and democratic groups. It coordinates health and education departments along the Burmese border and supports local border-based health groups through health policy and system development. The committee also supports ethnic health departments by providing training on various topics.

Ethnic health departments

Ethnic health departments partner with border-based health organisations by establishing health centres/clinics inside Burma, organising health training within Burma, developing health structure and management, recruiting and managing human resources and recognising health-worker status in the field. In addition, the departments manage supplies procurement and develop and maintain distribution to medics and health providers in the field. Ethnic health departments serve as centres of training and information about the health status of populations in their areas and provide valuable contact with the above-mentioned clinics and health centres operating in IDP areas.

An example of an ethnic health department working from the Thai–Burma border is the Karen Department of Health and Welfare (KDHW). The KDHW operates 33 mobile health clinics in Karen State, each of which serves approximately 3500–5000 people (Karen Department of Health 2006). Medics in these clinics, originally trained at the Mae Tao Clinic, can treat malaria, vitamin deficiency, intestinal parasites, landmine injuries and other common illnesses. Management of the mobile health clinics, as well as program design and monitoring/evaluation of other programs, is handled by a team based in Thailand.

Partner organisations

Several organisations—internationally and within Thailand—support the work of border-based organisations. This support ranges from financial to that of a more technical nature with regard to program design and implementation, as well as monitoring and evaluation. In addition, some groups specifically provide support to develop the capacity of these groups to grow and more effectively address the needs of their communities.

One example of a partnering organisation is the Planet Care/Global Health Access Program (GHAP; <www.ghap.org>), which has been working with local groups on border-based healthcare programs since 1998. Program staff and volunteers work closely with local groups operating programs in the IDP border areas by providing technical assistance and building local capacity in the area of public health program design, implementation, monitoring and evaluation. The GHAP also assists in the analysis and recording of program outcomes for improvement and advocacy work.

Case study: Border-Based Reproductive Health Coordination Group

In 2007, reproductive health coordinators from the BMA, the KDHW, the BPHWT, the Mobile Obstetric Maternal (MOM) Health Worker Project, the Karen Women's Organisation and the Mae Tao Clinic, together with members of GHAP, formed the Border-Based Reproductive Health Coordination Group. The group seeks to exchange ideas on reproductive healthcare provision in the conflict zones of eastern Burma.

In regular meetings, program coordinators discuss recent activities, share challenges and solutions and strategise about expansion and implementation within each organisation's reproductive health program. In this way, the coordination group brings about a better understanding of how collaboration between programs can strengthen the larger IDP community. Supply procurement, logistics, training and other issues are made easier as a result of the partnerships formed among the organisations. Finally, these regular networking meetings build capacity among local project coordinators, empowering them as leaders of their displaced communities.

Many of the organisations in the networking group are operating extensive TBA programs. TBA programs in this region have unique organisational goals and financial/human resources, but they share common goals of improving access to, and the quality of, reproductive healthcare for IDPs, as well as the collection and dissemination of vital maternal and neonatal health data. Because of these common goals, organisations have come together for program development and design on several occasions. One such example was the creation of a unique standardised pictorial TBA data-collection form, which has since improved data sharing and dissemination.

Given the difficulty of coordinating, supplying and training TBAs within conflict zones, it is essential that programs cooperate towards achieving common goals. As the example of the Border-Based Reproductive Health Coordination Group shows, networking and standardisation of data collection and future program design can strengthen border-based TBA programs. The success of this coordination should be a model for the future development of similar networks for other pressing issues such as malaria control and health education.

Case study: health information systems training

The efficient collection of data and the analysis of information are critical to the success of health organisations. The longstanding civil conflict in eastern Burma has effectively stopped any flow of official health information from the region. The ethnic health organisations serving IDPs in these 'black zones' are therefore the main source of data about health status in the region.

In 2006, an initial needs assessment found that the development of technical skills for data management and the creation of comprehensive border-wide health information systems (HIS) were among the highest priorities for border-based health organisations. The assessment also determined that a standardised data-management curriculum applicable to these groups did not exist. In response, four border-based health organisations—the BMA, the Mae Tao Clinic, the BPHWT and the KDHW—organised intensive HIS training. The specific objectives of the training were: 1) to build the capacity of organisational staff to manage HIS; 2) to standardise data-collection procedures and data management between border-based health providers; 3) to establish regular coordination and communication between cross-border health providers regarding HIS; and 4) to use data for targeted program planning and advocacy.

During the initial 10-week training period, 28 trainees from six different border-based health organisations were equipped with the basic skills needed to create data-collection forms, to calculate important indicators of health status, to manage databases and to analyse data for program planning and advocacy. Training was facilitated by a trainer from GHAP and by the Mae Tao Clinic HIS coordinator. Through monthly follow-up meetings, the trainees continue to coordinate their data-collection and reporting efforts, monitor progress on HIS projects, troubleshoot and upgrade their skills.

As a result of the initial training, organisations have updated their program databases, reducing data-entry errors and improving data quality. Some groups are in the process of updating their data-collection forms to more efficiently collect the information they need to calculate health indicators. This increase in local capacity for HIS reduces the need for outside technical advisors and greatly enhances program sustainability and ownership. Moreover, the coordination of data collection and reporting across multiple border-based organisations strengthens their program planning and advocacy abilities and generates new knowledge about the health status of the population in Burma's 'black zones'.

Success of border-based health programs

Case study: expansion of the BPHWT

The BPHWT faces a number of challenges in carrying out its work. Security risks and the junta's 'four-cuts' policy restrict travel, which hinders healthcare service provision in the field as well as the attendance of training sessions by BPHWT workers. Data records, training materials and supplies are sometimes lost when workers are forced to flee an attack, or are confiscated by the military. Some health workers have been arrested and even killed. For example:

> The SPDC attacked a village in Du Playa when they heard the BP team was treating villagers. The team and villagers fled to the jungle, one of the men taking care of BP security was shot in the shoulder. Later when it was safe to return, they discovered the house they had been treating patients in was burnt to the ground. (BPHWT 2001)

Despite these challenges, however, the BPHWT provides an indispensable service to IDPs in eastern Burma and has continued to grow. Through collaboration and mutual support from other border-based groups, the BPHWT has expanded greatly since 1998. In 1998, there were 32 BPHWTs; in 2007, 76 teams were working in 17 areas. The BPHWT now works in Karen, Karenni, Mon and Shan States in eastern Burma, as well as cooperating in an integrated program in Chin

State and a pilot program in Arakan (Rakhine) State. The total number of cases treated by BPHWT medics in 2006 was 71 789 (BPHWT 2006). The TBA program has grown extensively, from 55 trained TBAs in 2000 to 725 in 17 areas in 2007. An essential part of this program is the repeated follow-up training provided to TBAs trained by the BPHWT. TBAs supported by the BPHWT receive biannual training to improve skills, receive new knowledge regarding health interventions and discuss improvements to the program. This continued support and regular contact with TBAs supports the quality of the program and builds up TBA skills over time (see Table 12.1 on the growth of the BPHWT).

Table 12.1 BPHWT: number of teams and intended target population

Year	Number of BPHWT teams	Number of TBAs	Target population of IDPs
1998	32	-	-
1999	-	-	-
2000	56	55	100 000
2001	60	200	120 000
2002	70	200	140 000
2003	70	200	140 000
2004	70	230	140 000
2005	70	460	140 000
2006	76	720	150 000
2007	76	720	150 000

Sources: BPHWT annual reports and six-monthly reports, 1998–2007.

Case study: KDHW Malaria Control Program

The KDHW launched a Malaria Control Program (MCP) in 2003. Administered and managed from Thailand, the program consists of a team of medics, the members of which live and work in communities within Burma where they provide care. They return to Thailand every six months for refresher training, to restock supplies and share data. The MCP has grown extensively since 2003, with 50 medics and a network of village health workers providing malaria-control services to 40 859 people in 53 areas in Karen State (Table 12.2).

Table 12.2 KDHW MCP program expansion

	2003	2004	2005	2006	2007
Areas covered	4	5	17	36	53
Households	398	554	2041	5800	7501
Population	1868	3460	9798	31 646	40 859

The KDHW MCP conducts malaria-prevention education activities, vector control through insecticide-treated mosquito nets, early diagnosis with Paracheck diagnostic tests and Artesunate combination therapy for treatment. In addition, it includes 'directly observed therapy' for Artesunate combination therapy treatment and biannual population screening and treatment. Finally, MCP medics promote community participation by relying on the volunteer health workers that they recruit and train to conduct house visits to monitor mosquito-net use and provide education.

The KDHW MCP has shown enormous success since its inception in 2003. Approximately 90 per cent of people in the target area sleep under insecticide-treated nets every night and 95 per cent of those diagnosed with malaria have completed directly observed therapy. As illustrated in Figure 12.1, the prevalence of *Plasmodium falciparum* (*Pf*) malaria has decreased in each target area since inception of the MCP. The program also serves as a platform from which to gather essential data from the target population. For example, between 2002 and 2006, the KDHW MCP network and members of the GHAP conducted an extensive study on the prevalence of *Pf* malaria in Karen State (BPHWT 2006).

Figure 12.1 *Pf* malaria prevalence by term (KDHW MCP)

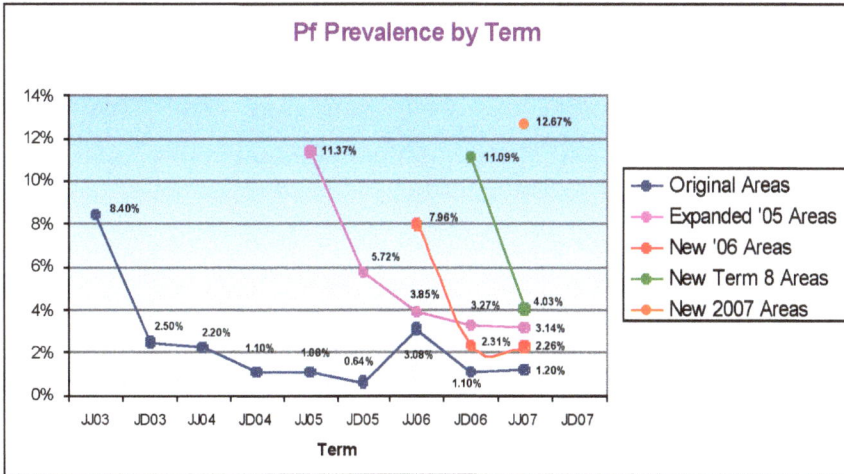

Conclusion

Continued conflict and consistent human rights violations have increased mortality rates and worsened the health status of IDPs and other vulnerable populations in Burma. Collaboration with and partnerships among border-based health organisations have proved to be viable solutions towards providing primary health care to these vulnerable populations, and should be a focus for the international public health community. Without an end to human rights violations in Burma, however, any improvements in health status are unlikely to be sustained.

References

Back Pack Health Worker Team (BPHWT) 2001 *Annual Report 2001*, Back Pack Health Worker Team, Mae Sot, Thailand.

Back Pack Health Worker Team (BPHWT) 2006 *Annual Report 2006*, Back Pack Health Worker Team, Mae Sot, Thailand

Backpack Workers Health Team, 2006 *Chronic Emergency: Health and Human Rights in Eastern Burma*, Open Society Institute, Bangkok Available at: www.geocities.com/maesothtml/bphwt/index.html.

Beyrer C, Suwanvanichkij V, Mullany LC, Richards AK, Franck N, Samuels A, et al. 2006, 'Responding to AIDS, tuberculosis, malaria, and emerging infectious diseases in Burma: dilemmas of policy and practice'. *PLoS Medicine* Oct;3(10):e393. \

Human Rights Documentation Unit, 2006 *Burma Human Rights Yearbook*, National Coalition Government of the Union of Burma. Available at: http://www.ncgub.net//BHRY/2006.

Fox, P. G. and Kumchum, S. 1996, 'Caring for Myanmar refugees in Thailand', *International Nursing Review* 43:154-8.

Karen Department of Health and Welfare, 2006, *Annual Report 2006*, Karen Department of Health and Welfare, Mae Sot, Thailand.

Karen Human Rights Group, 2006(a), *Less than Human: Convict Porters in the 2005 - 2006 Northern Karen State Offensive*, Mae Sot, Thailand.

Karen Human Rights Group, 2006(b), *Toungoo District: The civilian response to human rights violations*, Mae Sot, Thailand.

Karen Human Rights Group, 2006 (c), *Dignity in the Shadow of Oppression: The abuse and agency of Karen women under militarisation*, Mae Sot, Thailand Karen Human Rights Group, 2007 *Development by Decree: The politics of poverty and control in Karen State*, Mae Sot, Thailand.

Mae Tao Clinic, 2006 *Annual Report*, Mae Tao Clinic, Mae Sot, Thailand. Available at: www.maetaoclinic.org/publications

Mullany L.C., Lee C.I., Paw P., Shwe Oo E.K., Maung C., Kuiper H., et al. 2008 'The MOM Project: delivering maternal health services among internally displaced populations in eastern Burma', *Reproductive Health Matters*. May;16(31):44-56.

Skidmore, M. 2003, 'Medical assistance and refugee safety in contemporary conflicts', *Lancet*, 362(9377):75.

Stover, E; Suwanvanichkij, V; Moss, A. 2007, *The gathering storm: infectious diseases and human rights in Burma*.

Sullivan, T. M., Maung, C., Sophia, N. 2004, 'Using Evidence to Improve Reproductive Health Quality along the Thailand-Burma Border', Disasters, 28(3):255-268.

Endnotes

[1] They face a whole new set of issues, however, in terms of procurement and program management; sometimes they have an illegal status; and there are issues relating to security and payments required by local authorities.

Index

Union Solidarity and Development
    Association (USDA), 17, 25, 35, 37, 40,
    43, 44
United Kingdom, 130, 140
United Nations (UN), 4, 26, 54, 198, 207n
    Development Program (UNDP), 28n,
    43, 117, 120, 130, 163, 175n, 199
    Educational, Scientific and Cultural
    Organisation (UNESCO), 114, 117,
    120, 133, 163, 175n
    General Assembly, 13
    International Children's Emergency
    Fund (UNICEF), 118, 133, 152, 175n
    International Fund for Agricultural
    Development (IFAD), 68
    Office on Drugs and Crime (UNODC),
    199
    Secretary-General, 3
    Security Council, 33, 35, 44
    World Food Program, 212
United States of America, 35, 40, 47n, 74,
    92, 140, 186, 193
    financial sanctions, 23, 42, 81, 97
    sanctions, 88
    USAID, 68
Vietnam, 52, 93
Wa Special Region, 168, 200, 201
Win Myint, 28n, 37
World Bank, 14, 64, 127
World Health Organisation (WHO), 194,
    206n
World Trade Organisation (WTO), 127,
    130
World Vision International, 198–9
Yangon, 17, 27n, 28n, 30, 94, 98, 99, 129,
    181, 184, 189, 193, 198, 203, 207n
    curfew, 37
    education sector, 122, 128, 129, 132,
    133, 135–6, 137, 138, 140, 141–2,
    146–8, 166, 176n, 179, 180, 182, 184,
    185, 186, 187, 188
    markets, 201, 207n
    military violence, 37, 202
    non-governmental organisations, 155,
    160, 169
    protests in, 13, 16, 18, 19, 20, 21, 27n,
    38

security presence, 4, 23, 24
Ye Myint, 34, 38, 43, 44
Zaw Zaw, 39

www.ingramcontent.com/pod-product-compliance
Lightning Source LLC
Chambersburg PA
CBHW061245270326
41928CB00041B/3417